Providential Democracy

T0316194

Providential Democracy

An Essay on Contemporary Equality

Dominique Schnapper

Translated from the French
by John Taylor

Routledge
Taylor & Francis Group

LONDON AND NEW YORK

Originally published in French by Editions Gallimard, © Editions Gallimard, Paris, 2002.

Published 2009 by Transaction Publishers

Published 2017 by Routledge
2 Park Square, Milton Park, Abingdon, Oxon OX14 4RN
711 Third Avenue, New York, NY 10017, USA

Routledge is an imprint of the Taylor & Francis Group, an informa business

Library of Congress Catalog Number: 2008035479

Library of Congress Cataloging-in-Publication Data

Schnapper, Dominique.
        [Démocratie providentielle. English]
    Providential democracy : an essay on contemporary equality / Dominique Schnapper.
        p. cm.
    Includes bibliographical references and index.
    ISBN 978-1-4128-0869-9 (alk. paper)
        1. Equality—History--20th century. 2. Democracy—History—20th century. I. Title.

JC575.S3613 2006b
323.42—dc22

                                                              2008035479

    ISBN 13: 978-1-4128-0869-9 (pbk)
    ISBN 13: 978-0-7658-0306-1 (hbk)

This book is dedicated to the memory of my husband,
Antoine Schnapper, who shared my life—its joys and ordeals—
for more than forty-five years.

"The gradual development of the principle of equality is a providential fact. It has all the chief characteristics of such a fact: it is universal, it is durable, it constantly eludes all human interference, and all events as well as all men contribute to its progress.
—*Alexis de Tocqueville*

Contents

Introduction

The debates inspired by globalization and by the construction of Europe inevitably provoke thought about the very principles underlying how we live together in democratic societies. On both sides of the Atlantic, an increasing number of books, in political philosophy and the social sciences, deal with the aptness and effectiveness of so-called classical citizenship in an expanding world. Such writers inquire into the means by which all members of a society might be induced to participate in a genuine democratic project, as well as into those by which specific population groups might have their need to be acknowledged fulfilled. To the extent that no coherent critical systems (as was formerly the case with the ideologies of Fascism, Nazism, or Communism) remain directed against what English speakers call "liberal societies" (in French, this could literally be stated as "societies organized by means of citizenship"*), the problem of adapting traditional citizenship to the needs and demands of *homo democraticus* has now arisen.

I would like to contribute to this debate by extending the scope of a project begun over a decade ago. My ambition has been to respond, as a sociologist, to problems that have long been formulated by political philosophers; in other words, to base my response on an objective knowledge of modern society, the primary aim of a sociological study. It seems to me that political philosophers often fail to take historical experience sufficiently into account. They of course do not entirely exclude such experience from their purview, indeed in the sense that they themselves are historical individuals who intend to participate in public debates. Yet they do not systematically base their analyses on historical experience. They thus tend to generalize upon their own particular social and political experience, as

---

* Much misunderstanding between English and French speakers results from the different meanings respectively given to the term "liberalism" ("libéralisme"). In French, the term evokes economic liberalism and is connoted "right-wing," whereas in English it evokes political liberalism and is connoted "left-wing." In order to avoid ambiguity, I shall italicize liberal and liberalism whenever I use them in their English senses.

opposed to relativizing or criticizing it. Yet how can one appraise the appositeness of, say, a Marxist critique of "formal" freedoms without having knowledge of, and reflecting upon, the experience of societies whose leaders declared such freedoms to be useless or secondary and who claimed to replace them with "real" freedoms?

If theoretical thinking is to be renewed, it seems to me that a necessary prerequisite lies in the quest of the rational knowledge to which sociology aspires. By means of the factual knowledge provided by sociological studies, sociologists can legitimately test philosophers' meditations on democratic society. In any event, the conceptual constructions of political philosophy will never entirely satisfy sociologists, who consider empirical inquiry—and, more generally, the learning acquired through sociological research aimed at a rational and critical comprehension of historical societies—to constitute the basis from which they can only then attempt to render human relations intelligible. It is true that, until recently, sociologists have too often been divided into two groups: those who concentrate their efforts on establishing and criticizing the validity of their investigative results, rather than on participating in public debates; and those who restrict themselves to radically denouncing economic-liberal societies, rather than comprehending them. If one wishes to examine what the future holds in store and, in particular, the possibilities of constructing a united Europe, then one must begin with factual knowledge and meditate on what democratic societies have become.

A Sociological Project

The analyses developed in this book thus stem from a strictly sociological project whose essential steps I shall now outline. After investigating the history and processes of integration in French society,[1] I sought to understand the modern "community of citizens" or—to use the traditional French term—the "Republic" as it has existed up to now in the framework of the French nation.[2] Taking off from the knowledge of specific societies, which is provided by historical and sociological inquiry, I attempted to elucidate the idea underlying the republic (in the sense of Max Weber's "ideal-type")— a republic that was, and still is (for the time being), national. I perceived that the essential characteristic of the republic is an ambition to create an abstract political society by transcending, through citizenship, the specific roots and attachments of its members. Individuals are thus also citizens, regardless of their historical (in the

broadest sense of the term) or ethnico-religious origins,[3] and regardless of their social attributes. A democratic nation bases its legitimacy upon this abstract political society, a community of citizens
made up of individuals who are free and equal from the civil, juridical, and political standpoint. This community of citizens thereby
constitutes at once the principle of political legitimacy and the source
of the social bond—the social fabric. That tension arises between
the civic principle and the diverse manifestations of ethnicity—stemming from historical and religious heritages—is inscribed in this very
definition. In each nation-state, what might be called the "ethnic"
dimensions of collective living—the sharing of the same history,
collective mythology, language, and culture—exist side by side with
the citizenship principle, which proclaims the political freedom and
equality of all citizens. In a democratic nation, an oscillation or a
dialectic inevitably arises between political legitimacy—free and
equal citizens acting in political life as subjects of abstract rights—
and the ethnic, historical, or ethnico-religious realities of the society
at hand, which is made up of individuals differing in origin, religious faith, and material living conditions.

Having defined and described the ideal-type of the republic (in a
national context), I then set forth my thinking on these matters by study-
ing the effects, but also the limits of these effects as well as the lapses in
the principles of citizenship, that are revealed by the sociology of interethnic relations. This was the topic of *La Relation à l'autre*.[4] Throughout that study, I wanted to show that, even in the longest-standing democracies, the civic principle has never been powerful enough to prevent human beings from identifying with historical or religious particu-
lars—which is legitimate. Yet nor has the civic principle been powerful
enough to control prejudice with respect to certain groups of people
living within the same political society or to curtail discriminatory practices inherited from the past—both of which are contrary to collective
values. No society is, or can be, purely civic. Religious, ethnic, or historical realities—some legitimate, others illegitimate because of the civic
values at stake—persist or are revived. While references to historical
and religious particularisms are both inevitable and desirable as long as
they remain compatible with common values pertaining to the freedom
and equality of all citizens, the stigmatization of and discrimination
against certain groups are directly contrary to the civic principle shaping and structuring collective living. Alongside other striking examples,
this was indeed the case in the United States, where blacks were long

perceived, not as equals, but rather as descendants of African slaves and discriminated against because of their "race"; this was also the case in most European nations, where citizenship principles did not eliminate anti-Semitism, even though nearly all Jews behaved as loyal citizens.

In this new stage of my study, I would like to examine the impact of democratization on the community of citizens or, to use once again the traditional French term, on the "republic"; that is, a society shaped and structured by means of the principle, values, institutions, and practices of citizenship. By "democratization," I mean the extension of the idea of the equality of all human beings, as well as the impact of this extension to all aspects of social life. This specific sense is obviously derived from that used by Alexis de Tocqueville when he was analyzing the effects of equal social conditions on American society. This study will therefore analyze the consequences of universal citizenship on social institutions and human relations. Twentieth-century history has given a controversial meaning to the term "democracy." Totalitarian communist regimes claimed to be "democratic," and established a form of political government that developed, in monstrous fashion, the democratic aspiration to equality. It is under these circumstances that "democracy" was opposed, by some observers, to "totalitarianism."[5] Today, by looking back at historical events, we can resume the kind of reflection—at the very origins of sociology—which was fostered by the economic and political transformations of modern society: how can social bonds—the social fabric—be maintained or restored in societies based on the sovereignty of the individual? By using the term "democracy" to designate societies that have also been called "pluralist-constitutionalist" (Raymond Aron), or *liberal*,[6] I would also like to rekindle the debate about the links between "republic" and "democracy." Does not democratization tend to weaken the principle of political transcendence that was at the very heart of the republican idea, an idea formerly, and more or less strongly, inscribed in the institutions and social representations of every European nation?

The concept of *providential democracy* can likewise be analyzed as an ideal-type.[7] Concerning a unique "historic individual" or "historic individuality," the concept is directly inspired by Max Weber's elaboration of the ideal-type of capitalism—"significative in its singularity"[8]—and by the ideal-types subsequently worked out by other thinkers who borrowed the same conceptual model: "industrial society,"[9] "peasant society,"[10] and "post-industrial society."[11] According to this methodological approach, the originality of a unique historical event is defined and its "own individual character" (Weber) or essential trait is analyzed, which enables one to understand the social phenomena observed and analyzed by sociological studies. Daniel Bell made the same point with respect to his own ideal-type of a "post-industrial society," when he noted that the concept of post-industrial society was one of the tools that could enable us to better grasp the meaning of the complex changes experienced by the social structure of Western countries.[12] The concept of *providential democracy* has the same ambition. If a necessary prerequisite for providential democracy is the existence of a Providence State—the redistribution of part of a nation's wealth among the national population—then it is not a new political theory that is needed, but rather a thorough understanding of the traits of the social structure, as well as of the forms of social relations, that are characteristic of a democracy claiming to satisfy—all the while guaranteeing political freedom—the social and economic needs of all its members. I take off here from the idea that the spreading of the idea of democracy is, to cite Bell once again, one of the tools which should enable us to better grasp the complex changes experienced by the social structure of Western countries. Naturally, this viewpoint represents only one of several from which one can try to grasp the evolution of democratic societies. I of course do not mean to eliminate or discredit other "tools" that might also contribute to such an understanding.

As stated above, the essential feature of the ideal-type of a nation founded on the citizenship principle is the ambition to create an abstract political society by transcending, through citizenship, the specific roots and attachments of its members. What characterizes providential democracy is that priority is given to a search for real equality, no longer just for the formal equality of citizen-individuals. This tends to weaken the community of citizens or, to put it differently, the very principle of political transcendence.

The analysis developed in this book concern France, even though I have endeavored to elucidate specific French phenomena by implicitly referring to the experiences of other European countries. In reality, providential democracy takes on different forms in different historical societies. A comparison of the many diverse national societies of Europe—which are all, to different degrees and in different forms, providential democracies—greatly surpasses the scope of this book. In the future, however, such a comparison could constitute a new stage in this ongoing study. In the meantime, analyzing France, despite or because of its singularity—and each European nation is singular—represents a step in research focused on the evolution of the providential democracies which have united to form Europe. This analysis, moreover, enables one to formulate the more general problem, faced by all European nations, of the construction of a united Europe. The weakening of political transcendence, linked to the extension of democracy, raises even more political problems in that the project of a united Europe calls into question the historical ties between nation and republic. What remains of the national republic today? How can the idea of citizenship, which was conceived in a national framework—and citizenship indeed remains the only idea available at the moment for organizing collective living—effectively organize a post-national society? How can one conceive of a political society that would go beyond the nation-state in which political modernity was born?

A sociologist venturing into such topics, whose implications are as directly political as these, risks not being followed and acknowledged by colleagues—which is perhaps not too serious, except for the sociologist's personal comfort. Above all, however, the sociologist takes the risk of seeing analyses reinterpreted, indeed swept up into political strategies for which he or she feels little, or no, sympathy. With this new book, I have few hopes of avoiding the kinds of misunderstanding that were fostered by overly narrow, politicized, readings of *Community of Citizens: On the Modern Idea of Nationality*—misunderstandings that guaranteed the book's success at the same time. Both in France and abroad, that book was read, not as an attempt to acquire a rational knowledge of society, but rather as a political essay designed to defend and illustrate the virtues of the French Republic. It thus earned the support of those claiming to be "republicans" or anti-European "sovereignists," and the disapproval of those considering themselves to be more "modern" or "progressive"—the democratic virtue *par excellence* in societies aimed at the future—be they, by sensibility, favorable to a democratic, multicultural viewpoint or, rather, above all advocates of a united Europe. I have never concealed my "republican" convictions. However, in that book, I had no intention of giving my personal preferences—whatever they might be—a sociological underpinning. It simply seemed obvious to me that modern politics could be studied only through an informed and systematic reflection on historical societies: the sociological investigation could be carried out only on national societies. This approach did not imply that a republic was logically or necessarily national—an idea that was widely attributed to me. My approach simply took note of the fact that, up to then, this had been the case. For all such topics, it is difficult to separate sociological analysis from political commitment. Probably, for this particular topic, this is especially true. In France, creating a civic-nation utopia was proclaimed as a political ideal. It was probably inevitable that a purely intellectual analysis of the idea—indeed, in the sense of Weber's ideal-type—underlying a democratic nation would be interpreted, in social and political realms, as the same thing as formulating a political ideal.

I have neither the naiveté nor the pretentiousness to claim that I was fully objective. However, I persist in believing that the research scientist's efforts to keep universality in sight and to strive for objectivity—conceived of as a goal, an ambition, as well as a limit, not as a reality—continue to distinguish "academic" sociologists from intellectuals popularized by the mass media; that is, where both kinds of thinkers are taken as social types. In the hopes of avoiding new misunderstandings as much as possible, I would now like to outline my personal position on Europe and the notion of a nation. Experience shows that readers will not disregard the question.

Constructing a united Europe was and remains a grand political project. For more than fifty years, Europe as a whole has contributed to ensuring peace among European nations as well as to the victory of Western democracies over the Soviet empire. It has favored the prosperity of various peoples—which, like all kinds of prosperity, has been relative, yet nonetheless unquestionable. In this respect, Europe as a whole is to be praised. I personally hope that the project of a political united Europe will be achieved. No European nation is big enough to act alone in the world, and if European nations were united, Europe would take on a presence and possess a possibility of action that would be all the more desirable in that it would create a balance of power with our American allies. I hope that this political united Europe will be constructed, but the task is difficult. Advocates of a united Europe need to become fully aware of the difficulties in order to give themselves, and us, a better chance of overcoming them.

I have no intention of engaging in technical discussions about desirable reforms that could be undertaken by the Providence State,** nor of formulating what should be the policies of a Welfare State which, as everyone agrees, is in crisis. I have no intention of joining in on an "economic-liberal" (in the French sense) critique of the Intervention State—a critique to which I do not adhere. Nor do I intend to deplore the end of civic responsibilities and announce the weakening, or even the dramatic crumbling, of the republic. Instead, I attempt to comprehend the kinds of social bonds that are established, at least in part, by the democratic Social State. By analyzing debates revealing the typical kinds of tension or contradictions of providential democracy—debates in which I myself have taken part in other writings—I avoid presenting my own viewpoint here, except in a few questions raised in my conclusion. In this book, I desire to analyze the logic behind, and the meaning of, a providential democracy that is at once irresistible and protective, and to show that it is a necessary product of democratic values, of the aspiration of *homo democraticus* to equality in all dimensions of his life and social relations.

Tension and Criticism

In order to understand the evolution toward providential democracy, one must begin by analyzing the essential characteristics of political modernity and the criticisms that have been leveled—and continue to be leveled—against the traditional notion of citizenship.

** The term "Intervention State" ("*État d'intervention*") strikes me as preferable to "Welfare State" ("*État-providence*"), which suggests that the State intervenes only in favor of population groups that are underprivileged in one way or another. The phenomenon of intervention is actually much broader. Beveridge in fact preferred a more factual translation: "Social Services State." The translation of the English term "Welfare State" by the French term "État-providence" has been rightly criticized in this respect: it confines State intervention to its social-transfer dimension. It is of course impossible to correct this well-established linguistic habit. For purely stylistic or rhetorical reasons, "Intervention State," "Providence State," "Social State," and "Welfare State" will all be used here. The reader should understand that these terms cover all institutions—including local organizations and collectivities, and not just the administrative offices of the national State—associated with the social protection and wealth redistribution systems as well as with cultural intervention. The expression "Intervention State" does not necessarily imply that the State was the originator of all measures; often, the State only rationalized and organized measures that actually originated in civil society. The French Social Security system, for example, extends coverage originally underwritten by employers' emergency benefit programs ("Caisse de secours du patronat paternaliste") and by worker's mutual funding programs ("mutuelles ouvrières"). In this book, the term "Intervention State" designates all measures undertaken by political authorities.

Criticism has constantly been made of the formal aspect of a citizenship not taking into account the real economic conditions under which citizen-individuals live. Criticism has constantly been made of the abstract aspect of a citizenship not taking into account the real ways in which citizen-individuals can be deeply rooted in a particular history and culture. These criticisms, and the political responses given to them, contributed to the evolution of European societies and to the transformation of the eighteenth-century utopian idea of a republic into providential democracy.

By its very nature, political modernity is characterized by three kinds of tension which, indeed, were perceived and analyzed as early as the French Revolution and its subsequent debates: the tension between the autonomy of the individual, proclaimed sovereign, and the necessity of creating legitimate, constraining, collective institutions; the tension between the proclaimed civil, juridical, and political equality of all citizens and the inequalities of the economic conditions under which they live; and the tension between the abstract notion of "citizen" as a subject of law and the particular historical and religious roots of specific individuals. The concept of citizen, which was conceived at the end of the eighteenth century, indeed implies a principle whereby the individual is wrenched from his historical, religious, and social attributes. Important intellectual movements have denounced the consequences of these three kinds of tensions on modern societies.

The tension between individuals and political institutions was "resolved" by the republic by means of two important philosophical ideas. The first, whose development ranges from Socrates through Montesquieu, states that the freedom of individuals lies in respecting the law to which they have contributed; it follows that obeying the law constitutes the supreme form of political liberty. The second idea, fostered in modern democracy, states that it is legitimate for some citizens, who are elected through the vote of all citizens, to exert power in the name of all; the election has empowered them to embody the general interest: only a representative republic is legitimate. Thus, in a society born of political modernity, an individual entrusts representatives with the care of drawing up laws, and remains free by obeying the law. But what happens if the preeminence given to the individual is such that he no longer recognizes any outside authority, even when he is at the very origins of that authority?

The tension between the civil and political equality of citizens and the real, concrete, social inequalities of individuals was criticized by the social Christian movement before it was taken up, and orchestrated, by thinkers of a socialist and Marxist persuasion. Confronted with the gap, in historical societies, between a proclaimed equality of rights and de facto social inequalities—especially noticeable and revolting during the first industrial revolution—the latter thinkers denounced the impostures of "formal" bourgeois citizenship and called for the advent of "real" citizenship. The effect of these criticisms, even though it was postponed, was that both *liberals* (in the English-speaking world) and French republicans recognized the legitimacy of social rights and organized the redistribution of resources by means of the institutions of the Providence State. All citizens could thus be ensured of having living conditions that would guarantee their dignity. But what happens if the conditions established for the redistribution system constrain the production of wealth and the flexibility required for economic organization?

The tension between the abstract notion of citizen and the historical attributes of real, living individuals was criticized by counterrevolutionary thinkers. They criticized an abstraction wrenching the individual from nature and history; they impugned the idea of developing a society that they considered to be artificial, based as it was on the individual and not on the collectivity; they denounced the perverse consequences that would result from a rationalist political construction that violated the inevitably hierarchical nature of societies and the lessons of historical experience. In their view, both human and citizenship rights would be inefficacious and dangerous.[13] *Liberals* and French republicans "responded" to this critique by distinguishing between public and private spheres. The citizen-individual was accorded all rights to develop his historical and religious singularities in private, as an individual, all the while participating, as a citizen, beyond these singularities, in a unified public sphere or realm that was open to all and religiously neutral. But what happens if the border between public and private realms becomes so vague that the very principle of distinguishing between them becomes inoperative for organizing collective living?

These criticisms are inevitable, to the extent that they stem from the very characteristics of citizenship; yet they also surge forth in revived forms, depending on historical conditions and the responses brought to them. In France today, theoreticians who belong to the "left-wing of the left-wing" and who follow in the footsteps of Pierre Bourdieu, revive traditional Marxist criticism by analyzing the political marginalization or exclusion of the most deprived individuals,[14] or the ravages of globalization as it weakens the social and economic protection provided by the national Welfare State. In North America, communitarian thinkers[15] are inspired by criticism formulated by Edmund Burke as early as 1790; they invoke the value of historical roots and religious convictions of individuals, even if, with a modernized vocabulary, they demand that cultural rights be publicly acknowledged. In both cases, criticism is leveled today, no longer against democracy as such, but rather in the name of genuine democracy. The former thinkers criticize economic globalization because it calls into question the social protection provided by rights that were obtained, after political struggles, in Providence State societies. The latter intellectuals denounce the perverse effects of cultural and political homogenization as imposed by nation-states which, in their view, ultimately eradicate infra-national or transnational identities and cultures, and deny individual authenticity, which cannot be separated from an acknowledgment of an individual's culture.

Given these three kinds of tension, sociological analysis shows (as I have stated above) that national societies—in which the values and institutions organizing the practice of citizenship have been integrated—have never been totally civic, even if they have invoked civic values as the foundation of their political legitimacy. Ernest Gellner has rightly noted the paradox of nationalist ideology appealing to ethnic arguments—language, race, and territory—when putting forth a claim to national independence and to the right of a people to construct a civic nation-state.[16] Anthony Smith has pointed out that pre-national "myth-symbol complexes"—comprising specific myths, memories, values, and symbols—have not been eliminated by the founding of modern nations.[17] The latter inevitably oscillate between a "civic" pole of transcendence through politics (citizenship, the republic and its institutions, law) and an "ethnic" pole of concrete, down-to-earth concerns (the individual, economics, history). In providential democracies, the latter pole is always favored.

Of course, the forms taken on by these three kinds of tension, and the institutions and practices by which they are overcome or managed, are historical; they vary from one national society to the next and constantly change over time. This is why each European nation is singular, even if all European nations are shaped and structured by the values, institutions, and practices of citizenship. Each nation is the product of a particular history, the three essential factors of which are the birth of the nation as an independent political entity, the form of political centralization adopted, and the relations with the traditional institutionalized religions.

On a more abstract level, there are two overarching conceptions of citizenship: "English-style" and "French-style." The idea of transcendence through politics and representation was indeed legitimized by these two major intellectual traditions. One called for the separation and balance of powers, as invented and theorized by English thinkers following in the footsteps of John Locke and Montesquieu; the other argued for a fusion between the individual and society, as in Rousseau's conception of a "General Will," which is directly alluded to in Article 6 of the 1789 Declaration of the Rights of Man and the Citizen: "Law is the expression of the general will." These two currents of thought have fostered the development of two kinds of "citizen."

According to the British tradition, the diversity of specific individual attachments and community memberships or loyalties must be respected in order to ensure genuine freedom for individuals against a political power always threatening to become arbitrary. English democracy has retained the idea that freedoms are ensured through the creation of opposing forces derived from the political representation of the main social forces. Pluralism is perceived as the "natural" expression of public freedoms. One is a British citizen by virtue of being a member of a specific community.

In the utilitarian logic of British democracy, diverse social groups are represented in political life because of their very specificity; by defending their own interests, they contribute to the general interest and to the good working order of the entire society. In the pluralism of the English liberal tradition, there is room for particular groups, classes, professional bodies, and various orders; such pluralism is opposed to the totalizing and unitary conception of citizenship as was brutally imposed in France by the French Revolution.[18]

Indeed, in France, the "citizen" appeared on the political scene by means of a revolution that soon became violent. By proclaiming the new reign of the citizen, French revolutionaries were initially inspired by one of the intellectual movements stemming from Rousseau. For Rousseau, intermediary bodies between the citizen-individual and the State prevented man from being free, because the dependence linking human beings to each other was the source of inequality; in his view, these intermediary bodies should be destroyed. As a direct expression of the General Will, the citizen should be independent of all intermediary bonds and dwell in a close and direct relationship with the State. Although French revolutionaries, as early as 1789, raised the question of representation, they nonetheless essentially maintained Rousseau's conception of a unitary democracy wary of pluralism. For them, each citizen's will and interest identified with the collective will and interests. The general interest could not be deduced from the sum or composition of particular interests. Robespierre believed that he was fulfilling Rousseau's idea when he called for the general interest against all real, tangible, down-to-earth individual interests. Like the nation, citizenship was an indivisible whole; it needed to be organized and guaranteed by a centralized State, which was the expression of the General Will and the producer of the society.

This dual political heritage can be linked to the historical conditions underlying the birth of the citizen: on the English side of the Channel, the birth was progressive, liberal, and aristocratic, before becoming more democratic; on the French side, it was immediately revolutionary and democratic, before becoming economically liberal.[19] Today, are not these two traditions unequally adapted to the democratic society being put together on the European level? Indeed, the construction of a united Europe represents a challenge for all the European nations in which republican institutions were conceived and acquired legitimacy. The weakening of political transcendence, which can be observed in democratic societies, takes on a singular form each time, and the consequences engendered by the weakening vary with respect to the political project of each nation.[20] It is in France where the direct and widespread consequences of the weakening are the most noticeable. This is understandable because French society was built up, politically, around the utopian idea of the republic. The project of a united Europe deeply calls into question the entire political tradition developed by a nation, which explains the current wariness of the two most ancient nations, France and England. Is not a French-style republic—or "republic by divine right"[21]—ill adapted to a democratic society organized around the production and redistribution of wealth? Does not English-style citizenship respond better to the necessities of providential democracy?

The first chapter of this book analyzes the dynamics of democracy, as they are fueled by an ambition to ensure real equality, and no longer just the formal equality of individuals. The State henceforth intervenes ever more often in social relations; its action is ever more particularistic; by granting new rights to certain categories of the population, the State becomes one of the essential sources of social identities. The dynamics of democracy have increased the number of people possessing political rights and have stimulated a questioning of the meaning of citizenship. Confined to so-called "active" citizens in 1791, political rights have gradually been granted ever more widely. But the inevitable limits encountered by the definition of the body politic, or citizen body, are ever more contested. Through its universalist ambition, a democratic utopia gradually renders illegitimate all the boundary markers, or barriers, defining the exercise of political rights; it stimulates debate about the limits and the very contents of a citizenship still judged to be formal or insufficient with regards to the democratic ideal (chapter 2).

The dynamics of democracy have resulted in the development of a Providence State that intervenes ever more often to satisfy the economic and social needs of human beings. Considered to be sovereign, citizen-individuals have the right to a "normal" existence, all the more so in that efficient economic production has increased collective wealth. Modern society is organized around material prosperity and the search for private personal happiness. The link between citizenship and the economic conditions of existence characterize modern citizenship which, in this sense, differs fundamentally from citizenship in Antiquity; in modern society, only satisfactory living conditions guarantee autonomy to the citizen-individual, whose exercise of citizen rights depends on this autonomy. The Intervention State acknowledges and takes care of the rights of salary-earners: their rights to material subsistence, to housing, as well as to medical care and education or—to use the democratic term—to "culture," such as it is defined in France by the like-named Ministry (chapter 3).

The dynamics of democracy stimulate contemporary debates about the public recognition of cultural rights, which can also be called "ethnic" rights. The dynamics of democracy fuel the aspiration, of certain historical collectivities gathered within the same national society, towards a public recognition of their rights. This is the only way by which the dignity of each individual will be fully recognized, yet only to the extent that the dignity in question is inseparable from the kind of dignity publicly granted to the individual's original culture. This ambiguity has nourished the two-decade-long debate between communitarian and *liberal* thinkers (chapter 4).

Finally, chapter 5 analyzes the specific trials encountered by the French Republic as it is faced with democratization and the increasingly "providential" aspect of society, not to mention the challenge of the united Europe project. These difficulties are revelatory of the transformation of modern societies into providential democracies, as well as of the problems raised by the construction of a political united Europe. Indeed, a political Europe can only be based on, and organized around, the idea and the institutions of citizenship. Even as European nations were born, in essentially political forms, by demanding their independence against powers considered to be imperial and in order to establish democracy, how will they now—having become providential democracies—construct a political Europe?

More generally—and I will conclude with this question—, if the dynamics of democracy tend to exhaust or erode the forms of collective transcendence, be they of religious or political inspiration, how can societies continue to be held together?

*   *   *

As in my previous books, the analyses developed in this book were first worked out in my seminar at the École des Hautes Études en Sciences Sociales in Paris. The book benefited from the attentiveness and the objections of my students. Yet it would never have been written without the friendship, encouragement, and criticism of my closest interlocutors. By providing essential critical remarks, Pierre Manent led me to a better understanding and formulation of my own objectives. Serge Paugam and François-Xavier Schweyer constantly helped me to develop each step in my thinking. As before, Éric Vigne's attentiveness and high critical standards were inestimable. May everyone be heartily thanked.

Notes

1.   Schnapper, 1991.
2.   Schnapper, 1994.
3.   Schnapper, 1993.
4.   Schnapper, 1998.
5.   Aron, 1965.

6.   With the sense given to this term by Yael Tamir, who examines the compatibility between a national project and democracy in *Liberal Nationalism*. Cf. Tamir, 1973.

7.   For a development of these analyses, see Schnapper, 1999; in particular, pp. 29 ff.

8.   Weber, 1992 (1920), pp. 156-7.

9.   Aron, 1962.

10.   Mendras, 1995.

11.   Touraine, 1969; Bell, 1976 (*The Coming of Postindustrial Society*, 1973). "Postmodern" society, the term forged by the philosopher Jean-François Lyotard, has not been examined as extensively by sociologists, although Alain Touraine's expression "cultural democracy" perhaps comes close to it. Cf. Lyotard, 1979.

12.   Bell, 1976 (1973), p. 159.

13.   See Binoche, 1989, for a precise discussion of this matter.

14.   This is the case, for example, of Daniel Gaxie (1978).

15.   The term applies to authors such as Alasdair MacIntyre, Michael Sandel, Charles Taylor, and Michael Walzer. For an introduction to this debate, one can profitably consult Bertin et al., 1997.

16.   Gellner, 1983.

17.   Smith, 1986.

18.   Using another vocabulary, Pierre Rosanvallon evokes the democratic tension between a pole expressing the sovereignty of the people, with the risk of a totalitarian slide, and a liberal pole open to pluralism and diversity. Cf. Rosanvallon, 1998.

19.   Yves Déloye rightly comments that this conception was even achieved by a different way of carrying out the electoral ritual. Cf. the article "Acte électoral" in Perrineu-Reynié, 2001.

20.   On the concept of "political project," see Schnapper, 1994, p. 51. English translation: *The Community of Citizens*, p. 26.

21.   I borrow this expression from Yves Déloye and Olivier Ihl, "Deux figures de l'universel: la République et le sacré," in Sadoun, vol. 1, 2000, p. 149.

1

The Dynamics of Democracy

Modern citizenship has a universal vocation: all men are potentially free and equal citizens. This legitimacy principle fuels the dynamics of a democratic society. The idea that an individual is sovereign and that all men are equal permeates all social institutions and gives a singular style to the relationships between democratic individuals, since the relationships have to be founded upon the equal dignity of each member involved. And because *homo democraticus* is sovereign in this respect, he tends to accept no outside authorities, including even those whom he himself has freely elected as his delegates or representatives. He refuses the very idea of a hierarchy.[1] He tends to judge each distinction as discriminatory, each particular competence as illegitimate, in that they seem contrary to equality.

Today, the dynamics of democracy are best illustrated by the development of the social and cultural Providence State. Modern democracy breaks with the idea of political equality as instituted by the Greek *polis*, in which, according to Hannah Arendt, the isonomy guaranteed the *isstes*, or equality, not because all men were born or created equal, but rather, to the contrary, because all men, by their very nature (*phusei*), were not equal and needed an artificial institution, the *polis*, which by virtue of its *nomos* rendered them equal.[2] In contrast, modern democracy aims to ensure the real equality of citizen-individuals. The modern State has to attain certain goals; to use Bertrand de Jouvenel's terms, *telocracy* replaces *nomocracy*. It is not just a matter of ensuring the equality of all men before the law, but also of striving for the equality of all men through law.

"Economic liberalism logically leads to democracy by means of the principle of equality before the law."[3] In the first stage of the Welfare State, those in power sought to give a real, concrete sense to the equality of all citizens. Theirs was a universalist politics: formal equality had to become as real as possible. In the second stage—in the logical, more than the chronological, sense of the term, since the two political strategies are always more or less mixed in reality—State intervention, encouraged by the idea of a democratic utopia, is always more particularistic. The State becomes a protagonist intervening directly in social life. It is not equality, but rather equity that matters, and State intervention is considered necessary for achieving it. An inflationary number of providential measures builds up, in order to guarantee personal security and well-being. Once it has become an essential source of social identities, the Social State creates successive sedimentary layers of measures as it constantly develops new categories of beneficiaries and increases the number of ways of intervening. It seems that, whenever measures are needed, new rights and new categories can always be added on.

From Political Rights to a "Love of Well-Being"

Following from a conception of social justice based on equality, the Providence State is responsible for redistributing wealth in order to ensure the material, intellectual, and even moral well-being of individuals. The Welfare State regulates production and redistributes a share of the wealth produced. The education of individuals is organized by means of the school system, and cultural and athletic policies are carried out by the national State and by local collectivities. Individuals are ensured equal access to health care and provided with compensation in the case of accidents, unemployment, and retirement. The tax system and all the obligatory levies included in payments or withheld from income enable the State to carry out financial transfers from certain groups to others; the State thereby manages rivalries and conflicts in the name of social justice principles on which citizens agree. It is in this sense that one can speak of a social and cultural Intervention State.

The "taste for well-being," which forms the "prominent and indelible feature of democratic times"[4]—or, in sociological terms, the aspirations of citizens (as inscribed in the new principle of political legitimacy) to living conditions that are collectively judged to be decent (the very prerequisite of modern happiness)—was understood rapidly after the proclamation of the sovereignty of the citizen. As early as January 1793, Jean-Paul Rabaut Saint-Étienne expressed the tension, typical of political modernity, between the "political equality" of citizens and the "unequal personal wealth" of individuals: "Nothing better characterizes democracy than the tendency to equality and the passion and even violence required to achieve it. . . . Once political equality is established, poor people soon feel that it is weakened by the inequality of personal wealth, and since equality is required for independence, they are indignant and embittered against the men on whom they depend for their needs; so they then demand the equality of personal wealth."[5] Indeed, "having obtained political equality in terms of rights, the poor turn to that most natural and active desire: de facto equality. Even more, I would say that without this desire or hope for de facto equality, equality in terms of rights is only a cruel illusion which, instead of providing the promised enjoyments, submits the greatest and most useful share of citizens to the kind of torture that Tantalus experienced."[6] As Marcel Gauchet rightly notes, the future "social question" is already apparent in these words; so is the principle of the Intervention State.[7]

This explains why the tradition of human rights carries along with it two different elements: freedom-rights and claim-rights ("*droits-créances*," in French).[8] Established by the French Revolution of 1789, the former guarantee the rights of citizens against State power by ensuring the freedoms of thought, expression, and religious worship, as well as those pertaining to holding meetings, working, and doing business. These rights develop the inspiration of the 1789 revolutionaries in revolt against the arbitrariness of royal power (see articles 7, 8, 9, 10, and 11 of the 1789 Declaration of the Rights of Man and the Citizen). The entirety of these freedom-rights can be summarized by the definition provided in article 9 of the Declaration, which was used as the preamble to the Constitution of 1793: "The law should protect public and individual freedom against the oppression of those who govern." In other words, it is necessary to defend the individual—his rights and private life—against State intervention, and to preserve his autonomy. As to the second kind of rights, the claim-rights established by the revolutions of 1848 (following upon socialist criticism and the demands of both workers' and social-Catholic movements), they aim to ensure the real conditions underlying the practice of freedom-rights. They define the rights that individuals possess over the State, enabling them to oblige the State to provide services: rights such as those concerning work, material security, education, rest from work, and so on. As opposed to freedom rights, these rights imply State intervention in favor of individuals. As opposed to freedom-rights, which aimed to limit the possibilities of State intervention, claim-rights induce a reinforcement of State action so that formal citizenship can become real citizenship, and so that citizen-individuals can truly exercise their rights. Even as the Republic proclaimed political rights in 1789, the Providence State countries gradually shaped and structured the institutions— finalized after the Second World War—that enabled European peoples to benefit from the claim-rights whose legitimacy had been proclaimed during the revolutions of 1848.

In its current form, the Providence State was born of the dynamics of democracy, of the demands and instabilities typical of a community of citizens. Retrospectively, we can see that the Providence State was inherent in the very principle of citizenship—a fact of which the most clear-sighted revolutionaries were already fully aware. Political and juridical equality could not be made into the very principle underlying both political legitimacy and the social bond without simultaneously implying that action should be taken to make social and economic conditions less unequal. Mere political equality for all citizens could not help but appear insufficient for guaranteeing genuine citizenship. Because the citizen was sovereign in rich societies organized around production, he had the right to material living conditions susceptible of ensuring his dignity. He had the right to possess the necessary means for providing himself with food and lodging, as well as for decently raising his children, so that he would be able to—as Marxists put it—"really" exercise his political rights. Human beings are thus not just producers, but also citizens. In the name of the solidarity induced by the "community of citizens," the State henceforth had to compensate for any social consequences, resulting from a strict application of economic logic, that appeared contrary to social justice. The State was required to intervene because it was its duty to guarantee that each citizen enjoyed living conditions that were generally considered, at a given moment in time, to be normal. The European Court of Human Rights in fact followed this argument when it declared, in 1979, that it intended to provide individuals with material living conditions requisite to the exercise of their freedoms.[9]

Although the great Providence State institutions were established after the Second World War, the origins of the Providence State go back much earlier.[10] The contemporary Providence State belongs to the history of an Intervention State whose legitimacy and primary function originally were to ensure the security of society members. According to Thomas Hobbes, the contract (or "covenant," as he phrased it in English) should establish "a Common Power, as may be able to defend them from the invasion of Forraigners, and the injuries of one another."[11] Yet the protection of human beings is not the only thing at stake. "The great and chief end, therefore, of men uniting into commonwealths, and putting themselves under government, is the preservation of their property; to which in the state of Nature there are many things wanting."[12] In the second article of the 1789 Declaration of the Rights of Man and the Citizen, which enumerates the "natural and imprescriptible rights of man," "security" appears just after "freedom" and "property." The Providence State derives from a long process of collectivization of the various kinds of action that had been undertaken in favor of the poor, the sick, and the ignorant. The Providence State is not merely opposed to an ancien régime or to the "economic-liberal," or purely "regalian," Abstention State of the nineteenth century. No such simple opposition exists, neither in the realities of State institutions, nor in the conceptions of the State. As the protector of individual security and the guarantor of citizen equality, the State first became an "Ensuring" State, to use François Ewald's terminology (in French, "assurantiel"[13]); since the beginning of the twentieth century, the State had ensured that the risks of social life would be shared collectively. As the protector of the ignorant, the poor, and the sick, the State then took over and developed the role that had been played by charitable Catholic Church organizations as well as by the public solidarity institutions of the various socialist movements; the State likewise took over and developed the role played by educational establishments long organized by the Catholic Church.

What gives a singular character to the Providence State is the extent of its intervention, at a time when national wealth has considerably increased; but even more so, the Providence State is characterized by the political sense that it has been given. Having become "providential," the modern State has indeed developed, or recycled itself, according to the logic of political modernity: each citizen—being sovereign—has the right to have his social and economic conditions ensured in ways that respect his dignity and allow him to really exercise his political rights. After the Second World War, the State gave itself the legitimacy of correcting inequalities and favor-

ing equal opportunity, of guaranteeing—to all society members—
not only formal equality but also living conditions enabling them to
enjoy an equality that would be as real as possible. If the founda-
tions of what became the Providence State were actually established
before the Second World War, the Welfare State institutions created
in 1945 took on a directly political sense. The British public health
system derived directly from the perpetuation of the war economy.
In France, the important social-protection laws took over programs
developed during the French underground resistance movement.
These new institutions not only had a goal of correcting the often
painful short-term effects of the economic market, but also of in-
venting a new social and political form of intervention that would
go beyond the antinomies of economic efficiency and social justice. Even as economic liberals, ever since Adam Smith, had har-
bored the same thoughts with respect to the reconciliatory effects of
economic liberalism, the theoreticians of the Providence State, and
the politicians and administrators who established it, thought that
such a State would reconcile—thanks to analyses inspired by John
Maynard Keynes—economic efficiency and the demands of social justice. In their view, the Providence State would respond to
the demands inherent in democratic values and, in particular, to
the aspiration for a real, concrete equality for all citizen-individuals; that is, the State would respond to the passion for an egalitarian
utopia.

This is why, in all countries, including the most economic-liberal
democracies, the Providence State intervenes through the budget,
through fiscal and monetary policy, and through the organization of
public services—devoted to health care and education—which ensure minimal protection to marginalized or excluded citizens, be they
"poor people" or "ethnic minorities." Even in the United States, considered to be the archetypal economic-liberal State, the State intervenes through the tax system, the budget, and monetary policy;
through Medicare, Medicaid, and semi-public health-care schemes
such as Blue Cross and Blue Shield, the State guarantees a minimum
of resources and health care to the most underprivileged citizens;
through affirmative action policies, the State has intervened in racial
and ethnic conflicts and inequalities. Yet it is also true that, depending on the country, the State intervenes in unequal ways: the proportion of redistributed wealth varies between 20 percent and 57 percent of the Gross Domestic Product. Moreover, and especially, the

State intervenes on the basis of a "social contract" that varies from one national political tradition to the next, as Gosta Esping-Andersen has rightly shown.[14] According to him, one can distinguish an overall "[economic-]liberal" governmental system (to which the United States, Canada and Australia come closest), a "corporatist-state" system (as in Germany, Austria, France, and Italy), and a "social-democratic" system (of which the Scandinavian countries provide the best examples). In each of these systems, the family, the economic market, and the State enter into a different, specific structuring or configuration.[15]

In the "economic-liberal" Providence State, transfers of redistributed wealth essentially concern population groups whose income is weak and who depend on the State. Traditional and economic-liberal norms, as well as the work ethic, continue to dominate. The right to receive transfers, indeed limited, is strictly defined, and it moreover stigmatizes those benefiting from them. The State encourages the economic market either passively, by guaranteeing a minimum income to the poorest members of the society, or actively, by subsidizing private social-protection institutions. The beneficiaries of State social policy are also poor, and social stratification is defined with respect to the economic market; class dualism exists. In the "corporatist-state" system, encouragement of the economic market has never been as strong as in the economic-liberal system, and the idea of granting social rights has not seriously been called into question. What dominates is concern about maintaining status differences: social rights depend on class and status. This kind of corporatism is organized by the State, which has become the essential source of social protection: private insurance coverage plays only a marginal role. The redistribution capacity of this system is limited. Institutionalized religion continues to play an important role and acts to preserve the functions of the traditional family: the social-security system excludes non-working spouses and child-raising benefit payments are high; in contrast, measures encouraging women to work remain weak. The subsidiarity principle implies that the State intervenes only in aspects of social life where the family is considered to be deficient. Finally, in the "social-democratic" system, Providence State policies are applied in a universalist manner and extend to the middle classes. The social-democrat political party represents this collective political project. Rejecting the dualism between the State and the economic market, between the working class and the middle class, social democrats have aimed to establish a Providence State ensuring the equality of all citizens at the highest level possible. All social classes are integrated into the same system of universal insurance coverage; everyone pays contributions to the system and everyone is dependent on the State. The State thereby emancipates individuals from both the family and the economic market; the State takes care of children, the elderly, and the poor, as well as encourages work for women. What characterizes this kind of system is that it is based on the fusion of work and social protection. It thus closely depends on maintaining full employment: first, because employment gives one the right to social protection; and second, because the kind of universal redistribution involved requires limited social problems and high contributions.

This ideal-type analysis enables one to explain differences among countries with respect to social rights, social stratification, the extent of transfers, and, more generally, the diverse relations among the family, the economic market, and the State. Such an analysis prohibits one, however, from making simplistic, "more" or "less" comparisons between diverse Providence State countries. According to Esping-Andersen, the differences among the three systems essentially derive from three factors: the nature of class mobilization, in particular the working class; the structures of class coalition during the transition of a rural economy into a middle-class society; and the heritage of the political system's institutionalization modes. In the "economic-liberal" system, the middle classes are linked to the economic market. In the "corporatist-state" system, social insurance has cemented the ties of the middle classes to the Providence State. In Scandinavia, the success of social democracy has been closely linked to the establishing of a middle-class Providence State, which benefits from the support of both the traditional working class and the new "white-collar" class. Private social protection was nonexistent, and it was possible to establish a level of protection high enough to satisfy the middle classes. Yet the cost of such a social protection system is particularly high. Class coalitions not only explain the past, but also predict the future, of such regimes. It should be clear by now that the Intervention State, in the countries participating in the construction of a united Europe, has become an essential dimension of the national State.[16]

Although throughout the nineteenth century the criticism stemming from social Catholicism, workers' movements, and the different currents of socialist thought—all of which denounced the gap between the proclaimed equality of civil, juridical, and political rights and the reality of social and economic inequalities—was a necessary factor behind the establishment of the great social-protection institutions after the Second World War, historical conditions have also favored the rise of the Providence State. The protection of children, the sick, the jobless, and the elderly, as well as the redistribution of the benefits of economic growth, certainly appeared to be legitimate tasks after the sacrifices that had been made by the population during the war. Yet the Welfare State was also a means of responding to Communist criticism, and its overall challenge. This can be observed during the debates that took place in France as the Social Security system was being created, a period of time when almost a third of the electorate was voting for the Communist Party, which, moreover, managed to impose its ideology well beyond its electoral influence. The Welfare State intended not only to compensate for inequalities considered to be excessive in terms of social and economic living conditions, but also to respond to thinkers and politicians who claimed to draw their inspiration, more or less directly, from Marxism, and who had criticized bourgeois or formal citizenship. Created in response to the challenge and corresponding values of Soviet military power, the Providence State came to the fore during a time of history when democracies were confronted with the political and ideological threats of the Communist world. In this respect, the Providence State was a specific "political form" with its own logic and coherence: that of "compromise."[17] If, as Esping-Andersen shows, the Providence State instituted new forms of relations among the family, the economic market, and the State, it was also a response to the great ideological and political debate—which marked the second half of the twentieth century—between economic-liberal democracies and communism. This explains the nicknames often given to the Providence State: "the third way," the "crutch of capitalism," or the compromise that would "reconcile, for a while, the necessities of regulating an inegalitarian society and the citizenship demands emanating from dominated groups."[18] During the years of the ideological cold war, the Providence State appeared to be the means of reconciling, or going beyond, the ideological and political conflict between "capitalism" and "communism." This being said, it is important to remember that the Providence State is also linked to instabilities inherent in modern citizenship and democratic demands.

The Action of the Providence State

Toward the Particular

"I have shown how the dread of disturbance and the love of well-being insensibly lead democratic nations to increase the functions of central government . . ."[19] The vocation of the Intervention State is to extend itself without limits, to the extent that the needs to which it attempts to respond and the inequalities that it claims to correct are unlimited. Democracy bears the promise, as well as the illusion, of equality for all citizens. All human needs are legitimate as such. By definition, human needs possess no intrinsic limits when human aspirations—numerous, possibly contradictory, and ever revived—turn into rights: the rights to security, to work, to leisure, to education, to health, to bear children, and so on. In the highest social categories, needs can even be considered as extending to domestic animals, who in turn become the object of intensive care as regards nourishment, hygiene, and health. "To feel good . . ." becomes everyone's goal. In terms of health, education, and culture, "well-being" is essentially a relative notion. It results from the trends and values of a society that is organized around production and its corresponding values, as well as permeated by the idea of an egalitarian utopia. The aspiration to well-being can never fully be satisfied. By definition, resources are and remain limited. The deficit of the Social State not only fluctuates, but indeed is structural. It depends on the object of State intervention and on the aspirations that it intends to satisfy. The increasing number of ever more specialized service professions for helping people offers a prime example. The only possible argument for limiting the transfer of resources is financial; yet in the value system dominating the world of the Providence State, such an argument is considered to be illegitimate.

In order to understand the specific forms of Intervention State action, it does not suffice to invoke the aspirations, which have become natural for *homo democraticus*, to greater security and ever better living conditions. Intervention State action belongs as well to the history of the State in each national society. By definition, the Providence State works out categories of contributors and beneficiaries, and endeavors to take into account the diversity of social situations. In France, the inevitable bureaucratization that results from these activities is combined with "state-corporatist" management inherited from history[20]—or "corporatist-state" management, to use Esping-Andersen's typological terminology. The Social State acts in the same way as the State does in all circumstances, in other words in a formal, bureaucratic manner.[21] This is not, however, the case in Germany, where the Federal State dating from 1945 is weaker. The social-protection system, inherited from Bismarck, is also, to use Esping-Andersen's typology, "corporatist-state," but social action, essentially carried out on the *Länder* level, adapts aid to the needs of individuals; attribution of aid is examined case by case and is controlled by people in direct relation with those requesting it. As to the French Providence State, it stems from a long history of State policy: the State has indeed built up a national society by instituting a common language and culture, as well as by developing a national army, national industries, and a State administration, all of which are based on powerful professional corps made up of military officers, civil servants (functionaries), and engineers. The role of the State, in the definition of non-State professions, has also been considerable. Even "independent" professions—consisting of tradespeople, salespeople, or those belonging to "liberal" professions (such as doctors and lawyers) have modeled themselves on the civil-servant professions by preventing outsiders from participating freely in the economic market, by restricting competition, and by organizing themselves into self-managed professional groups. Their independence is guaranteed by the State.[22] High-level private-enterprise management has likewise adopted the professionalization models provided by the national engineer corps and high-ranking State functionaries. The big business firms and corporations have taken on the same kind of hierarchical organization, based on diplomas, as the civil service. The new professional corps of the Social State, and the new kinds of social professions, have similarly followed suit by adopting the models provided by already-established professions and State professional corps. Social-protection and resource-redistribution institutions in fact perpetuate the history of a State whose first elements go back to Philippe le Bel, even if the daily management of protection and redistribution is carried out by organisms (Social Security, Family Child-Raising Benefits Office ["Caisses d'Allocations Familiales"], National Employment Agency ["Agence Nationale Pour l'Emploi," ANPE], Unemployment Benefits Office ["Association Pour l'Emploi dans l'Industrie et le Commerce," ASSEDIC]) run by representatives of workers' and employers' unions. The bureaucratic logic of the Intervention State reinforces the management techniques typical of the French State, thus giving a singular character to the ways in which a republican political society has been transformed into a providential democracy.

The ambition of making living conditions more equal has the objective consequence of transforming the logic behind the action undertaken by the Republican State, ideally a neutral and rational arbitrator with a universal purview. The Republican State had always intended to surpass the particularisms inherited from feudal society. It had been built up in order to embody the general interest against particular interests, to guarantee social cohesion and, at a later stage, to reduce inequalities.[23] State organizations allowed a principle of (an at least relative) autonomy to be maintained, and they kept alive the idea that the general interest does not reflect the interests of any particular group. Sociological analysis certainly underscores the limits of this kind of transcendence, put forward as an ideal. The conception of the State as neutral and universal has always been a regulating idea as well as a principle of action, not a description of how it functions daily. In an study made during the 1960s, Pierre Grémion showed that prefects did not mechanically apply instructions emanating from the central authoritative power. Although prefects are the agents *par excellence* of the Republican and Jacobinic State, they have nonetheless always negotiated with local politicians and other important local personalities, so that their power would be established in close cooperation with them.[24] In the same spirit, "criss-crossed regulation" emanates from local elected officials and State civil servants in the management of local collectivities.[25] Pierre Bourdieu has highlighted the fact that the king's jurists and agents, once they became functionaries, not only set forward the project of the monarchic, then republican, State in order to impose universal values over particularisms, but also in order to establish their own power. Yet projects are not without influence on modes of behavior. Even if a reference to a universal value is not independent of the particular interests of a particular social group (notably the one that Bourdieu calls "the State nobility"), it is nevertheless true that "the symbolic universalization of particular interests, even if it is undertaken with ends of legitimation or mobilization in mind, inevitably makes the universal value progress."[26]

As to the Intervention State, it attempts to reconcile the principle of treating individuals in a formally equal way—the founding principle of political legitimacy—with practical management that cannot avoid the necessity of taking into account individual cases, specific situations, and particular conditions. This is especially true when the State endeavors to correct the social and economic conditions— by definition, particular—in which individuals live.

Once the State intervenes to correct social living conditions, it cannot help but increase the number of categories of "entitled parties" (or beneficiaries), and control the allotment of whatever funds are redistributed. Dividing up the population into categories is inevitable. This can especially be observed in the administration of social affairs, the favorite tool of the Intervention State; the production of texts defining new categories is particularly prolific. Ever-finer categories of beneficiaries are created as particular population groups publicly express their needs, and new plans of action are drawn up to respond to these needs. The vocabulary of the Providence State is at once abstract (as it applies to categories), inventive (as it creates new, ever more specific categories), and esoteric. Only specialists can master the neologisms, to which one refers with acronyms.

Eight social minima thus exist today, each new category having been added to the preceding ones as the years have gone by. The first, established in 1956, concerned elderly people; their living conditions were considered intolerable—the retirement benefits system instituted after the Second World War had not yet developed its effects. The extension of the salaried class then led, in 1975, to allocations for the physically or mentally handicapped who could not exercise a profession in the normal job market. During the 1980s, the economic crisis, which increased the number of jobless people and weakened social bonds, inspired new measures for new categories of beneficiaries: minimum compensation for unemployed young people and long-term unemployed people, followed by minimum compensation for people with dependent children who possessed few financial resources because of their economic and geographical isolation. In 1988, a Minimum Insertion (or Inclusion) Income ("Revenu Minimum d'Insertion," RMI) was established for "everyone."[27] By creating a category for all individuals of at least twenty-five years of age who did not benefit from any other form of social protection, the Minimum Insertion Income extended the policies already adopted in that it defined an ultimate category susceptible of benefiting from national solidarity. Below, however, the reader will see that the Minimum Insertion Income also constitutes a rupture in the social philosophy underlying the legitimacy of the Welfare State.

The management of the economic crisis has revealed the logic specifically informing the French Intervention State. On the one hand, successive governments have increased the number of jobs in the State sector (taken in its broadest sense); on the other hand, they have ensured replacement incomes to population groups temporarily or definitively excluded from the job market. Governments have developed a series of intermediary, juridical, economic-status categories that belong, strictly speaking, to neither employment, nor welfare, nor unemployment; and governments have also increased the number of types of precarious employment or—to use statisticians' terminology—"special other kinds of employment." Categories such as the following have been created, each depending on the work and contracts involved: Contracts of Limited Duration ("Contrats à durée déterminée," CDD), Job-Qualification Contracts ("Contrats de qualification"), Job-Adaptation Contracts ("Contrats d'adaptation"), Training-Occupation ("Formation-occupation"), Jobs Useful for the Collectivity ("Travaux d'utilité collective," TUC), Training Sessions for an Initiation into Professional Life ("Stages d'initation à la vie professionnelle," SIVP). These were followed by Job-Orientation Contracts ("Contrats d'orientation"), Contracts for a Return to Employment ("Contrats de retour à l'emploi"), Employment Initiative Contracts ("Contrats d'initiative emploi"), Local Insertion (or Inclusion) Programs for Women ("Programmes locaux d'insertion pour les femmes," PLIF), Programs for Local Insertion or Inclusion ("Programmes pour l'insertion locale," PIL), Employment-Solidarity Contracts ("Contrats emploi-solidarity," CES), Consolidated Employment Contracts ("Contrats emplois consolidés," CEC), Youth Employment Contracts ("Contrats emploi-jeunes"), to which one must add, to fully describe the juridical world of temporary and precarious kinds of employment, part-time contracts, school-firm training sessions, and so on. Common to all these kinds of employment is that the State takes on all or part of the social costs normally paid by the employer (as is also the case for apprentices in trades or in firms employing less than ten employees) and that the share of salaried-employee rights is reduced for jobs not based on a standard job contract. This creation of multifarious State-assisted jobs gave substitution statuses to those who were deprived of jobs, and it blurred social categories and hierarchies. The thrust of these kinds of State intervention was to share out the costs of the economic situation over diverse social groups, as well as to reduce at once the number of population groups risking to find themselves in a state of anomy and the political consequences of increasing unemployment figures. Set forward by diverse parliamentary majorities, this policy had a short-term positive impact as regards managing the economic crisis, at least from the social and political viewpoint. By increasing the number of intermediary status categories between employment and unemployment, the policy objectively increased the number of people employed in the Providence State professions and reinforced the dissociation between employment directly linked to the economic market and the rights born of the redistribution of resources.

The limits of individual-oriented policies have stimulated a type of State action with more wide-sweeping intentions. Beginning in 1981, another kind of intervention was developed in order to fight against social exclusion and violence in the suburbs of large and even medium-sized cities. Without claiming to be exhaustive, one can list the successive creation of the National Social Development Commission for Urban and Suburban Districts ("Commission nationale de développement social des quartiers," DSQ), the Housing and Social Life Operation ("Opération habitat et vie sociale"), Priority Education Zones ("Zones d'éducation prioritaires," ZEP), Information and Orientation Centers ("Permanences d'accueil, d'information et d'orientation," PAIO) as well as Local Missions for the Social and Professional Insertion of Youth in Difficulty" ("Missions locales pour l'insertion sociale et professionnelle des jeunes en difficulté"), Urban Area Contracts for the Insertion of Immigrants ("Contrats d'agglomération pour l'insertion des immigrés"), the National Deliquency Prevention Council ("Conseil national de prévention de la délinquance"), Urban Free Zones ("Zones franches urbaines"), Local Programs for Housing ("Programmes locaux d'habitat"), Family Contracts ("Contrats familles"), the City Contract ("Contrat de ville"), and so on.

Surely it is true that, by their very education, French high-ranking civil servants are particularly fond of refinements in the elaboration of new categories. Yet their creativity also reveals the logic guiding the Providence State. Administrators and politicians in power attempt to respond to the immediate needs of individuals, as these needs are formulated by the various protagonists acting in public life and then are collectively recognized as legitimate. It is no coincidence that the concept of "responsiveness" was developed by specialists of American political science: providential democracy is required to "respond" to the needs of members of a democratic society. In France, for example, the 1975 orientation law in favor of handicapped persons was passed in order to respond to claims put forward by the leaders of associations of parents with handicapped children—a cause subsequently taken up by politicians. Through the work of politicians and association members, the idea came to be accepted that the tangible living conditions of handicapped people represented a dysfunctioning of collective life; this, in turn, imposed upon the State the duty of intervening in order to correct the conditions. The State administrative agencies concerned with social needs respond to such claims by trying to adapt themselves to the ways in which the demands of the civil society evolve. Yet, at the same time, social agencies work under the threat of being accused of acting in an arbitrary and inegalitarian manner. One cannot claim simultaneously to take into account the particular needs of a particular population group and to ensure the equality of all individuals as regards the Providence State. Each city's specific policies, for instance, are inevitably different, and thus unequal on the national level. How can a policy take into account local specifics and be carried out in exactly the same way all over the national territory?[28]

State intervention is of course not limited to underprivileged categories of the population; it concerns all dimensions of life. The private sphere is also invaded and controlled by the Welfare State. At the end of the nineteenth century, the first legislative measures adopted involved child protection: keeping children at home (so as to limit their being placed with nannies), teaching mothers how to raise children, and limiting child labor. Today, such intervention continues to be reinforced. It has been extended by means of the ever-increasing medicalization of pregnancy and infancy, and by the determining role played by State-organized schooling in the destiny of individuals and families. In fact, intervention exists throughout one's lifetime, through regulations concerning public hygiene and the prevention of illness, as well as through increased medical consumption.

On the one hand, the State has taken note, through law, of the growing individualization of social relations; on the other, it has sought to compensate for the effects of this individualization on the weakest members of society, notably single women and children. As for the former, family law, which was deeply reformed during the 1970s, no longer tends to favor the so-called "traditional" family; the rights of individuals are given priority, even sometimes at the expense of the family's interest. Rights are granted to a partner living with an individual, to children born out of wedlock, and to all single-parent families. Contraception and abortion laws have similarly given women the right to take charge of their own fertility. At the same time, individualization has weakened the situation of the socially most underprivileged women; it is strong institutions that protect the weak. General social protection, which compensates for the risks of illness and pregnancy, and which includes special measures in favor of families (child-raising benefits, familial income quotient, parental leave, and so on), has been further reinforced with other specific measures such as the child support benefits which are allocated to single mothers. In an apparently paradoxical manner, the individualization of relations has thus increased State intervention. The instability of couples—which, today, is essentially based on the quality of the marriage relationship—leaves room for the intervention of judges, social workers, and psychologists; a judge defines the rights and obligations of each divorced parent, even as social workers and psychologists handle the misery or illness resulting from a divorce.[29]

The Intervention State has diminished individual dependence on close-at-hand or face-to-face kinds of solidarity, such as come from a family or neighbors. It has limited the power of the *pater familias* over his wife and children; it has ensured increased autonomy for women, even if the autonomy remains—depending on the social category—in fact unequal. At the same time, the Intervention State has increased individual dependence on the State and its agents—judges, doctors, psychologists, teachers, and social workers—each of whom is responsible in diverse ways for regulating family life according to collective values.[30]

Categories and Identities

By intervening ever more extensively and minutely in social life, by regulating work and family relations, by redistributing a great share of the national resources, the Intervention State has indeed become one of the sources of status* and social identities.

In a productivist society—that is, one organized around the production of wealth and its corresponding values—the social statuses of individuals are first linked to their place in the production system, as indicated by their employment. During the Thirty Glorious Years of economic development, professional activity as evaluated by a series of Socioprofessional Categories ("Catégories socio-professionnelles," CSP) defined by the Institut National de la Statistique et des Études Économiques—in 1982, these Categories were rechristened Socioprofessional Groups ("Groupes socio-professionnels," GSP)—was rightly held to be the best indicator of an individual's social position. Professional activity appeared to be the most revealing indicator of social stratification and the most effective means of measuring inequality. Yet this means of measuring was not exclusively typical of the Thirty Glorious Years period. In a productivist society today, as in the past, social status is closely tied to the ways in which one participates in economic life. Because modern societies give great importance to economic activity, it is first and foremost by participating in production that an individual seeks, and establishes, his social and personal identity.

Yet status and social identity are likewise linked to the economic status juridically conferred by the individual's *relation to employment* and by the *social protection system*. Indeed, the Intervention State structures an individual's *relation to employment* by regulating access to the job market and by establishing the legal conditions under which a professional activity can be exercised: collective bargaining agreements and labor laws define the rights and obligations of employers and salaried employees. All employer-employee relations are mediated by labor legislation. The Intervention State also ensures *social protection*, in the broad sense of the term, by defining the categories of individuals to whom can be granted the rights to benefit from social transfers. From this viewpoint, it is the State that makes the essential decisions, even when daily management is entrusted to organisms jointly run by union representatives. Working

---

* The term *status* is here used in its classical sociological sense, designating the more or less systematized and relatively stable set of complementary behavioral modes that one can expect, first, of an individual placed in a given situation, and, second, of the society with regards to that individual. All of the behavioral modes are recognized as legitimate by the individual as well as by the society.

or "active" citizens now out of work (the unemployed) and "inactive" citizens (schoolchildren, students, retired people, the handicapped, or welfare recipients) have the right to various forms of transfers, paid in coin or even in goods, and justified, in certain cases, by past (retired, unemployed or disabled persons), future (schoolchildren, students), or indirect professional activity (spouses of salaried employees or former salaried employees), as well as by, in still other cases, the mere idea of national solidarity (the handicapped or welfare recipients).

Job-holders possess a series of obligations and rights linked to their salary. This is why a salary has become much more than a simple remuneration for work accomplished. The Social Security system and the important collective bargaining and salaried-employee-representation laws, which rounded out labor legislation in general, have caused "gross" income (in other words, income directly corresponding to the work furnished) to be replaced by a "social" salary consisting of a set of rights and obligations. A permanent job-holder must work, respect work legislation, and pay his social-security contributions. In return, he benefits not only from a salary, but also from an entire series of rights for the present and for the future, for himself and for his family. Legislation protects him against work accidents and establishes all his working conditions, which include the duration of his employment and his rights to holidays, sick leaves, and retirement; legislation moreover ensures his right to continuing education and to benefits in the case of sickness, pregnancy, or unemployment. A salaried employee also possesses political rights: the right to elect personnel delegates ("délégués du personnel") and workplace-committee representatives ("représentants au comité d'entreprise"), the right to be elected, the right to benefit from the social and cultural projects of the workplace committee, and so on. It is in this sense that Sabine Erbès Seguin considers a salary to be the equivalent, up to the 1980s, of an entire set of rights demanded and granted, and that Yves Barel views work as the "great integrator."

A permanent job-holder possesses a status that does not directly depend on his immediate activity. Up to a certain point, the Intervention State dissociates activity and remuneration. The Intervention State grants rights that do not depend on an individual's current employment or on his or her direct relation with the economic market. A salary is no longer merely justified by its relation to the system of production, but also by rights—of a political nature—which are given to individuals by the social protection system, in the broad sense of the term (labor laws, social security). The relation to the social protection system henceforth constitutes an essential dimension of social status. This was illustrated by the Interprofessional Agreement of 14 October 1974, which created a special one-year indemnity (90 percent of gross yearly income, thus an amount approximately equal to net income) for salaried industrial and commercial employees, aged less than sixty, who had lost their jobs for economic reasons. This decision implied that a salary would be paid entirely during a period marked by the absence of work. This measure was abrogated in 1982 because of its unbearably high financial cost, but its extreme character reveals the logic underlying the action of the Providence State; only economic constraints prevented the measure from being perpetuated. At the same time, the measure shows how the Intervention State feeds on itself. In 1975, the Administrative Job-Dismissal Authorization measure was introduced by Jacques Chirac's government to control an individual's access to the status of "unemployed" (which had by then become extremely favorable) and to avoid a situation whereby the generous unemployment-benefit legislation, "which is very expensive for the Union Nationale pour l'Emploi dans l'Industrie et le Commerce (UNEDIC), would be deviated from its goal and become the object of abuse."[31]

This also explains why civil-service employment is an extreme and revealing form of this same logic. Functionaries are granted a status that is almost independent of their productivity. In their case, the growing dissociation between work and income is particularly noticeable. Hired on young and for their entire working lifetimes, and thereby possessing a clear-cut social identity, functionaries are ensured of having a minimal career defined from the onset of their entry into professional life and almost independent of the work that they will actually perform. Their juridical status guarantees them the benefits of a genuine plan for their professional life, as well as a status of a political nature. As for the private economic sector during the Thirty Glorious Years, the very notion of employment guaranteed by a Contract of Indefinite Duration ("Contrat à durée indéterminée," CDI) also long tended to imply an entire career project, even if such was fully achieved only in the ideal-type case of civil servants.

The different projects involving a "universal (or unconditional) minimum income" or a "universal allocation (or allowance)" that would be guaranteed, unconditionally, to all society members, enter into these same dynamics: this universal, unconditional income would have no other justification than the political right of all citizens and even non-citizens (because nationality would not be a condition) to receive an income independent of all relation to production.[32] In fact, the right to a Minimum Insertion Income (RMI) already adopts this logic: no condition stipulating previous employment, a specific handicap, or childcare responsibilities is required; the rights created by the legislation are purely political. In universal minimum income projects, the separation between economic activity and income is complete. Economic income is replaced by a political status derived from the Providence State.

Whereas the State in its exercise of regalian functions is formal in principle if not always in practice, and intervenes rarely in human relations, the Welfare State, on the contrary, contributes to the development of new statuses and social identities. The "social" identities constituted by social-protection legislation in the broad sense of the term, contribute to the development of "social" identities as attributed and recognized by society. The experience of unemployment, for example, derives from the creation of a social category that was needed to designate persons without employment—and possessing for that same reason certain rights—at a time when regular employment was defined by the administration of the State and put forward as a social norm. This occurred toward the end of the nineteenth and beginning of the twentieth centuries: up to then, those who did not have a job did not consider themselves to be "unemployed," "out of work."[33] During the past twenty years, we have similarly witnessed the development of the category of the "excluded."[34] With the development of the social protection system, holding down a permanent job (whether public or private), being retired, or being unemployed implies, in each case, rights, statuses, and disparate social identities. The relation to employment gives a different sense to the same categories or social qualifications: being an engineer with a Contract of Indefinite Duration (CDI), a Contract of Limited Duration (CDD), or an engineer out of work, do not have the same significance. Obviously, within the same status defined by the social protection system, the Socioprofessional Groups criterion continues to be a good indicator of social position. Even if they are both civil servants, a mailman does not enjoy the same status as a member of the Council of State. Even if all three have a Contract of Indefinite

Duration, a superior technician and a factory worker cannot be confused with a high-level manager. An unemployed person who has accumulated financial and cultural resources because of past employment does not have the same experience of unemployment as a jobless person without any resources, and so on. By defining new categories susceptible of benefiting from social transfers, the Intervention State inevitably classifies. It divides up the population into categories of "contributors" to and "beneficiaries" of the redistribution of wealth; it develops new categories, devoted, for example, to the jobless, the disabled, or the "nearly retired."

Studies of how unemployment or retirement is experienced show the impact of this categorization on the consciousness of individuals and on the manner in which they are perceived by others. An unemployed person does not dare behave in ways considered legitimate for a retired person, who, with a clear conscience, can tend to his garden or watch television in the middle of the afternoon.[35] The same objective situation of involuntary non-work takes on a different sense, and implies different kinds of behavior, when an individual moves from the status of jobless to that of "nearly retired" or retired. Young people feel that their dignity is respected more if they are enrolled at the National Employment Agency (ANPE), in other words if they are defined by a status referring to the job market, even in negative terms. By making ambiguous the significance of job experience and social identity, temporary jobs (belonging to the intermediary status categories such as have been described above) have permitted such people to better manage their lack of permanent employment (that is, contracted for an indefinite duration).[36] However, at the same time, by trying to make social conditions more equal, the Providence State creates new forms of inequality, notably those concerning the relations between individuals and the social protection system.

In France, an Intervention State concerned with culture and an Intervention State concerned with sports must be added to the Social Intervention State that shares out produced resources. The foundation of the Cultural Providence State was laid by the policies of the Popular Front and the Vichy government, then built up, during the immediate postwar period, by policies concerning the theater. Its existence was definitively established in 1958, when a Ministry of Culture was created for André Malraux. More than elsewhere, the State directly intervenes in cultural life. The political sense of cultural intervention henceforth belongs to official ideology; the ministry's policies are increasingly assimilated to "purely social" policies, because, as one culture minister himself puts it, they are linked to educational and training policies, to policies carried out by social workers, to employment policies, to regional and national economic development, and to policies concerning the publication and circulation of scientific research.[37] The same stages are visible in the development of the Sports Providence State. Once again, the Popular Front marked a decisive step. Intending to democratize athletics, Léo Lagrange (then State Under-Secretary of Sports, Leisure, and Physical Education) developed policies that had first been adopted after the First World War. These policies were taken up again after the Second World War and extended during the Fifth Republic. Like André Malraux, Maurice Herzog was assigned a national mission in 1958. The State has contributed to the construction of sporting facilities, institutionalized and inspected the practice of sports, overseen and organized the diverse national athletic federations as well as local athletic associations, and financed championship-level athletics. As in the case of culture, the same ideology underlies public policies concerning sports—policies that are reaffirmed with every new law.[38] Like the Cultural Providence State, the Sports Providence State henceforth puts itself forward "as an element of solidarity, social cohesion, and territorial structuring."[39]

In countries that have adopted an official policy of multiculturalism, such as Australia and Canada, measures are also undertaken so that the cultural specificities of diverse population groups will be preserved and perpetuated. These measures consist of supporting professionals and specialized institutions so that particular cultures and identities will be safeguarded. According to advocates of these measures, this is the best means of reinforcing social bonds in a genuine democracy. In the United States, affirmative action policies aim at compensating for historical discrimination against certain population groups, notably Afro-Americans. This could be called the Ethnic Intervention State. In France, one speaks of "republican integration," according to which historic and religious singularities are not acknowledged in the public realm; an official politics of multiculturalism has not been adopted. Yet we will see that State intervention takes ethnic specificities ever more into account.[40]

Between the Universal and the Particular

With the consent and cooperation of the various "social actors" (as one says in French, thereby indicating all the interest groups, associations, unions, lobbies, or individuals who can take political action with respect to socio-economic policy), the Social State increases the number of its intervention measures and develops ever more diversified categories and categorial rights. It seems that the State must inevitably move from a logic of formal citizenship to diverse forms of ever finer categorization. Even as the Providence State had been created on a universal basis in order to be a tool of political solidarity, an individual's sources of income are ever more often examined before he is allowed to benefit from a wealth redistribution policy—which raises the question of the "republican pact" and increases the risk of giving birth to a "dual" society. The financial crisis is obviously responsible for this evolution, which affects all Providence State countries. Yet there is still more to this situation. More deeply, if a logic of formal equality were strictly followed, then the State would always risk only sprinkling out redistributed wealth, which is limited by its very nature: transfer benefits, insignificant for the well-off, would remain insufficient for the poorest people. From this observation stems the idea of adapting intervention to the diversity of cases. Should this logic be extended, as suggests Denis Olivennes, the goal of social policy thereby shifting voluntarily and politically from equality to equity? According to Olivennes, universalism based on the abstract principle of equality must be abandoned if a genuine redistribution of wealth among social groups is to be achieved; universalist rules must be discarded and replaced by "moral magistatures" that would appraise individual cases, as is, in fact, already the case with the Minimum Insertion Income (RMI). This would imply reserving socialized expenditures for the poorest people, suppressing free university schooling for all citizens, and granting familial advantages and reimbursing healthcare expenses only with respect to level of income.[41] It would be necessary to make room for particular cases and for direct relations between individuals, which would imply breaking off from the French tradition of State action.

Yet particularistic policies have their own social costs. How may the notorious perverse consequences of individualized social policies be avoided—the "threshold effects," the stigmatization of the social-policy beneficiaries, the inevitable re-creation of new categories of excluded persons? A particularistic policy inevitably tends to validate the failure of the beneficiaries and risks imprisoning them inside their marginality.[42] No social policy can totally avoid what sociologists call "labeling," which reduces individuals to the category in which they are classified. Welfare policy always risks contributing to the locking up of some welfare receivers into careers of being poor people, accentuating their disqualification, and increasing their sentiment of social inferiority. Through intervention, the Providence State strengthens an individual's belonging to the categories that it creates; it inevitably validates inferiority or, in any event, the particularity of those whom it protects. Providential policies risk fostering a welfare-assisted mentality and, in the case of ethnic intervention, fueling a victimization culture that assigns individuals the role of victims and prevents them from taking their social destiny into their own hands. Necessary in themselves, providential policies create welfare beneficiaries who risk adapting, at least partly, their behavior to the role that has been established for them by the social intervention policies and to the expectations of the social workers responsible for applying them.

This is why the legislation establishing the Minimum Insertion Income (RMI) sought to break off from the logic behind and perverse effects of welfare assistance, by linking the allowance to an inclusion project. The legislation provided for universal coverage and for giving resources to any person who did not enter into the extant categories of welfare-assisted population groups. Yet beneficiary categories had nonetheless to be developed. Nor did the Law Against Exclusions, which also intended to take universal measures, escape from this rule; it, too, was ultimately aimed at certain categories. Otherwise, how can public wealth be justifiably transferred? In the case of the Minimum Insertion Income (RMI), as in that of any social policy, the inevitable perverse effect is to create new excluded persons at the same time; in other words, those who cannot benefit from the Minimum Insertion Income (for example, young people who are less than twenty-five years old and who have no financial resources) or who do not want to submit to bureaucratic inspection rules (the homeless, called in French the "*sans domicile fixe*" or "SDF"). This, indeed, is the argument used by advocates of a universal, unconditional minimum income. But even in this case, would it not be necessary for beneficiaries to at least make themselves known, and thus to enroll in an administrative category? Such has been the experience of managers of the Restaurants de Coeur (charity restaurants offering free meals to the poor); they have been obliged to control the number and verify the social identities of the people regularly eating there.

However, criticism of social policies should not be simplistic. It is true that a "positive discrimination" (or "affirmative action") measure benefiting some society members is necessarily "negative" for all the other members. For example, it is true that "ethnic" job recruiting risks engendering a dual society in which population groups progress at different speeds. It is true that the Providence State inevitably creates forms of clientelism and bureaucratization. As mediated by Providence State institutions, interdependence and solidarity among human beings have become abstract relations. Yet neither the critique, denouncing these damaging effects, that emanates from an economic-liberal position, nor the radical critique, from the 1970s, that denounced the "social control" function involuntarily exerted by Providence State agents and, in particular, social workers, is sufficient.[43] The material and symbolic acknowledgment of each person's right to decent living conditions and to the expression of his or her singularities also contributes to preservation of the social fabric. The Providence State permeates the life of citizens through meetings and exchanges between its agents and those seeking out, or benefiting from, its intervention measures.[44] Teachers, psychologists, doctors, educators, social workers, and social-program athletics coaches establish bonds with their diverse "clients." It should not be forgotten that Social State intervention measures follow the logic underlying democratic aspirations. The daily action of the Providence State responds to the demands of *homo democraticus*, who is concerned about his well-being.[45]

This is why Social State authorities try to intervene in ways avoiding both the limits of universalist policies and the perverse consequences of particularistic policies. In countries where State intervention is customary, as in France, one senses the limits of universalist policies. Yet the American sociologist William J. Wilson, who has analyzed the perverse effects of particularistic policies in the United States, suggests adopting a European-style universalist Providence State.[46] This proves that the Intervention State engenders its own kind of aporia, and that no policy can avoid producing perverse effects. However, when the costs of a universalist intervention policy become too high, shifting from one type of intervention to the other risks becoming inevitable. Given the nature and goal of State intervention in France, will the Providence State be able to remain based on universalist principles?

Because of these aporias, intervention policies often end up being closer to each other than the social and philosophical conceptions on which they were originally based. In all cases, the Providence State attempts to correct the inconvenient aspects and inevitable limits of the policies that it carries out. To take the example of the integration policies that have been carried out in Europe with respect to population groups of foreign origin, one notes that certain countries proclaiming universalist principles are inevitably led, when actually dealing with the question, to take into account population-group particularities, though perhaps in an indirect way; other countries, attached to particularistic policies, nonetheless reorient their measures in the direction of universalism. During the 1990s, the French thus adopted policies that were more particularistic, via diverse policies concerned with large cities and schooling. After extensive debates, the Germans, in contrast, decided to abandon the idea of providing special (particularistic) education for foreign children.[47]

This being said, internal dynamics nevertheless lead to an individualizing of Social State action, which tends to particularize its action and to "ethnicize" it, thus taking into account the diversity of individual cases. In chapter 4, we will see that the most recent policies concerning large cities move in this direction. Through its own dynamics, the Providence State tends to shift from social insurance to redistributing wealth and to solidarity, from equality to equity, from the formal to the individual, from the universal to the singular. In responding to the demands and needs of democratic citizens, intervention policies—economic but also cultural—inevitably tend to particularize social relations.

Irreversible?

These dynamics induce a process whose steps progress in a manner appearing at once necessary and irresistible to the various social actors. It is this—to all appearances—irreversible aspect that explains what Pierre Rosanvallon calls the "sociological resistance" to Providence State reforms.

Economic-liberal thinkers of the last century had already analyzed the non-reversibility of the State when it takes positive measures.

Wilhelm von Humboldt underscored the growth dynamics of the State when it intervenes in the living conditions of individuals: the administration feeds on itself. His view was that the State should preserve only one function, that of protection and security; it should "confine itself to preventing evil," for "it wrongly meddles in the private affairs of citizens." Should one thus concur with the economic-liberal critique from the last century, and conclude that a Providence State necessarily suffers from inertia and is unable to return to an earlier, smaller size? In the 1980s, those two great theoreticians and practitioners of economic liberalism, Ronald Reagan and Margaret Thatcher, stabilized and limited the Providence State, even corrected certain peripheral aspects of it, but they did not dismantle it. Even in the United States, where the Providence State is limited, what Democratic Party policies had established was preserved by a Republican president elected on an economic-liberal platform.

The internal dynamics of the Providence State derive not only from the force of inertia inherent in all bureaucratic organizations and from their capacity to persevere even when the object of intervention tends to disappear—the Ministry of Veterans in France and the Ministry of Colonies in Italy are two telling examples. The internal dynamics of the Providence State also originate in the typically democratic ambition to ensure, beyond formal equality, real equality, which is a horizon impossible to attain, a plan of action impossible to achieve. The dynamics are furthermore linked to the democratic logic according to which diverse social groups possess both the legitimacy and the tools necessary to claim recognition of their acquired social, as well as political, rights.

The "Generations" of State Intervention

In State intervention, two "generations" (as in the "generations" of computers) can be observed. In a first stage, the State intends to ensure citizens with living conditions enabling them to truly exercise their political rights. The scope of State intervention is universalist. However, given the limits of policies aimed at all citizens, another, ever more particularistic, type of intervention develops; this is the second stage.

As regards social intervention policies, Robert Castel has thus described this succession of two policies as that of "integration" followed by "insertion" (inclusion). The former "are inspired by the search for overarching equilibriums, the homogenization of society, beginning with the center. Policies are carried out through general directives on a national level. Examples are attempts to provide access for all citizens to public services and education, as well as programs to reduce social inequalities and better share out opportunities, to develop a social protection system, or to consolidate the working conditions of salaried employees." As for "insertion policies," they appeared at the beginning of the 1980s, when the social rights linked to employment, complemented by Social Aid (a welfare program designed for citizens not protected by the Social Security system), no longer responded to social problems as they were perceived by politicians and the public opinion. The policies obeyed "a logic of affirmative action [or "positive discrimination," as the French put it]: certain population groups and particular sectors of the social sphere were targeted, for whose benefit specific strategies were employed."[48] The Minimum Insertion Income (RMI) law illustrates this shift from one policy to another: for the first time, a welfare measure required that an inclusion contract be negotiated with the beneficiary—an inclusion contract that, each time, would be adapted to the particularities of the beneficiary's situation and capacities. This represents a rupture with the logic guiding formal and general measures, and is the sign of a shift to another generation, "age," or era.

With respect to the Cultural Intervention State, two successive eras also exist. According to an already "classic" distinction, one is called "cultural action," the other "cultural democracy."[49] In the former, which dominated the period 1958-1981 and directly perpetuated the overall cultural policy of the Popular Front and the Vichy government, action was taken in order to democratize access to culture and, in this respect, to enable all citizens to enjoy equal, and real, rights with respect to gaining access to cultural practices. The State gave itself the goal of ensuring the real equality of all individuals with respect to cultural practices, even as Social Security system guaranteed that all citizens could benefit from the same health care. With this aim of democratizing culture, the organizers of the Youth Cultural Centers ("Maisons des Jeunes et de la Culture") especially sought to allow members of the lower classes to attend cultural events from which they were excluded de facto. This policy was also inspired by the project of Popular Universities ("Universités populaires"): thanks to the Youth Cultural Centers, located both geographically and symbolically near areas where the economically

weakest population groups lived, it was thought that works of art—
and culture in general—would become accessible and, ultimately,
familiar to everyone. State intervention targeted particular population groups, yet in order to help them become like the others. The
policy did not call into question the universalist principle behind
State action.

Beginning in 1981, the new Minister of Culture, Jack Lang, ushered in a second era of Ministry policy, defined by specialists as
"cultural democracy."[50] The overall policy has been maintained by
all successive left-and right-wing ministers. In this second era, the
State acts in order to animate and incite artistic creation (in all cultural fields). It no longer only aims at ensuring access to culture—
thus at influencing "demand"—but also and especially at favorizing
and encouraging creativity—thus at influencing "supply." With respect to creative artists, writers, musicians (etc.), the State no longer
contents itself with fulfilling traditional roles of sponsorship, of preserving cultural heritage, of teaching, and protecting professions. It
intervenes directly into cultural life. It buys and commissions works
of art; it gives employment and financial resources to creative artists
of all kinds; it builds up and validates reputations, thus going well
beyond its duties as the overseer of the national cultural heritage. Its
intervention measures break with the conception of an economic-
liberal State. Indeed, in this second era of cultural policy, it is impossible not to take into account the value of the works of art, literature,
music (and so on) involved in cultural policy—a necessity that contradicts, by definition, the rules guiding a State that must respect the
principles of formal equality and universalism. Not all creative artists can be helped, so it is impossible to help certain, selected, creative artists without taking into account the value of their production. By financing certain composers or musicians, by buying works
produced by certain artists or sculptors, by granting research or travel
scholarships to certain writers, by providing grants to certain drama
troupes, the Cultural Intervention State selects certain aesthetic values; it favors certain creative artists and certain artistic teams, not in
order to make them become like the others, but rather in order to
assert their originality.[51] The State intervenes in the literary and fine
arts world in the same way that art gallery directors, literary critics,
or art collectors intervene. The State takes sides: how can the equality of all creative artists be respected? The significance of State intervention is not the same when the State is concerned not only with

the material living and working conditions of artists, but also directly with the works of art; it is not the same when it organizes not only the democratization of "cultural consumption," but also promotes certain kinds of "cultural production." Beginning in 1981, State intervention—both in quality and quantity—in cultural life constituted a rupture in the very conception of State action.

The evolution of cultural intervention policy raises the question of highbrow culture in a democratic society. When status inequalities are rejected, when a society based on honor is transformed into one based on the equal dignity of all citizens, then how can highbrow culture be maintained, in other words a culture implying that value judgments are made which are based on the idea that cultural production results in works of art that possess unequal values, worth, or qualities? Whence the dilemma analyzed by Pierre-Michel Menger: is the goal of cultural policy to favor the access of the greatest number of citizens to the works of art produced by highbrow culture, by encouraging creative artists and by ameliorating their working conditions?—a goal that was not contested during the first era or "generation" of cultural intervention policy. Or should the goal of cultural policy be to encourage, primarily, the creativity of all citizens, by abolishing the distinctions among the different kinds of cultural expression—a goal which is achieved by direct or indirect aid provided by the Ministry of Culture to crafts, fashion, photography, advertising creativity, industrial aesthetics, circuses, puppet theaters, popular song, rock music, and cartoon drawing?[52] In the United States, the extremism of certain critical movements is revelatory of this democratic idea, which is supported by "deconstructionist" literary critics: all texts are considered to be equal or, at any rate, their quality depends on their political meaning and their capacity to convey the fate and revolt of underprivileged groups such as women or Afro-Americans. For such critics, traditional highbrow culture is antidemocratic.

The shift from an equal-opportunity policy to the various affirmative-action policies aiming to ensure no longer merely equal opportunity—thus an inequality of results—but indeed also equal results, also illustrates the dynamics of democracy and the move from one form of intervention to another. The former policy consists of ensuring that equality, for all individuals, is applied. The State tries to fight against all forms of discrimination in education, employment, and housing; it tends to limit economic inequalities by increasing the number of social protection measures with respect to the poorest citizens. For measures taken in favor of population groups socially defined because of their "race," one speaks of "color-blind" policy since it is directed at all citizens. This universal-type policy is adopted in all democracies. Yet the limits of the results obtained by such a policy increasingly motivate the adoption of affirmative action, or positive discrimination, measures. For example, the practice of busing was adopted so that the school population in each American school would proportionally reflect the national proportions of Black and White citizens; the measure was gradually suppressed, but its very existence is telling. In the universities and business firms of the United States, Canada, and Great Britain, recruiting students and employees belonging to certain ethnic or social groups has become mandatory. In California, legislation requires that half of the public construction projects put up for open bidding must be assigned to firms managed by members of minorities. The French parliament has modified the Constitution in order to allow the voting of a law designed to ensure an equal representation of men and women in political institutions: it is not only equal opportunity, between men and women, that is guaranteed, but indeed an equality of results: an equal representation of men and women. The idea that a formal inequality is justifiable is increasingly accepted, assuming that the formal inequality is motivated by the imperative of attaining de facto or real equality.

Even if State universalism was obviously an idea or an ideal and not a practice—yet ideas and ideals are not without consequences on practice—the recent stages of social intervention no longer merely aim to give a real, concrete, sense to the equality of all citizens. In the first period, in the logical sense of the term, the State had a universalist vocation. The intention to ensure more real equality among citizens, beyond their formal equality, could be seen especially in a social insurance system that limited the risks of those possessing less material security, but also in the organization of an overall social protection system as well as in the carrying out of cultural and athletic policies. In the second period, State intervention became particularistic, creating ever-finer categories; the State became a protagonist intervening directly in social life as a whole, as well as in specific social milieus. No longer was it founded on the principle of equality but rather on that of equity, and positive-discrimination (affirmative-action) measures were correspondingly justified. Another social philosophy was at work, and it is a direct product of the dynamics of democracy.

Social Milieu and Vested Interests

This new kind of social philosophy becomes all the more imperative in that each new specific act of State intervention shapes and structures a new social milieu that contributes to the inertia of the overall providential system. A public intervention measure is aimed at a particular population group: handicapped persons or beneficiaries of the Minimum Insertion Income (RMI), for example. The measure modifies the relational system within a social sub-system and responds to the demands of the various social actors who have established the legitimacy, in a given sector of social life, of public measures that will enact a series of norms and allocate resources. The intervention measure defines "targets," "clients," "recipients," "beneficiaries," and "contributors." Inevitably, a corps of administrators, social workers, and cultural mediators is created; they are given the task of distributing the resources and inspecting the ways in which the resources are used. Because public funds are at stake, various persons (including independent or civil-servant sociologists and psychologists) are instructed to evaluate the impact of the new measures. This explains why the creation of a Minimum Insertion Income has spawned an entire milieu consisting not only of beneficiaries, but also of social workers, administrators, and researchers, whose material and symbolic interests depend on the continuation of the program. Among these different groups, a relational system is established and stabilized; everyone contributes to its perpetuation. By shaping and structuring a new field of solidarities and rivalries, a public measure thus inevitably induces a form of bureaucracy and clientelism; or, to use the terms of certain polity specialists, "neo-corporatism"[53] or "ethnization." By its very existence, the milieu created by a protection measure contributes to the definitive institutionalization of the measure. Georg Simmel had already noticed that welfare was aimed at reinforcing the social structure: "Welfare is based on the social structure, whatever form it might have; it is in total contradiction with any socialist or communist aspiration aimed at abolishing social structure. The goal of welfare is, precisely, to mitigate certain extreme manifestations of social differentiation, so that the social structure can continue to be founded on that differentiation."[54]

The creation of the Social Security system itself offers an example. Even in the momentum caused by the Liberation of France at the end of the Second World War, Pierre Laroque did not succeed in reorganizing into a single system the various insurance schemes already existing for specific social categories. He had to content himself with adding, to the extant schemes, the so-called "General Scheme" concerning salaried industrial and commercial employees (three-quarters of the working population). The specific insurance schemes, inherited from the prewar period or created in the immediate postwar period, were maintained: the "special" schemes for salaried employees and civil servants working in mines, for the national train system (SNCF) or the (EDF-GDF) national gas and electricity utility (10 percent of the working population); the special schemes for farmers, farm workers (10 percent of the working population), and non-salaried, non-agricultural workers (called the "non-non's") who represented 5 percent of the working population.[55] Well-organized professional milieus managed to maintain or create their own specific insurance schemes. They acted as lobbies defending the rights that they had acquired, in most cases, before the institution of the Social Security system in 1945.

Another example occurs in the case of the Cultural Providence State. In his 1982 policy speech in Mexico City, Jack Lang, at the time Minister of Culture, announced a new era in cultural intervention policy. This was the birth certificate of "cultural democracy." He proclaimed the union of artistic activity, the business spirit, and production, thus breaking spectacularly with the conception that had dominated ever since the nineteenth century, according to which the art world was, and should remain, remote from the financial world.[56] This new policy was accepted by all cultural milieus, first because it was formulated by a left-wing politician who was a member of the first Socialist government to govern France in decades; and, second, because it was accompanied by a doubling of the Ministry of Culture budget and by a valorization of culture in all political and mass-media events. The characteristics of the Providence State—creation of a milieu and bureaucratization—were then accentuated. Public intervention, here as elsewhere, constituted a social milieu made up not only of creative artists of all kinds, the proclaimed beneficiaries of this policy, but also administrators, cultural mediators (critics, cultural-event organizers, impresarios *et al.*), and even sociologists and the administrators commissioning sociological studies. The Ministry of Culture became the Ministry of Creative Artists and, perhaps even more so, of All Culture Professionals; in other words, of all mediators whose existence was linked to the new policy. "Unburdened by the stakes of a credible social project and of those involving the aesthetics of modernity, the action of the Ministry clearly shows itself up for what it is: a system for the allocation of public funds to the professional art, music, literary, and theatrical worlds."[57] The situation had become one where "the autarchy of the artistic circuits that are aided can favor aesthetic research that has no other outlet than in institutions themselves financed by the State."[58]

The Sports Intervention State has not escaped from this rule. Maurice Herzog and his successors have increased the number of new participants, professionals and various other "actors" in the athletic policy world by instituting fifteen specialized committees, by mobilizing researchers in order to evaluate athletic policies and produce statistics about all those who practice sports, by creating civil-servant positions in order to inspect the administrative management of the sports federations and the use of subsidies, by professionalizing athletic jobs that up to then had been filled by volunteers, and finally by organizing and subsidizing sports at the championship level. According to newspapers, the agents of the Sports Intervention State—administrators, coaches, doctors, physical therapists, psychologists, and cooks—outnumbered the athletes who went to Australia for the 2000 Olympic Games in Sydney.

In the same way, the "Ethnic" Providence State, instituted in Australia and Canada after the announcement of a policy of multiculturalism, has established a milieu in which specialized social workers, school and university teachers, the organizers of cultural, religious or folkloric associations, radio and television professionals, and official interpreters all now share a material and symbolic interest in the perpetuation of so-called "ethnic" culture, ever more deeply informed by local culture, ever more remote from the original culture of the emigrants and, even more, from the culture

Even in the United States, where the Social State is reduced, vested interests are well defended. The dynamics of democracy are also at work there. Affirmative action policy is significant in this respect. Measures taken in favor of certain population groups have often been presented as temporary. They have been adopted in order to resolve a specific historical situation, notably the heritage of slavery, and to accelerate an equalizing of conditions between whites and blacks. Yet the measures have not been curtailed; they have been extended, despite opposition, to other human categories, such as women, Native Americans, Hispanics and, in certain cases, Asians. Each intervention policy creates a social milieu that is directly interested, materially and symbolically, in its perpetuation.[60] Like all intervention policies, an ethnic intervention policy structures social identities and is rarely called into question. The Ethnic Providence State is also irreversible.

In France, it is unanimously considered illegitimate to reconsider "positive" benefits once they have been granted by the Intervention State. This is true both of rights concerning the defense of professional groups (farmers, hunters, and the diverse corps of civil servants and assimilated functionaries provide prime examples) and of measures as symbolic of "social progress" as the official number of weekly working hours. From this viewpoint, the support given by the majority of the population—including employees in the private sector—to the long public-employee strikes that took place at the end of the year 1995, demonstrates the intensity of general public's reaction when acquired rights are to be defended—even if the rights in question belong to other groups and, indeed, objectively threaten their own rights.[61]

It is through this matter of acquired rights or vested interests—the economic resource of a social group—that one simultaneously perceives all the dimensions of the professional, statutory, and even familial identities of the group members. By regulating the relations between individuals and groups, the Providence State is an essential source of the sharing out of individuals into categories, of the development of their social status and their identities. Through their right to retirement at fifty years of age, members of certain professions benefiting from "special social security schemes" surely defend their material acquired rights, but also their individual and collective identity, built up through all the experiences and representations of a career defined, among other characteristics, by retirement at the age of fifty. This explains why even the attempt to modify the rights of newly recruited persons, without changing the status of those already working in a given career, have also met with failure. Newcomers needed to benefit from the same juridical status so that the identity of each and everyone in the given profession would continue to be fully acknowledged. In a democracy, it is difficult to call into question acquired rights or vested interests, in the material sense of the term, but one calls even less into question the forms of the relationships that come to exist between individuals and groups, as well as the modes of social recognition. It seems that the Social State can act only by adding on new rights, without being able to reconsider those that have already been granted.

"Hence it is natural that the love of equality should constantly increase together with equality itself, and that it should grow by what it feeds on."[62] An inflation of Social State intervention is inscribed in its very project. Neither material well-being nor an aspiration to equality have inherent limits. Moreover, it is impossible to reconsider acquired rights—nor the benefits of economic growth—that allow more material goods to be granted to individuals and more equality to be created among citizens. Once established, the social effects of State intervention appear so obvious that their necessity is imposed absolutely. What indeed might call into question what seems—to the sovereign individual—to reflect the very vocation and values of providential democracy? The legitimacy of the Social State is to "respond" to the needs of individuals as they are expressed in the public sphere. Even State management methods seem difficult to reform because they are so firmly linked to the existence of a social milieu and, in France, to State institutions. Studies show that efforts undertaken to reform the action of the Social and Cultural State, to decentralize it, to increase negotiations with associations and beneficiaries, and to make it more experimental or creative, meet with little success. "The weight of centralism and bureaucracy, as well as the categorial definition of problems and the failure to enter into dialogue with all social actors,"[63] all contribute to a consolidation of the bureaucratic structures of the Providence State. Measures accumulate like layers of sediment; the process is denounced by all the various social actors, but no one attempts to call it into question. According to Claus Offe, the Providence State has become, in one sense, an irreversible structure, whose suppression would entail no less than the abolition of democracy and unions, with fundamental modifications of the political party system.[64]

Notes

1. It is obviously Louis Dumont's work that must be evoked here. Cf. Dumont, 1967 and 1977.
2. Arendt, 1990 (1963), pp. 39-40.
3. Aron, 1976 (1965). pp. 138-9.
4. Tocqueville, 3, I, 5, edition of 1868. English translation: II, p. 27.
5. Cited by Gauchet, 1989, p. 212.
6. Harmand, cited by Gauchet, 1989, pp. 213-4.
7. Condorcet also develops the idea of the gap between political rights and the "real" exercise of these rights, pointing out that the gap runs the risk of ruining the Republic: "By reviewing the history of societies, we have had the opportunity of seeing that there often exists a wide gap between the rights that the law acknowledges for citizens and the rights that they actually enjoy; between the equality that is established by political institutions and that which exists between individuals: we have pointed out that this difference has been one of the main causes of the destruction of freedom in ancient republics, of the turmoil that shook them, of the weakening that delivered them into the hands of foreign tyrants. These differences have three principal causes: an inequality of wealth; an inequality between those whose means of subsistence, ensured by themselves, are then passed on to their family, and those whose livelihood is dependent on their life span, that is on that period of their lives when they are capable of working; and finally an inequality of education. Cf. Condorcet, 1988 (1794), p. 216.
8. This distinction was clearly formulated by Luc Ferry and Alain Renaut in Ferry-Renaut, 1985. Legal specialists speak of political rights and social rights, of first-generation and second-generation rights. One can associate the same inspiration with the distinction between the PFRLR ("Principes fondamentaux reconnus par les lois de la République," "Fundamental Principles Recognized by the Laws of the Republic"), which concern political freedom, and the PPNNT ("Principes particulièrement nécessaires à notre temps," "Principles that are Particularly Necessary for our Times"), which concern claim-rights.
9. The examples are many. In France, the Preamble to the 1946 Constitution underscores the legitimacy of social rights. The Spanish Constitution declares in Article 9.2 that "all public authorities must work to promote the necessary conditions enabling individuals, and the groups to which they belong, to enjoy a real and effective freedom and equality." The Italian Constitution declares in Article 3.2 that "it is the duty of the Republic to remove obstacles of an economic and social nature which, by limiting de facto the freedom and equality of citizens, prevent full individual development and the genuine participation of all workers in the affairs pertaining to the political, economic, and social organization of the country."
10. For a sociological history of the birth of social protection institutions, see De Swaan, 1995 (1988).
11. Hobbes, 2000, p. 117. English original: *Leviathan*, Dent, 1973, p. 89.
12. Locke, 1977, p. 146. English original: *Two Treatises of Civil Government*, Dent, 1924 (1975), p. 180.
13. Ewald, 1986.
14. Esping Andersen, 1999 (1990).
15. Like all typologies, this one would need to be qualified and refined so that it could take into account the national diversity of providential societies. The Canadian Providence State, for example, is more developed than that of the United States. Although they are classified in the same type, France and Germany organize their social protection system differently. And so on.

16. This is no simple presupposition born of purely historical or philosophical thinking. As indicators of the importance of the Providence State, one can variously cite the size of the social budget, superior in France to the State budget; the extent of the population that participates in it; the massive and consistent attachment of the population to the Social Security system; and the protest against projects designed to reform it, of which the 1995 strikes in France offer the most spectacular example.
17. Bergougnoux-Manin, 1979.
18. Bruno Jobert, "Les politiques sociales et sanitaires," in Grawitz-Leca, 1985, p. 315.
19. Tocqueville, 3, IV, 4, edition of 1868, p. 492. English translation: II, p. 318.
20. As Pierre Rosanvallon (1990) puts it.
21. Serge Paugam and François-Xavier Schweyer, "Transformations et inerties de l'État-providence," in Galland-Lemel, 1998, pp. 146-180.
22. Dubar-Tripier, 1998, *passim* and in particular p. 193.
23. Badie-Birnbaum, 1979.
24. Grémion, 1976.
25. Dupuy-Thoenig, 1983. See also Durand-Thoenig, 1996.
26. Bourdieu, 1989, p. 559.
27. Minimum incomes for the elderly and the handicapped were instituted by means of the supplementary allocation of the National Solidarity Fund ("Fonds national de solidarité"), established by the Law of 30 June 1956; the allocation for handicapped adults, the AAH ("Allocation aux adultes handicapés"), by the Law of 20 June 1975; the allocation for isolated single parents, the API ("Allocation de parent isolé"), by the Law of 9 July 1976; the allocation of widowhood insurance by the Law of 17 July 1980; the allocation for insertion, as well as the allocation of specific solidarity, the ASS ("Allocation de solidarité spécifique"), in 1984; finally, the Minimum Insertion Income (RMI), by the Law of 1 December 1988. The increasing number of agents and categories has led to a situation where, in 1980, experts once found a case where twenty-two different people were working to solve the problems of a single family (see Bruno Jobert, "Les politiques sociales et sanitaires," in Grawitz-Leca, 1985, p. 382). In 1998-9, 5.5 million people were covered by social minima, in other words nearly 10 percent of the French population. Cf. *Études et résultats de la DREES*, Ministère de l'Emploi et de la Solidarité (Ministry for Employment and Solidarity), No. 67, June 2000.
28. This is the criticism formulated by Jean-Paul Fitoussi and Pierre Rosanvallon in Fitoussi-Rosanvallon, 1996 (pp. 90-1), and it is a little facile, for there exists an objective contradiction between establishing equality for everyone and taking into account individual cases. From a juridical viewpoint, one endeavors to combine the State's obliging of local collectivities to take social aid measures with Article 72 of the Constitution, which grants freedom to these same local collectivities with respect to their administration of such affairs.
29. A National Council of National Mediation was created, in 2001, by the Ministry of Justice and the Ministry of the Family, "to favor the organization of familial mediation and to promote its development, especially as regards a professional code of ethics, the education and the qualification of mediators, the official approval of centers, and the financing of mediations" (*Bulletin quotidien*, 10 October 2001).
30. The increasing role of the State in solving family problems has been demonstrated by numerous studies. A summary of these studies can be found in Singly, 1993, for example.
31. According to the expression formulated by the Minister of Social Affairs and Employment in a speech, on 29 May 1986, given before the National Assembly to justify the suppression of the Administrative Job-Dismissal Authorization (*Journal officiel*, p. 1445). I am grateful to Olivier Dutheillet de Lamothe for having drawn

my attention to this.

32. For an overview of this debates, see *Vers un revenu. . .*, 1996, as well as Ferry, 1995, and Ferry, 2001, chapter IV.
33. Topalov, 1994.
34. Paugam, 1996.
35. Guillemard, 1972; Schnapper, 1994 (1981).
36. For a development of these analyses, see Schnapper, 1989.
37. Pierre-Michel Menger, "L'État-providence et la culture," in Chazel, 1987, p. 50.
38. Thus Article 1 of the Modified Law of 16 July 1984 emphasizes "the development of physical and athletic activities" as an "important factor in individual equilibrium, health, and development," and adds that it is therefore "in the general interest," the practice of sports being "a right for everyone regardless of sex, age, individual capacities or social conditions." Cf. Éric Bournazel, "Institutions et droit du sport," in Arnaud, 2000, pp. 32-3. This is indeed the ideology of the Providence State. See also Callède, 2000.
39. Callède, 2001, p. 76.
40. See below chapter 4.
41. Denis Olivennes, "La société de transferts," in *État-providence. . .*, 1996, pp. 389-411.
42. See also Serge Paugam's studies, especially Paugam, 1991.
43. See, for example, Verdès-Leroux, 1978. For this topic, one can also read Donzelot, 1977.
44. De Swaan, 1995 (1988), p. 316.
45. There is a genuine market of "wellness" in which participate not only medical doctors and psychologists, but also the organizers of various local or oriental spiritualist movements. Radios have increased the number of broadcasts open to the public in which listeners, who remain anonymous by using their first name only, call in and describe their problems to a psychologist and thereby give themselves the feeling, for a moment, of being a famous mass-media star.
46. Wilson, 1987.
47. A 1999-2000 study commissioned by the European Commission—concerning the children of immigrants settled in France, Great Britain, and Germany—showed that the differently motivated, respective public policies of these three countries each resulted in a massive cultural integration of immigrant children to the norms and values of the society at hand. However, marked differences separated the Muslims of Great Britain from other Muslims, and less strong differences distinguished the children of Muslim immigrants from those of European immigrants (Portuguese and Yugoslavs). Cf. Report on the "Effnatis" study that was submitted to the European Commission in March 2001, under the direction of Friedrich Heckman, Roger Penn, and Dominique Schnapper.
48. Castel, 1995, p. 418.
49. See the validation of these terms by Pierre Moulinier, in the "action culturelle" article in Waresquiel, 2001.
50. Philippe Urfalino distinguishes three periods: the "action culturelle" ("cultural action") carried out by André Malraux, which begins to "crumble" in 1966; then the "développement culturel" ("cultural development") adopted by Malraux's successors until 1981; and finally the "démocratie culturelle" ("cultural democracy") undertaken by Jack Lang. From the viewpoint that I have adopted here, the second stage directly continues Malraux's policies and does not imply a rupture, which only occurs with Jack Lang's new policies in 1982. Cf. Urfalino, 1996.
51. The same kind of intervention occurred in 1991 when the Scientific Director of the

Department of Human and Societal Sciences of the CNRS (the French "Centre National de Recherche Scientifique") declared that methodological individualism was an antiquated paradigm. He thereby no longer limited himself to ensuring the formal conditions of scientific debates and intervened as one of the participants in this debate.

52. Menger, 1987, p. 45.
53. Jobert-Muller, 1987.
54. Simmel, 1998 (1908), p. 49.
55. Fournier-Questiaux, 1984 (fourth edition), p. 560.
56. This conversion accompanied that which most socialists made in favor of the values of business firms and the economic market.
57. Urfalino, 1996, p. 345. See also Schnapper, 1994/5.
58. Menger, 1987, p. 40.
59. Hawkins, 1982. For a development of these analyses, see chapter 4 below.
60. In the United States, specialized law offices devoted to "diversity counseling" and to the management of diversity has become one of the topics of business corporation literature. Cf. Oudghiri-Sabbagh, 1999, p. 455.
61. It should be recalled that Alain Juppé, the then Prime Minister, proposed in particular to gradually equalize the retirement conditions of functionaries and quasi-functionaries possessing a "special status" (Paris métro and national train company employees, for instance), and those imposed, by Édouard Balladur's government two years previously, on the salaried employees of the private sector depending on the General System of the Social Security System. For a long time, the majority of private sector salaried employees were not hostile to the strikers. In October 1995, 53 percent of the private sector salaried employees supported the strikers and 30 percent expressed their sympathy for them, although the majority were favorable to the project presented by the Prime Minister. Cf. Stéphane Rosès, "La popularité des mouvements sociaux ne se dément pas depuis 1995," *Le Monde*, 7 March 2001.
62. Tocqueville, 3, IV, 3, edition of 1868, p. 483. English translation: II, p. 312.
63. Paugam, Schweyer, in Galland-Lemel, 1998, p. 178.
64. Claus Offe, cited in De Swaan, 1995 (1988), p. 305.

2

An Impatience with Respect to Limits

Although it is the action of the modern Providence State that best illustrates, today, the dynamics of democracy, it was on a political level that the universal vocation of modernity, as well as the exigencies of democracy, were first expressed. Both ran up against extant limits, or barriers, induced by social and political institutions and, more generally, against everything that had been inherited from historical societies. Even revolutions with the most radical intentions take place in societies that are already constituted. The modern definition of the body politic, or citizen body, collided with conceptions inherited from the past, notably those in which women, the poor, aliens, and native population groups from colonies, were considered not to possess the qualities necessary for exercising citizen rights.

Yet heritage is not the only limit. A universal political project comprises its own inherent contradictions. Even as it proclaims the universality of citizenship, a democratic society necessarily specifies the number and quality of those allowed to possess citizenship rights. Suffrage can never be, literally, universal. Democracy "attributes sovereignty to the people, which presupposes that the people is defined, that is limited."[1]

The pressure exerted on the frontiers or boundaries of the body politic can be illustrated by the history of suffrage rights, inasmuch as elections lie at the heart of political legitimacy. History reveals a gradual extension of "the people," in other words those who, because they are entitled to the entire set of political rights, constitute the community of citizens. Yet today, criticism is leveled no longer just at the definition of the body politic, but also at the contents and, more widely, the meaning of citizenship.

The Extension of the Body Politic

Modern society is based on a principle of essentially universal inclusion: citizenship is open to all individuals, regardless of their historical, social, biological, or religious characteristics. By definition, a citizen is an abstract individual who is not otherwise identified or qualified by his particularities: all individuals are thus susceptible of becoming citizens. Because the community of citizens is defined in juridical and political terms, its vocation is to open itself to all people likely to participate in political life, beyond their particularities or particularisms.

"Actives" and "Passives"

After asserting the universality of the citizen, and after drawing the necessary conclusions of this assertion by granting citizenship even to Protestants, Jews, actors in theatrical troupes, and executioners, French revolutionaries—as is well known—then limited the exercise of citizenship by distinguishing "passive" citizens from "active" ones, the latter being the only group authorized to fully exercise political rights. The community of citizens was historically conceived as a community consisting of male proprietors and heads of the family, who at the time were considered to be the only kinds of people who were autonomous and responsible—in other words, fully human. The 1791 Constitution granted active citizenship to four-and-a-half million of the six million men of more than twenty-five years of age who were then living in France. The right to vote was subject to various conditions: one had to be born (or to have become) French, to be more than twenty-five years old, to have lived in a given town or canton for at least a year, to pay—in any locality of the country—a direct tax contribution equal to at least three days of work, not to be an indentured servant, to be registered—in the municipality of one's place of residency—in the national guard, and to have taken the civic oath. Moreover, the Constitution stipulated that accused, bankrupt, or insolvent persons automatically lost their civic rights. As the first revolutionaries worked out the notion of "active citizen," they excluded from a full exercise of citizenship—thus from the rights to vote and to be elected to public office—children, the insane, the poor, the unsettled (servants, nomads, and vagabonds), women, those under legal supervision and forbidden to enjoy free use of their possessions and even of their own person, aliens, and slaves (thus Black people from the French West Indies). All passive citizens were judged incapable of delivering an independent and competent judgement on public affairs.

The value of *individual autonomy* justified these kinds of exclusion. Minors, people under supervision, the mentally insane, women, servants, and slaves were not considered to be autonomous, either for biological reasons or because of the social conditions in which they lived. Yet the overall idea of universality was not contested. It was not a matter of segregation or exclusion. "The great majority of Constituents imagine that political equality has been achieved. Those who exclude a third of the citizens from the primary assemblies speak as if they had instituted universal suffrage."[2] To the Constituents, it did not appear contrary to the universality of citizenship to prohibit a part of the population—because of "weakness of age, sex, or condition," as Louis de Bonald puts it—from enjoying the right to exercise all the prerogatives of citizenship. It was, rather, a question of "purifying" the Republic by granting to the best of its members, detached from their particular roots, the responsibility of expressing the General Will and of defining a general interest that would not be summarized as the sum of particular interests. According to the utopia of representation, which will be analyzed in the final chapter of this book, the Constituents were supposed to embody the very idea of the political transcendence on which the legitimacy of "delegation" is founded.[3]

Among the de facto limits, or barriers, established in 1791, some have become illegitimate, enabling members of categories formerly excluded from active citizenship to possess citizen rights today; other limits are still debated, in ways revealing the very logic behind modern democracy and its vocation to extend itself ever further.

The distinction between active and passive citizens, as it was formulated in 1791, is now *illegitimate*. Everyone knows the famous dates which, in French history, marked the extension of the body politic: in 1848, the right to vote was granted to men belonging to low socio-economic categories (such as workers, peasants, and servants, as well as former slaves liberated by the abolition of slavery in Guadeloupe, Martinique, and Réunion); in 1944, to women; in 1974, to young adults between the ages of eighteen and twenty-one, as well as to newly naturalized citizens. Until this date, newly naturalized citizens—despite the theoretically indivisible quality of citizenship—received the right to vote only after five years and, only after ten years, the right to be elected.

The inclusion of the diverse categories of passive citizens in "active" citizenship has each time proved to be an ordeal, insofar as—

in each case, and in different ways—the extant social order, perceived as being natural, that is in conformity with nature, did not seem to contradict the proclaimed ambition of universality. Women, members of the so-called "dangerous" classes, and the native population groups of the colonies were obviously not, in the eyes of their contemporaries, human beings endowed with autonomy and reason. Yet once made, the decision to add a new category to the citizen body was always put into effect in an obvious and imperative manner. This initial rejection, then ultimate acceptance, of a decision henceforth perceived as irresistible even by those who had fought against it, is revelatory of the dynamics of democracy.

The Poor

Granting political rights to the economically weakest individuals is perceived, today, as self-evident. We have seen that, as early as 1791, revolutionary orators had understood that the proclamation of the sovereignty and the civil, juridical, and political equality of citizens could not help but incite them to demand an equality of "wealth." Yet the type of suffrage (proclaimed in 1848), which at the time was called "universal," was not really accepted by everyone until after the Law of 30 November 1875, which established voting for males of twenty-one years of age or more, with no tax-contribution quotas to meet, and with only a six-month residency requirement. At the time the right-wing, hostile to republican values, resigned themselves to this change with a feeling of ineluctability: "We'll have to live with it."[4] As for those who, like Jules Ferry, viewed universal suffrage as a "sacred, sovereign institution" and celebrated it as "the Fact that is Right and Just" (in French: "le fait, le Droit, le Juste"), they also felt that it was "inevitable."[5]

In order to sense the evolution that has led to today's democratic sensibility, it is necessary to recall the revolutionaries' argument: only an individual possessing mental and economic autonomy can fully exercise his rights and citizen prerogatives. In consequence, after the revolutionary period, the political rights of poor people remained in abeyance, even though Article 21 of the 1793 Constitution declared that "the society has the duty of giving subsistence to wretched citizens, either by procuring work for them or by ensuring a livelihood to those unable to work." That the exclusion of the lower classes from citizenship seems, today, so obviously illegitimate is partly due to an internalization of democratic ideals. Yet this is also because the condition of the lowest socio-economic categories has been transformed by labor law and the social protection system. Workers no longer loom as barbarians in the phantasms of the well-off; they participate in the entire social protection system instituted by a salaried-employee society. Democratic ideals have gradually eliminated the kind of personal-service jobs that implied an inequality in social status—and not just an economic inequality—between "master" and "servant."[6] Servants as a social-status category and "dependants" in general have become fewer and fewer in democratic societies, while personal-service jobs—-the entire fields of health care and education—have become professions defined by statutes.[7] Personal-service jobs are now contracted between legally equal parties. More generally, the rise in the average educational level of the population, and the extension of salaried-employee protection, have ensured the rights, and thus the dignity, of every citizen. How indeed would a salaried employee, whose professional qualification and rights are guaranteed juridically, accept having the exercise of his or her political rights denied? As for those who no longer have salaried-employee protection, such as long-term unemployed people, Minimum Insertion Income (RMI) beneficiaries, or the homeless (the "sans domicile fixe," SDF)—in other words, people who are described as being "excluded" or "disaffiliated" (Robert Castel)—they retain their citizen rights and are allowed to sign up as voters by using the address of a humanitarian association. Social marginality cannot justify exclusion from citizenship.

We are probably still informed by the idea, of revolutionary inspiration, that an individual not possessing dignified living conditions cannot be a genuine citizen. However, despite the fact that revolutionaries interpreted this postulate as excluding the poor from active citizenship, modern democracy has taken on the mission and assumed the legitimacy of turning the poor into true citizens by organizing education for all and by guaranteeing minimal living conditions through the systems of social protection and collective-wealth redistribution.

Women

"Reason desires each Sex to be in its place, and remain there. Things go bad when the two Sexes encroach upon each other. . . Reason requires that women hold the scepter of politeness, without aspiring to that of politics."[8] Sylvain Maréchal's remarks, made in

1801, were reiterated in various forms throughout the entire nineteenth century. Women were not autonomous individuals, but rejected as being unqualified for this attribute. Today, the idea that women belong to a specific natural species is depreciated. If the idea still persists, it is no longer expressed. As in the case described above, this evolution results from an internalization of democratic ideals which, moreover, now enter into relationships between parents and children as well as into those between husband and wife.[9] The autonomy of the citizen has gradually become the model for the autonomy of each spouse in a married couple, and thus for women in general.

This is not to say that this effect has been either simple or immediate, nor that it has been totally acquired. In France, it took more than one hundred fifty years for women to be granted the entire gamut of universal political rights. In the Preamble to the 1946 Constitution—thus two years after the passing of the right to vote for women—besides "principles that are particularly necessary in our times," it is asserted that "the law ensures that women be provided with rights equal to those of men." Until then, the disjunction between the Polis and the family, between the public realm of men and the private realm of women, had justified the increased separation of the sexes during the nineteenth century. The principle that a distinction should be made between public and private spheres had legitimized the difference in the political rights that were accorded to the two sexes. The Polis was restricted to men. Until the end of the nineteenth century, a marriage did not unite two autonomous individuals—which would have implied the possibility of divorce—but rather constituted a living organism considered to be in conformity with nature. It thus seemed natural that a marriage was represented in the Polis by its natural "head"—the man—and that the woman was reduced to social dependence and to the juridical and political status of a minor. Comte claimed women were children by nature.

It is true that the contradiction between democratic values and this conception came to be inscribed in the Civil Code when birthright (primogeniture) was abolished and the law established equality between sons and daughters with respect to inheritance.[10] Yet legal equality, between men and women, was acquired only belatedly. The stages are well known.[11] First, through their professional activities, women demonstrated their ability to participate in public life. In this regard, the First World War represented a breakthrough, when women took on tasks that had been considered specifically masculine. Between 1924 and 1970, education for women was gradually made to conform to that existing for men. Beginning in the 1970s, as women gained control of their bodies and their fertility—through the use of the pill and the right to abortion—they further acquired the means of social autonomy. As Geneviève Fraisse remarks, "democracy is exclusive, yet it does not officially exclude, in that it does not state its exclusion rules. It produces exclusion by means of a series of real or imaginary, juridical or medical, literary or philosophical, impediments. . . . There is no exclusion statement, for it would too powerfully contradict the principles of modern democracy."[12]

Today, the "gender" limit has become illegitimate. Whenever de facto limits are held up to the social and statutory equality of women, they appear intolerable and are strongly denounced.[13] Yet studies reveal that only a very few women, despite qualifications that are at least equal to those of men, hold down positions of political or—in the big business firms and corporations—economic power; that women, in all professional fields, are proportionately fewer as the level of responsibility rises; that women are the first to be affected by unemployment and precarious employment; that they continue to take care of most of the domestic chores. This situation appears so antagonistic to proclaimed collective values that, in French, various grammatical possibilities are often appealed to so as to fictively erase, from social and academic life, gender differences and the discrimination from which women indeed continue to suffer in the job market. It has been shown, for instance, that the Book Union ("Syndicat du Livre") members who slowed down the entry of computer technology into the printing trade were also struggling, as men, against the employment of female workers; the men were concerned about asserting their male and professional superiority, as well as defending their jobs against all forms of competition.[14] That women are relegated to the modest jobs of the Providence State, which extend their traditional familial roles, and that they remain outsiders in the places where important political and economic decisions are made, are considered to illustrate the deeply antidemocratic nature of so-called classical citizenship.

Thus, in the overall movement toward an equality of political rights and statuses, persistent de facto limits become untenable, according to the law formulated by Tocqueville, even as they continue to be attenuated. This impatience with respect to every de facto limit—

and no longer merely with respect to a limit in political rights—impeding the equality of men and women explains the reappearance in another form, through the instituting of parity in politics, of the taking into account of gender in public life. Gender had been invoked in order to eliminate women from political life; now it is used in order to encourage their participation.

Colonists and Natives

The dynamics of democracy have also made it illegitimate in principle, and impossible in fact, to perpetuate any political situation based on an inequality of civil, juridical, and political statuses. Colonial Algeria offers a telling example. The theoretical means of conciliating the principles of liberty and political equality existed at the time: it would have been necessary to give to both colonists and native Algerians the same full and equal citizenship, to equally acknowledge all inhabitants of Algeria in regard to all aspects of the public realm, perhaps while simultaneously authorizing natives to preserve their particular personal status; in other words, to take what is called an "integration"—in French, "assimilation"—policy to its logical conclusion. Few contemporaries understood that this solution was not only logical, but also in fact the only one compatible with democratic values. In 1887, for example, two extreme left-wing deputies submitted, to the House of Deputies, a proposition calling for the naturalization of all native Algerians. In 1890, the Martineau Project called for gradually attributing political rights to native Algerians; yet this proposition was not even discussed by the deputies. Jurists and legal philosophers regularly pointed out that citizenship should be the ultimate goal of colonization. However, until 1940, they remained prudent about applying the principle: "The civilizing mission of the State requires that natives should not indefinitely be maintained in a legal situation ensuring them fewer guarantees."[15] According to jurists, since the concept of assimilation implied the non-separation of private rights and public law, the full exercise of citizenship was denied to "natives" because, in their private lives, they obeyed Islamic law. The Ordinance of 7 March 1944, adopted by the Provisory Government of the French Republic, granted access to citizenship and ensured the respect of individual rights. Yet this decision concerned only certain categories: Muslims who had distinguished themselves academically, in the military, or in public or electoral capacities. French citizenship acquired in this way could not automatically be passed on to children. Moreover, the Fourth-Republic Constitution, in an extension of the Provisional Government ordinance, indeed granted citizenship to all, yet distinguished the citizenship of French Republic citizens from that of French Union members.

This dual citizenship, which created two categories of citizens and thus two distinct electoral bodies in Algeria, contradicts the very idea of citizenship. As one jurist logically remarked, "common citizenship should normally lead to universal suffrage and especially to a single body of voters, because it should not be possible to distinguish among citizens as regards their public rights."[16] Yet the policy of assimilation ran up against an objective dilemma. The colonized natives did not want to lose their identity; out of dignity, they rejected the idea of taking on the conqueror's nationality. In the colonial context, naturalization inevitably meant treason. As for colonists, whose status was based on dominating natives, they refused to consider the very notion of an equality between themselves and the natives. The successive governments of mainland France, often little interested in colonial problems and divided as to their appreciation of the real situation, were, in the majority, of the opinion that citizenship was incompatible with a preservation of Islamic laws concerning marriage, repudiation, divorce, and the civil status of children. During a period marked by the philosophies of positivism and evolutionism, French governments fully participated in the idea of the technical, but also political and moral, superiority of Western civilization. With such policy at work, democratic principles could not help but be betrayed. This explains the creation of that juridical monstrosity with respect to the principles of modern democracy: nationality without citizenship. In 1862, the Algiers Court ruled that "a native person is French, though not, at the same time, a citizen."

School policy lay at the very heart of this contradiction. All projects designed to extend the French school system to native Algerians collided with the position of the colonists, for whom "it was necessary to combat the absolute evil: French-style primary-school education provided essentially by mainland teachers working in the egalitarian and assimilationist tradition."[17] The fact that French schooling could not help but mold second-class individuals who would then claim political rights, was a constant theme among French nationals living in Algeria. Whence their support for an Islamic education of the most orthodox and traditional kind, and their willingness that religious and technical schooling be maintained in Arabic.

At the same time, Catholic missionaries feared that public education carried out in the spirit of Jules Ferry would rivalize with their own schools. Finally, Muslims saw in French-style public education "a sort of trap designed to rob them of their nationality and religion."[18] The application of the Decree of 1883, which extended new French school legislation to Algeria, was so postponed in the colony that, by 1889, the number of Muslims enrolled in school was still not higher than it had been in 1870. In 1890, a new school program asserted that "France by no means intends to turn Arabs into resigned subjects, but rather into citizens who accept its authority"—a generous statement which nevertheless graphically illustrates the contradiction of French policy: education ultimately led "Arabs," having become citizens, to contest, rather than "accept," the authority of the foreign country. The famous Islamist William Marçais did not hesitate to assert that "French schooling is aimed at population groups that are politically French but in fact foreign. Its purpose is to educate subjects, not citizens."[19]

Retrospectively, it seems obvious that a policy aimed at transforming "natives" into French men and women could not, at the same time, deny them citizenship rights. However, most contemporaries did not perceive this as a contradiction. A few voices emphasized the fact that France was betraying human-rights imperatives by imposing its domination over other peoples. In the columns of *L'Intransigeant*, Henri Rochefort regularly wrote satire about this theme, but such criticism emanated exclusively from left-wing, and extreme left-wing, groups on the political fringe.[20] Otherwise, nonradical advocates and adversaries of colonization attempted to discern, through discussion, the genuine interests of France. Should French grandeur be restored by conquering vast overseas territories or should all the energies of the nation be mustered in preparation for the vengeance that would one day be taken out on Germany? Would colonial expansion encourage the industrial development of the country by ensuring the control of natural resources and of the outlets for its production, or would it instead slow down industrial development and become a financial burden on the national community? The argument and firm belief, shared at the time by all French people, that French civilization reflected universal civilization and that "natives" were not yet worthy of participating in it, sufficed to eliminate any discussion about the right of France to impose its domination over other peoples.

However, the dynamics of democracy were at work. Despite local opposition, French-style public schooling educated a generation of Muslims, who especially consisted of future schoolteachers thus inculcated with republican values. It was among these schoolteachers that the first generation of nationalist thinkers and militants were recruited; they would demand that the principles which were emphasized by the French school system (and which they had internalized) be applied to the colonized natives. At first, they asked for political equality and citizenship within the French system. When this demand was rejected by colonial authorities, nationalist militants from the next generation (who had also received a French-style education) put forth a claim to national independence. In their writings and speeches, one finds the same themes which Eastern European nationalists developed during the nineteenth century and which Élie Kedourie has also pinpointed in the writings of nationalist thinkers from Asia and Africa: on the one hand, the search for authenticity, the exaltation of a common past, the elaboration of a creation myth underlying the origins of the country; on the other hand, a demand for independence in the name of equality and the right of peoples to self-determination.[21] As in other colonized countries, Algerian intellectuals educated in the schools of the Republic played an essential role by appealing to ethnic sentiments that would build up a collective identity and, at the same time, by throwing back in the face of colonists the same values which colonists supported in mainland France yet which they had never applied, and did not intend to apply, to the "native" peoples of the colonies.[22]

The illegitimacy of the colonial situation thus depends not only on the *fact* that European colonial empires were disappearing, but also on the internalization of the universal vocation of citizenship and on the intolerable existence of a dual political status within the same society. It was in the name of equal political rights for both colonists and colonized peoples that independence struggles were waged everywhere. As early as 1821, when José de San Martín proclaimed the independence of Peru against Spanish domination, he declared that the name "Indians" or "Natives" would no longer be given to original peoples of the area; they were the children and citizens of Peru, and they would be called "Peruvians."[23] Regardless of what the future held in store, San Martín could not proclaim the independence of the Peruvian nation without asserting at the same time the universal vocation of citizenship, even with respect to the native, original peoples of the country. Today, the contradictions and illegitimate aspects of a political system based on an inequality of juridical and political statuses seem so logically and morally obvious to us that analyzing the arguments formerly put forward to justify them leads us into a strange and remote world.[24] Beginning with the end of the Second World War—which enables us to date the moment when democratic ideals were internalized—the claim that equal citizenship should be given to all, that is to both colonists and colonized natives, was judged to be legitimate, at least by a part of the mainland public opinion. Until then, as has been noted above, opponents of the colonial project had remained on the fringes.

The gradual extension of the citizen body has always been linked to the power relations existing among the diverse social groups. It has always run up against the interests of the most powerful citizens, and against the ethnico-religious emotions of individuals. American historians and sociologists show how, in the United States, WASPs managed to exclude from voting rights autochthonous population groups as well as those perceived, not as American citizens, but rather as descendants of African slaves: the American political project concerned immigrants. After the Civil War, and for generations, Whites especially could not admit that the dignity of Black people was equal to theirs; they could not accept the fact that Black people had been granted, and possessed, citizen rights. Whites subsequently carried on illegal practices, the condemnation of which was always ambiguous or belated because judges, even at the Supreme Court level, shared the same sentiments and kept legitimizing a policy of de facto exclusion. The citizenship principle is not susceptible of transcending each and every particularism that exists in any given historical and social condition. Yet it is important to note that Afro-Americans, after a century of fruitless political struggles, finally managed to exercise their rights by appealing to the meaning of citizenship. Because of their struggle, a new policy began attempting, in the 1960s, to compensate for the fate which, up to then, had been theirs. This policy allowed some Blacks to integrate into the middle class and most Blacks to exercise their political rights. Many large American cities today have an Afro-American mayor. Although proclaiming juridical and political equality is insufficient for eliminating racist practices and modes of racist thinking, an assertion of citizenship does not long remain ineffectual in democracies.[25]

The Limits of Reason and Mental Sanity

Some of the limits established by the French revolutionaries still seem *legitimate* to us, notably whenever we share the same conception of full "autonomy" or full "sanity" (in French, "raison," that is the "powers of reason"); in other words, whenever there is an absence, perhaps temporary, of these qualities in an individual. Individuals provided with a judiciary counselor (adults with a legal guardian) cannot be elected and cannot be city-council members. Article L.5 of the Electoral Code stipulates that certain sentenced persons, or certain persons forbidden to enjoy free use of their possessions and even of their own person (such as adults under police supervision), cannot sign up to vote. Yet new measures concerning imprisonment, adopted in 2001, recall that all convicts whose sentence does not include losing their civic rights can indeed exercise their citizen rights.[26] Similarly, insane people who have been declared "unfit civilians" are not allowed to vote or be elected. According to Article 18 of the Decree of 2 February 1852, psychiatric-hospital patients are not allowed to vote. However, modern criticism of this topic has now made the border between sanity and insanity seem less clear. As in the other cases evoked above, one senses a growing aspiration to extend voting rights. In Canada, for instance, fifty-thousand psychiatric-hospital patients were able to vote in the 1988 legislative elections, after a Federal Court decision declared it unconstitutional to deprive them of their right to vote.[27]

Today, a similar lack of autonomy still justifies the absence of political rights for children. Yet in this case as well, one again perceives the same impatience with respect to limits that so characterizes *homo democraticus*, and, more generally, the predicament of facing up to an inequality resulting from an age difference: how can one treat equally a person who temporarily possesses neither economic autonomy nor the full mastery of his or her reason? The 1989 International Convention on the Rights of the Child proclaimed the rights of children to be fed, well treated, and educated, all of which are self-evident rights in our societies, but it also granted them rights to freedom of expression (Article 13), association and peaceful assembly (Article 15), and access to information (Article 17). These are specifically political rights.[28] Although Article 12 specifies that these rights should be granted to a child "capable of forming his or her views" and in regard to "any matter affecting the child," the majority of children's rights advocates, when interpreting the Convention, pass over these restrictions. In "liberating" children from parental authority (as women were liberated from the authority of fathers and husbands), by considering them to have attained the maturity of an adult and by proclaiming that they should therefore possess all rights corresponding to this state, the Convention validated a conception according to which children, like adults, should possess genuine political rights. "Children are perceived as being persons. In this sense, the Convention turns to the twenty-first century. One moves away from the idea that children are fragile human beings who need to be protected from others, and acknowledges a sort of citizenship for them. People say: 'Children need to be prepared for becoming citizens.' The Convention says: 'No. Children are citizens.'"[29] This explains why it has been proposed to extend the 1974 voting-rights reform and grant voting rights to sixteen-year-olds, perhaps even to younger individuals. More generally, the idea is spreading that children should be fully acknowledged as genuine citizens, in all dimensions of their existence, even if they do not possess the right to vote. In the name of pre-birth citizen rights, some people defend embryo rights and thus oppose abortion.[30]

Claiming democratic rights is an endless process. The de facto barriers encountered induce one of the constitutive tensions of democratic society. This, moreover, explains why several recent critical studies have primarily focused on the limits—with respect to race, national or ethnic origin, or gender—that were established for citizenship in the past, as well as, for some limits, in the present.[31]

The Nation-State and the "New Citizenship"

Today, the impatience we have been discussing is primarily aimed at the national and political limits of citizenship. Up to now, societies based on citizenship have always been national societies, thus particular by definition. They have tried to conjugate the universal vocation of citizenship and the finitude of national societies. It is the form taken on by this union between the universal and the particular that is now contested, at once in public debates, academic studies, and theoretical treatises in political science.

The debate is all the more heated in that two down-to-earth political problems are at stake. How should nationality law evolve, and what policy should be adopted as regards the numerous permanently settled residents who are not citizens? Should laws be modified so as to extend nationality more widely to legally settled foreign residents or, instead, should alien residents be given specific political rights on a local or national level, yet not nationality?[32] By debating both nationality law, which has indeed been modified during the past decade in most European countries,[33] and the political rights of alien residents, one also implicitly or explicitly questions the meanings of citizenship and nation, their evolution, and the social philosophy underlying this evolution. By separating citizenship and nationality, does one not take the ultimate step in a democratic process aiming at ensuring full autonomy to individuals regardless of their belonging to a specific national society?

National Integration and Citizenship

The French revolutionaries had proclaimed that participating in the values and acts of the Revolution provided sufficient proof of citizenship. They therefore granted French citizenship to heroic foreigners such as the American Thomas Paine. Until the First World War, in twenty-two American states, aliens could vote in local, state, and federal elections, and this was a period of time when neither Blacks nor American women had the right to vote. Yet nationalism, as well as the growing "nationalization" of societies throughout the nineteenth century, gradually created a juridical distinction between nationals, to whom citizen rights were granted—in particular the right to vote and to be elected—and alien residents, who did not possess such rights.[34] Nationality and citizenship thereafter tended to become one, all the more so in that the number of nationals not possessing citizenship rights became fewer and fewer as the different categories of passive citizens—going back to 1791—were gradually included in the body politic. Only colonial societies represented an exception to this process whereby nationality and citizenship merged.

Today, with the objective weakening of nation-states and of the links—as regards law and identity—between individuals and their nation, this evolution is called into question. With the delegitimatization of national ideals and the creation of political entities surpassing a national framework (such as the European Community), the refusal to grant citizenship rights to non-nationals appears more and more illegitimate. Some thinkers have begun reflecting on the elaboration of new rights that would emanate from European Community institutions.[35] Others have, instead, examined the consequences potentially arising from the presence of population groups, of foreign origin, who have settled in Europe and who desire to be "citizens in a different way." The two approaches come together in proposing a new conception of citizenship, which is taking shape at the European level.

The national limits of citizenship are in the process of shifting from a legitimate, to an illegitimate, status. One now thinks of national citizenship as an exclusion principle for non-nationals, instead of considering it as a dialectic between exclusion and inclusion. It is true that any organization, whether political or not, by definition includes some people and excludes others. A democratic State cannot escape from this rule, because it is founded on the principle whereby citizen-nationals are included in, and non-nationals excluded from, the practices of political citizenship. The State includes the former by ensuring their equal participation, through citizenship, in political life; it excludes the latter from the rights that are directly linked to citizenship, because non-nationals already possess citizenship in another society. According to Article 15 of the 1948 Universal Declaration of Human Rights, everyone has the right to a nationality and to the corresponding civic rights. What characterizes modern citizenship, with respect to other political organizations based on religious, dynastic, or ethnic principles, is its potential openness, which is linked to its abstract nature.[36]

However, this potential openness is increasingly judged to be insufficient, insofar as it is based on nationality. It no longer suffices that a democratic society is, by definition, more open to foreigners than are other forms of political organization; and that one may acquire, say, French, Swiss, or German nationality through naturalization, or through rights deriving from birth or schooling in the adopted country. It no longer suffices to adopt the traditional, or "classic," solution established in all countries with a large immigrant population, such as France in the nineteenth and twentieth centuries: that is, a solution based on a strict distinction between citizen-nationals and aliens, with access to nationality facilitated for children (of immigrant parents) who are born and schooled within the borders of the national territory. It no longer suffices that a national democratic State provides for a foreigner's being able to benefit from the right to enter the political community, in exchange for his respecting a certain number of conditions established by nationality law. Today, it is considered important that a "new" kind of citizenship be fully

acknowledged, indeed the currently developing notion of a citizenship based on individual rights and no longer on a bond with the
national collectivity.[37]

Criticism leveled at the traditional, obligatory link between nationality and citizenship merges with the reflections of those who
intend to elaborate what, today, could be the contents of a "new
citizenship." Some critics impugn traditional citizenship because
it ignores the new conditions of collective life; other critics impugn it because it is linked to the nation and nationality. The "new
citizenship" would thus at once surpass a national framework and
renew the contents of the "old citizenship"; it would become social and economic, instead of political. It would henceforth be tied
to the individual and not to the relationship between an individual
and a State. These two critical currents of thought can be distinguished analytically, even if a given author combines them in his or
her own personal ways and even if both lines of argument often
tend to coincide.

The Limits of Politics

Advocates of a social and economic citizenship point out that
foreigners who have legally settled in European democracies, and
who have not become citizens of their adopted country, nonetheless
possess the civil, social, and economic rights of the country at hand.[38]
In their view, civil, social, and economic rights no longer merely
define the conditions underlying the exercise of political citizenship; such rights themselves have become the true political rights.
"Classical" political citizenship is accordingly disparaged, for the
genuine citizen rights today are considered to be social and economic rights. Consequently, argue these advocates, law should be
made congruent with facts, and citizenship—which should hereaf-
ter become a human right belonging to each individual—should be
granted with respect only to an individual's place of residency and
to his or her de facto participation in the adopted society.

According to these theorists, the distinction between citizens and
non-citizens is becoming less and less clear. Surely, only the citizens
of democratic nations fully benefit from the entire gamut of political
rights, including especially the right to vote in national elections and
to be elected to any position of authority associated with the sovereignty of the nation-state. Yet although legally settled aliens are not
citizens and thus do not enjoy political rights in this strict sense of

the term, they nonetheless possess—at least in European nations, and in accordance with legislation gradually elaborated ever since the end of the Second World War—the same civil, social, and economic rights as nationals. They enjoy individual freedoms and civil rights. They have the rights to come and go as they please, to marry, to be presumed innocent until they are proven guilty (if they are arrested by the police and brought to court), to be defended by a lawyer, and so on. Social and economic rights can be added to these civil rights. Although the first social protection measures were reserved for nationals, the juridical status of foreigners in Europe has gradually been assimilated, ever since the end of the Second World War, to that of nationals, as far as salaries, labor law, retirement rights, unemployment benefit rights, and social protection benefits are concerned. All European countries give aliens the right to vote in workplace-related committees and labor unions. They have the right to meet and form associations. Even when foreigners are illegally present or settled, they have the right to receive medical care and their children have the right to attend school. All the national legislation devoted to the social rights of aliens was sanctioned by European legislation during the 1960s. Indeed, European institutions have developed social law: they define the status of "salaried employee" and the salaried employee's corresponding rights; they guarantee the freedom to work, the civil and social rights of foreigners, and gender equality. They deal with problems of poverty, employment, education, as well as rural and urban renewal. The European Court of Human Rights would condemn, by appealing to the European Convention on Human Rights, any State whose practices did not conform to the principle that civil, social, and economic rights should be equal for everyone, that is both nationals and legally settled aliens.

In societies dominated by economic activity, political citizenship has thus become depreciated or "devalued," to use a term frequently employed by new-citizenship theorists, who indeed favorably view this evolution. According to them, being a citizen has become less significant than having a regular job and thus possessing all the corresponding rights. During the 1980s, it was often said that "it is better to have a job as a foreigner in Germany than to be an unemployed citizen in France." As societies become less political, legally settled foreigners possess the essential means for participating in collective life. They are entitled to the same rights as citizens, with the unique exception of the right to vote in national elections—yet national elections now play a secondary role, since the power of the national State, essentially devoted to assisting the production, then the redistribution, of wealth, has diminished. Moreover, national citizenship has become increasingly less significant because the essential role of the national State is no longer military and political. Its essential action is devoted to regulating the production and redistribution of collective goods by organizing the job market, the educational system, and social-protection services, and by sharing them out among citizens and foreigners.

The construction of a united Europe and the rights granted to foreigners who are citizens of European Union countries contribute to this evolution. European Community citizens possess not only the same civil, social, and economic rights as nationals, as do all legally settled aliens, but also a certain number of political rights related to European citizenship, in particular the right to vote in local elections. The momentum gathering towards granting political rights to aliens is becoming irresistible. At present, only Sweden, Denmark, Norway, Belgium, and two Swiss cantons give non-European-Union aliens the right to vote, and at that only in local elections. No European country gives foreigners the right to vote in national elections— even foreigners who are citizens of the European Union. Yet this resistance is not destined to last, given the transformation of the contents of citizenship. Elizabeth Meehan shows that a new conception of citizenship is in the process of being elaborated; it is based no longer on the juridical and political bond of individuals to a State, in the traditional sense of the term, but rather on a set of values and social practices developed and guaranteed by the European Community institutions, and in particular by the legal rulings of the European Court of Human Rights.

Meehan argues that European institutions are in the process of elaborating a new citizenship which not only calls into question the historical bond between a nation-state and citizenship, but also and especially creates a new form of citizenship. Considering social and economic rights to be simply conditions underlying the exercise of political citizenship is to continue to think in terms of classical citizenship. In reality, social and economic rights underlie the "new citizenship" insofar as they also have consequences on the political status of individuals. The rights grant a specifically political status to European citizens as well as to foreigners who are legally settled in Europe: rights, practices, and loyalties are now expressed on the level of a political united Europe. European Community law is thus in the process of giving birth to a specific citizenship based on a conception of solidarity and social justice that is common to all Europeans. Surely the national State remains the only authority that can give an individual, through the intermediary of nationality law, the status of European citizen; but such a citizen can plead before the European Court of Human Rights, even against his own national State. On several occasions, national States have been condemned by the Court in the name of the rights of European citizens and foreigners. The European Convention on Human Rights now prevails over national law.

Multiple identities are thereby being forged, as well as diverse rights and duties which are expressed through increasingly numerous institutions: a new configuration is being elaborated in which regional, national, and European governmental bodies, as well as transnational interest groups, come together in complex ways. The new citizenship emerging from these measures, institutions, and actions is no longer national or cosmopolitan, but rather multiple. Already, both national and European citizenships exist. According to Meehan, European citizenship is the product of the very history of the construction of a united Europe. Establishing economic unity has logically led to political unity: lower customs levies necessarily induced a common market, then a common currency, a common economic policy and, finally, a common political authority. Transnational economic interest groups have formed, and they act in the same direction. The Maastricht Treaty represents a new phase, inasmuch as it grants local political rights to all Europeans, establishes the principle of a uniform method of electoral balloting, and provides for the right to make petitions. It is no longer national States, but rather European institutions and regional powers, which deal with problems of poverty, employment, rural and urban renewal, and gender equality. In the European Parliament, a Committee of the Regions has the power to grant regions "a legitimate right to self-determination."

This is why the claim of residency—thus to the entire set of civil, social, and economic rights related to an individual's legal residence—put forth by all those who actually reside in a national territory appears more and more legitimate. Germans did not send back foreign *Gastarbeiter* ("guest workers") when the economic crisis made their presence unnecessary, although signed job contracts authorized this: everyone admitted that *Gastarbeiter* belonged, de facto, to German society.[39] Their presence and their work had given them the right to remain in Germany. Political refugees who no longer have a State to protect them nonetheless retain their human rights. The increasing number of people with dual nationalities represents another sign of the new citizenship mobility. Turkish *Gastarbeiter* who have settled in Germany have the same rights in Germany as in France, because their rights are guaranteed by European legislation and no longer merely by national legislation.[40] They can exercise their political rights in either country. More generally, those who were once called "guest workers," in English and German, in fact no longer exist. Immigrants are no longer mere "workers" who are temporarily present in order to fulfill a well-defined economic role before returning to their home country; instead, they are individuals entitled to civil and social rights: the right to residency; civil, social, and economic rights; the right to political activity through the creation of associations and interest groups; the right to contribute to the institutions of social and economic democracy by participating in labor-union activities and in workplace-related committees. The legalization of clandestine alien immigrants who are present in a national territory, a process regularly carried out by all European governments, is another indicator of the weakening of national citizenship. Hollifield remarks that foreigners in France have not suffered more from the economic crisis than nationals.[41] As for those "without legal papers," called "les sans-papiers" in French, did they not make a genuine political struggle in the public sphere in the name of their lack of rights?

A significant example of the new forms taken on by modern citizenship is considered, by some observers, to lie in the relations that immigrants who have settled in European countries since the end of the Second World War maintain with the citizenship of their adopted society. These former "guest workers" who have permanently settled in Western European countries and who, without being citizens in the same juridical sense as nationals, possess the entire set of civil, social, and economic rights established by European legislation, have not—and do not wish to—become national citizens. Moreover, it is with seeming reluctance that even their children adopt the nationality of the country of their birth—a nationality to which they are legally entitled because they have been born there. It is thought that such individuals embody a new way of being citizens in the adopted society, all the while representing a new status: that of "denizens," as Tomas Hammar has phrased it.[42]

These analyses are closely linked to political demands. The new-citizenship theorists take note of an evolution that they judge to be positive and recommend adopting legislation that would definitively establish these changes. Indeed, giving foreigners the right to residency, and guaranteeing their exercise of civil, social, and economic rights, without granting at the same time the rights to vote and to participate in political life (in the strict sense of the term), imply giving birth to second-class citizens who cannot, as others can, defend their rights and interests. According to this view, alien immigrants originating from outside the European Community represent a new version of the "passive" citizens of 1791.[43] Principles of equality and freedom should apply to all, including aliens: what can justify their exclusion from full citizenship, and the discrimination of which they are thus victims? Extending citizenship—thus voting rights—to aliens would moreover, according to this argument, simply set forward the history of suffrage law and accomplish the final phase of the potentially universal vocation of modern citizenship.

National Limits

The nationality limit has become illegitimate. This is why the most progressive theorists contend that nationality should be dissociated from the exercise of citizenship: equating nationality and citizenship characterizes the age of nation-states. In their view, de facto participation in a society should suffice to give one the right to citizenship. According to this argument, from the very moment that individuals are present, they are integrated: what can justify demanding more of them than that which permits them to live in a given society? It follows that is unworthy of a genuine democracy to lay down requirements for obtaining citizenship, with respect to individuals who desire to exercise it. An individual who is born in, or who emigrates at an early age to, a given society should automatically have the right to become a citizen, as well as those who have remained (even illegally) for more than five years in the country: they have been de facto participants in society. Residency alone should give one the right to citizenship, to the exclusion of all other requirements of compliance or willingness. Joseph Carens remarks: "I want to propose as a principle that people have a moral right to be citizens of any society of which they are members."[44] The naturalization candidate's only obligation should be to prove that he has been present in a national territory, even irregularly, for five years.[45] It follows, from this standpoint, that all prohibitions concerning dual, or multiple, nationalities should be suppressed. Acquiring a nationality should be a tool of integration, not its validation. "Foreigners have gradually acquired, not without struggles, an almost complete juridical equality in the fields of civil and social rights. In the process, civic rights stand out as the final kind of discrimination still separating French nationals from immigrants. Generally equal in all other ways, immigrants remain unequal in only one respect: citizenship, around which nationality erects a barrier whose existence has become problematic for the very reason that it constitutes an obstacle to the equality and freedom of those living in the national territory (. . .). This is why it is now acceptable to substitute residency for nationality as the basis of citizenship."[46] For such theorists, any condition laid down for obtaining a nationality, especially as regards cultural integration or the willingness to participate in a historico-political collectivity, is unjustified.

The extreme version of this conception is formulated by writers who contend that the very word "citizen," with its specific political connotations, is no longer meaningful and that the genuine social protagonist is the "taxpayer" (in French, "contribuable") or "user" ("usager"). According to this viewpoint, aliens have the right to acquire a nationality because they pay taxes. "The day could thus come when propositions such as a 'resident right,' based on the fact of living and working in society, gradually replace the notion of citizenship considered as a corpus of rights and duties linked to a territory and a State (. . .). Hence the suggestion to define the 'new citizenship' as the gradual replacement of the vague concept of citizen by the more precise notion of 'taxpayer' and, even better, 'user' (. . .). Does not the presence of a large population consisting of immigrants and young people stemming from immigration lead to the creation of a new conception of citizenship, pertaining to the existence of minority ethnic communities settled in a society in the process of becoming pluralist? This would be a non-territorial citizenship, granted to residents and not just to nationals, or based on the notion of acquired rights or vested interests. In other words, a resident right replacing the dated conception of citizenship and removing the sacred aura of 'nationality.' Thus, some people suggest replacing the vague concept of 'citizen' by the more precise notion of a 'user' who is responsible and who knows how to assert his or her rights."[47]

Political philosophers working on the idea of a social and economic citizenship thus concur with the theorists of European citizenship (as evoked above), who analyze and advocate a European citizenship based on participation in social and economic life and on a common conception of solidarity and social justice. According to these theorists, the specifically political nature of citizenship was linked to the age of nationalism and to the building of nation-states. However, even as during the nineteenth century the new citizens of national States were liberated from shackles inherited from feudal societies that had become obsolete, the construction of a united Europe is in the process of liberating economic "actors" from restrictions imposed by borders and by legislation inherited from the age of nations and nationalism.[48] National citizenship is no longer alone in giving a legal status and rights; European institutions are in the process of constructing a new citizenship that calls into question the historical link between citizenship and nation-state.

Yasemin Soysal is representative of radical thinking about the broken link between citizenship and nation-state.[49] According to her, the case of "denizens" (to use the term popularized by Hammar), whose status lies between those of nationals and foreigners, is merely a special case of a new conception of citizenship. She contends that this new conception is now based on the universal rights of individuals, or human rights, and is independent of an individual being registered in any territory, as well as independent of his or her belonging to, or participating in, a particular nation-state. This citizenship, which she calls "post-national," bases its legitimacy on the universal (thus transnational) ideology of human rights. It is established by international agreements which guarantee human rights, without individuals having to be linked to a particular nation-state. Moreover, today the role of national States is reduced to applying transnational decisions. National public policies no longer aim to transform immigrants, and their children, into citizens, but rather to favor their integration into the institutions of the Social Intervention State. This has led to the existence of "identity politics," which involve invoking human rights in order to demand, in European Community institutions, the creation and application of measures favoring manifestations of a particular identity, even at the expense of the rights and interests of national States. According to this view, we are heading toward a situation in which each person will have the right and the duty to participate in the political life of the nation-state (or "polity") in which he or she lives, regardless of his or her historical and cultural links (in other words, "national links") with the nation-state. It follows that the very principle of nationalism is being weakened and surpassed; that is, the legitimacy of the demand to make political organization congruent with national or ethnic links; or, as Ernest Gellner puts it in *Nations and Nationalism*, "nationalism is primarily a principle, which holds that the political and the national unit should be congruent."[50] On the national organizational level, tension exists between the universal vocation of citizenship—based on human rights—and the particularity of each nation-state. Today, according to Soysal, individual rights are being reinforced, at the expense of the interests of national States. She thus concurs with other theorists who believe that the Internet—by establishing an extension of political rights beyond all limits—at last allows direct democracy to be organized.[51]

Despite differences that should not be underestimated, the theorists of, respectively, European citizenship and social and economic citizenship both criticize political and national citizenship and both base their ideas on a conception of society conceived not as a historical and political community, but rather as a system organizing the production and redistribution of wealth in the name of common values—an organizational system complemented, or compensated for, by universal aspirations and regulations. They posit that all partners in this system are no longer united by a contract of a political nature, but rather by their participation in social and economic life. What in French republican thought, or in Anglo-Saxon *liberalism*, was a means—ensuring living conditions for citizen-individuals so that they could truly exercise their political citizen rights—tends to be transformed into ends: the legitimacy of a political society is henceforth based on the project of enabling all members to have living conditions that guarantee their dignity. In this perspective, the Providence State becomes one with the political society and ultimately defines itself without appealing to any political dimensions. The distinction, classical in Antiquity, between *ethnos*—the real, concrete society—and *polis*—the self-conscious political society—tends to fade. Between social and economic participation, linked to immediacy and locality, and the universal values pertaining to all human beings, political society no longer has a precise definition, nor limits.

Human Beings and Animal Species

This same impatience with respect to limits is revealed by the topicality and vigor of the growing transnational debate about the relations between human beings and animals.[52] The debate extends well beyond the circle of Deep Ecology theorists. Yet it is the latter who, by theorizing an extreme conception of political rights, most clearly reveal the dynamics of democracy.

They indeed plead for the granting of rights to "forests, oceans, rivers, to all 'natural' objects in the environment, even to the entire environment."[53] What is significant is the main argument formulated by one of the most widely acknowledged deep-ecology theorists: after giving citizenship rights to women, children, Blacks, Indians, prisoners, insane people, and embryos, it is necessary, Christopher D. Stone maintains—as a logical consequence of this process—to recognize "nature rights" both for animal and plant forms. A similarly inspired thinker intending to combat the exclusion suffered by animal species ("speciesism") puts it this way: "It is because we are antiracist and antisexist that we should be anti-speciesist and proclaim: 'all animals (including human beings) are equal.'"[54] In fact, in 1979, a Universal Declaration of Animal Rights was proclaimed, echoing the various Declarations of Human Rights. On an international level, militants for the political rights of animals gather under the banner of the Animal Liberation Movement and are inspired by the utilitarian philosophy of Peter Singer. He denounces a "speciesism" that would be of the same nature as racism and sexism, because it makes the limit of the right to life coincide exactly with the barrier of the human species.[55] However, according to him, if one accepts the equality principle as a solid moral foundation of our relations with other members of our own species, one must also accept the fact that it regulates our relations with other species, namely non-human animals.[56]

The international Great Ape Project has the intellectual and political ambition of including chimpanzees, gorillas, and orangutans in the political community. After the publication of Paola Cavalieri and Peter Singer's book, *The Great Ape Project*,[57] and the international coverage that it received, the contributors to a special issue of the review *Etica e animali* attempted to show that the project of including great apes in an extended community of equals, in other words a *polis*, was not only "theoretically sound," but also that it had today become "practically viable."[58] Indeed, Paola Cavalieri and Will Kymlicka contended that philosophical reflection is emerging about how moral and political equality for all may be ensured, when human beings who are increasingly different from each other are being integrated into the same society. The project of including great apes in the political community is an integral part of this indissolubly moral and political ambition. Indeed, one must never forget that "humanism has two sides: an inclusive side, which holds that all human beings have equal moral status, and an exclusive side which holds that only human beings have equal moral status."[59] According to this viewpoint, the differences separating great apes from human beings is not of a different order than those distinguishing human beings from each other. For, they ask, are not children, senile elderly people, and mentally handicapped individuals—none of whom are fully endowed with reason—inferior to monkeys in every respect? Such thinkers go on to argue that non-human animals on the one hand, and young children and mentally retarded human beings on the other, belong to the same category; that chimpanzees, dogs, pigs, and the adult members of numerous other species, greatly surpass a child with brain damage, from the viewpoint of their capacity to reasonably give meaning to life, because, even with the most intensive care, certain gravely deficient children will never be able to attain the intelligence level of a dog.[60] No solution of continuity would therefore exist between humanity and the animal kingdom. Man is above all a living creature who belongs to the whole world of living creatures.

This conception is indeed founded on the idea that there is a continuity between human beings and the animal, even the plant, world. Humans are living beings among other living beings; they are not fundamentally different from chimpanzees. Singer further contends that, among the ape population, humans are by far the most numerous[61]; following upon the rights granted to Black people, animals too should have the right to benefit from democratic rights: animals should have rights if human beings have them.[62] So it is no longer just a matter of asserting that humans have duties in regard to animals, namely those of protecting their existence and not making them unduly suffer, a proposition about which all humans—regardless of their personal philosophies—can today come to an agreement. It is no longer just a matter of claiming that animals have rights as "moral patients," even if the rights are not "identical" to the

rights enjoyed by humans.[63] What is significant is the development
of the idea that animals, like humans, are for that very reason entitled to political, and thus democratic, rights. This idea is based on
the utilitarian philosophers' position that human rights do not depend on reason and language, but rather on the capacity to suffer.
More generally, democratic rights put forward as demands are based
and legitimized by taking interests into account. It is the interest that
founds the right: great apes and even trees have interests that authorize them—or authorize those who speak in their name—to institute
legal proceedings and obtain compensation. In the name of democratic rights, the limit of humanity, defined—according to the heritage of Christianity and humanist thought—as a human being's freedom and responsibility, is now contested, if not denied.

Between Utopia and Self-Criticism

Impatience with respect to the limits defining the boundaries of
the body politic and the practices of citizenship does not only derive
from the fact that democracy has been exercised in the framework
of national historical societies marked by traditions, institutions, and
conflicts. Impatience also derives from the democratic utopia itself,
in other words the ambition to construct a political order that will
overturn the social order while asserting the civil, juridical, and political equality of all individuals—even though individuals are diverse in origins and beliefs, even though their social conditions and
their capacities are unequal. Is not, as Louis Dumont suggests, the
equality of all citizens, which is at once the principle of political
legitimacy and constitutes the passion of *homo democraticus*, contrary to the very nature of human societies, which are inevitably
hierarchical? According to Dumont, this utopian character explains
why democratic societies are fated to see phenomena develop, such
as racism, which stand in opposition to their own values; the phenomena result from a re-emergence of repressed sentiments.[64]

The principles and values to which societies based on citizenship
refer—an equality of civil, juridical, and political rights for all citizens beyond their historical diversities and social inequalities—are
of course often violated in the reality of social practices. The sociology of interethnic relations can be entirely interpreted in this sense:
it demonstrates the limits of the impact of citizenship on social practices; it unveils the ways in which a democratic society betrays the
principles from which it draws its inspiration. These lapses are not

caused by some institutional defect or by the willing malice of human beings, but rather by the utopian dimensions of citizenship (even if the utopia is creative), that is by "the very nature of this ideal, which can only serve as a regulator."[65] Given the utopian character of citizenship, social practices in societies shaped and structured by citizenship are, by nature, imperfect in regard to asserted values and unworthy of the ideal put forth as a claim. The universal vocation of citizenship—be it inscribed in the nation or in individual rights—and the affirmation of equal civil, juridical, and political rights for all individuals, necessarily engender lapses with respect to the proclaimed principles and thus justify criticism. By their very nature, modern democratic societies foster impatience and dissatisfaction, because they are necessarily unfaithful to the values that they invoke. Even as they proclaim the sovereignty of all free and equal individuals, democratic societies are imperfect and inevitably unworthy of the values that they put forth.

However, at the same time, democratic societies also accept criticism, even if often with reluctance. The acknowledgment of pluralism is institutionalized; it is admitted that no society reflects the absolute good and that, consequently, an objective should be relative and limited, with priority given to what is just over what is good—to recall Kant's conception. Democracies define themselves by the limits that they bring to politics, whenever they recognize the existence and the value of aspects of the "private" sphere. Taken as a whole, *liberal* political institutions—called "republican" political institutions by the French—organize political-institution plurality, limit each institution's power and base each institution's legitimacy on the ideas of pluralism and the separation of powers, as well as on the acknowledgment that, within society, there is a multitude of values and groupings of people. Even countries which, by tradition, are French-style in their conception of citizenship have evolved in such a way that pluralism is now inscribed in political institutions. The right to strike is guaranteed by the French constitution. More generally, the elaboration and development of social law as a whole reveals that the interests of various social groups are divergent. It is acknowledged that conflicts of interest among individuals and groups represent an unavoidable dimension of the way human beings live in society. The existence of opposition forces, such as the press, is considered to be necessary to the practice of democracy. It is asserted that it is necessary to structure and regulate conflicts, not deny or ignore them.

Advocates of democracy refuse, or should refuse, Utopias of General Reconciliation which, throughout twentieth-century history, have led to various forms of totalitarianism. In philosophical terms, they admit that the "conflict of needs and insatiable desires is inseparable from our freedom and our creativity."[66]

Democratic societies are characterized by a tension between—on the one hand—the utopia of citizenship and—on the other—the limits established for the democratic project and its univeralist ambition by the realities of historical societies as well as by those resulting from various kinds of heritage, from social representations, and from ethnico-religious feeling. However, the national State—the form that, up to now, has been taken on by democracy—is not the only cause of this tension. How can a society shaped and structured by citizenship be constituted, if there is no place—in both the abstract and real, down-to-earth senses of the term (and thus a place defined by limits)—for debates and criticism, when at the same time the impatience with respect to every limit is constitutive of the dynamics of democracy? Does not one enter here into one of the tensions constitutive of democratic society, which the post-national State, or any other form of transnational power, will experience as much as the national State?

By asserting that no society coincides with the good, and by recognizing that it is, and knows itself to be, imperfect, a society based on citizenship integrates its members in a paradoxical way. Because it is carried out in the name of the regulating idea of citizenship, self-criticism probably ends up, in the long run, being more effective at getting humans to live together than are political regimes who claim to strive for unity. This is because self-criticism acknowledges the multifarious, even contradictory, dimensions of the human condition. The republican-style "order," that is the republican organizational system (which, in French, is called the "ordre républicain"), actually refuses the mythical ideal of order and recognizes the meaningfulness of a creative disorder, which better suits the freedom of human beings. The republican order refuses the ideal of unity so as to recognize the diversity of individuals and the pluralism of their moral and historical references. At the same time, the tension between a recognition of limits and the creative utopia of citizenship which tends to push back every limit—not to mention the inevitable failures encountered by this utopia when shaping and structuring collective life—lies at the heart of the dynamics of democracy.

However, it is never a given that, under the effect of the dynamics of democracy, democratic societies remain aware of the "principial character of limits."[67] There is always a risk that limits foster dreams of organizing the good rather than guaranteeing the just, and thus of abandoning the dynamics of creative self-criticism for utopias positing absolute revolution and the forging of a new kind of human being—a tabula rasa type of utopia from which it is thought that a new order can be constructed that is based on human reason and autonomy, all the while neglecting the force of heritage and the weight of history on the life of societies.

The extension of political rights has always provoked resistance, even sometimes violent rejection. However, once obtained, the extension soon seems "natural" or "obvious." It has become self-evident. Calling rights back into question, once they have been acquired, is perceived and understood as a purely reactionary project, and thus one destined to fail: we live in societies aimed at the future. De facto limits that are maintained—such as those deriving from economic inequalities or from the nationality requirement imposed on aliens before they obtain citizen rights—are reinterpreted in terms of exclusion and appear intolerable from the standpoint of democratic values. Individuals susceptible of invoking multiple references, identites, and allegiances have become more and more numerous, not only for objective reasons—the growing mobility of population groups—but also because multiple, ambiguously mixed, references are now appraised positively. Those who, during the period when nation-states were triumphant, would have forgotten their remote origins in order to willingly adopt the surrounding society as their sole reference, today are more likely to maintain transnational references, identities, and allegiances. The term "diaspora," which once entailed suspicion, if not persecution, during the days of triumphant nation-states, has now taken on an essentially positive sense: it is in good taste to insist on the transnational bonds maintained among dispersed groups. Putting down nationality—or in certain radical ecologists' dreams, humanity—as a prerequisite of citizenship is now perceived as the sign of national—if not nationalist or "speciesist"—withdrawal, inciting the kind of debates, criticism, and self-criticism that are typical of democracy. Any condition restricting the exercise of a right seems contrary to the very vocation of democracy.

Notes

1. Dominique Colas, "La citoyenneté au risque de la nationalité," in Sadoun, 2000, vol. 2, p. 116.
2. Rosanvallon, 1992, p. 80. Just after becoming independent, the United States maintained the requirement of property for electors, which allowed the exclusion of "people in low circumstances." Cf. Wood, 1969, p. 168. The latter became members of the voting body in England only after the reform of the male vote, in 1867.
3. See chapter 5 below.
4. Rosanvallon, 1992, p. 331.
5. Rosanvallon, 1992, p. 342.
6. Tocqueville, 3, III, 5, edition of 1868, p. 285. English translation: II, p. 187.
7. See chapter 3 below.
8. Quoted by Rosanvallon, 1992, p. 132.
9. Tocqueville had already observed this in America. Cf. Tocqueville, 3, III, 12, edition of 1868, pp. 342 ff. English translation: II, pp. 222 ff.
10. Geneviève Fraisse, "Les deux gouvernements: la famille et la Cité," in Sadoun, 2000, vol. 2, p. 49.
11. Women obtained the right to go to court (as plaintiff or defendant) only in 1938; the right to vote, only in 1944. Marital tutelage for the husband existed until 1965. Parental authority replaced paternal authority in 1970. The right of a woman to exercise a profession without the authority of her husband exists since 1966; divorce by mutual consent dates to 1975; and the joint income tax declaration to 1983.
12. Fraisse, in Sadoun, 2000, vol. 2, p. 41.
13. This is the topic of feminist literature. Fundamental texts can be found in Carter *et al.*, 2000.
14. Mariani and Nicol-Drancourt, 1989.
15. Lampué-Rolland, 1940, p. 212
16. François Luchaire cited by Sylvie Guillaume, "Citoyenneté et colonisation," in Émeri-Zylberberg, 1991, p. 135.
17. Ageron, 1968, p. 97.
18. Ageron, 1968, p. 340.
19. Cited in Ageron, 1968, pp. 939-40.
20. Girardet, 1983 (1972), p. 92.
21. Kedourie, 1971.
22. The same educational effect was observed in Black Africa, even though the white population was much smaller. Despite being behind schedule, schools gradually educated the children of the agents of the white population: militiamen, postal workers, guards. They, too, were Westernized "lettrés" or educated people who believed in the myth of assimilation (integration) and claimed equality and citizenship for themselves. The French schools had taught them its value. This is why, at the beginning of the First World War, they increased their declarations of loyalty to France and participated in the fighting. When they were victims of flagrant inequalities, they appealed to the Ligue des droits de l'homme (the Human Rights League). Black Africans who had been colonized demanded independence only when a genuine citizenship policy had failed. They turned the colonists own values against them. Cf. Brunschwig, 1983. Note that Australian aborigines obtained the right to vote only in 1962 and were counted and noted as such in the national census only in 1967.
23. Anderson, 1996 (1982), p. 61.
24. A long and pertinent analysis of these arguments is found in the aforementioned article by Dominique Colas.

25. A development of these analyses can be found in Schnapper, 1998, especially pp. 472 ff.

26. The number of people deprived of civic rights because of a court sentence is approximately 500,000 in France. Cf. Jean Claude Masclet, article "électorat" in Duhamel-Meny, 1992.

27. Rosanvallon, 1992, p. 417.

28. Roussel, 2001, p. 192.

29. J.-P. Rosenscweige, in *Libération*, 21 November 1989, writing about the Convention on the Rights of the Child. Cited in Kaltenbach, 2001, p. 52. The lowering of the age of "childhood" can be observed in all fields, even as violent behavior and questioning of parental authority appear ever earlier. In divorce proceedings, a child's opinion is solicited at an ever earlier age.

30. Christine Boutin, while defending the rights that in her view should be acknowledged for children before their birth, and while advocating the prohibition of all abortions, entitled her book *L'Embryon citoyen* (The Embryo Citizen). Cf. Boutin, 2001.

31. For example, Spinner, 1994; Sadoun, 2001, vol. 2. Rogers M. Smith (1997) offers the same kind of analysis as regards American nationality legislation. Twelve years earlier, he had published a book of a very different persuasion, advocating the restriction of the simple right to nationality because of birth on national soil. Cf. Schuck-Smith, 1985.

32. According to the Maastricht Treaty, community residents in European Union countries possess the right to vote in local elections where they reside and in European elections. Before the Treaty, communal consulting councils were created for foreigners in Belgium (in 1972), as well as in Germany and the Netherlands (1975), and the right to vote in local elections was granted to foreigners in Ireland (in 1963), in Sweden (1976), in the Netherlands (1985), in Denmark (1981), in Norway (in 1982), as well as in Switzerland, in the cantons of Neufchâtel (in 1948) and the Jura (1879). Norway granted the right to vote to all Nordic citizens in 1978 and Finland in 1981. In general, voter turnout by foreigners has been inferior to that of nationals and it is regularly in decline. Cf. Wenden, 1997.

33. This was, for example, the case in Great Britain, Sweden, Belgium, the Netherlands, and France.

34. The nationalization of European societies has been studied by Gérard Noiriel; see especially Noiriel, 1991.

35. For a good example of this argument, one can consult Meehan, 1993 a and b.

36. Schnapper, 1998, pp. 446 ff.

37. Dominique Colas attributes to their colonial past the reticence of the French to grant political rights to foreigners, and points to a "homology of attitudes as regards yesterday's natives and today's foreigners" (in Sadoun, 2000, vol. 2, p. 126). This appears correct. This does not mean that everyone's situation is the same. Those who were colonized in the past found themselves governed by an outside authority; they were French subjects without possessing citizen rights. Foreigners came freely and they possess the citizenship of another country (except those benefiting from a right of asylum).

38. One can find, for example, a good expression of their arguments in the contributions gathered in Brubaker, 1989.

39. This argument is invoked especially by W. R. Brubaker, in Brubaker, 1989, p. 19.

40. Soysal, 1994, p. 141.

41. Cited by Soysal, 1994, p. 33.

42. Hammar, 1985 and "State, Nation, and Dual Citizenship," in Brubaker, 1989, pp. 81-95.

43.   Pasquale Pasquino, article "Sieyès" in Perrineau-Reynié, 2001.
44.   Joseph Carens, "Membership and Morality: Admission to Citizenship in Liberal Democratic States," in Brubaker, 1989, p. 32.
45.   In the Netherlands, ever since 1985, the right to participate in local political life is based on the notion of "country of residence," not on "country of birth." Cf. Jan Rath, in Le Cour Grandmaison-Withol de Wenden, 1993, p. 102.
46.   Olivier Le Cour Grandmaison, "Immigration, politique et citoyenneté: sur quelques arguments, in Le Cour Grandmaison-Withol de Wenden, 1993, p. 102.
47.   Wenden, 1987, pp. 71-3.
48.   Dahrendorf, cited by Meehan, 1993a, p. 179.
49.   Soysal, 1994.
50.   Gellner, 1983, p. 1.
51.   See chapter 5 below.
52.   In France, Goffi (1994) and Fontenay (1998) need to be cited, not to mention all the debates that occurred when entire herds of cattle were burned in enormous bonfires in order to eradicate the mad cow disease. The importance of the economy of the pet industry, and the specialized press, are both well known.
53.   Ferry, 1992, p. 22. For the rights of nature and the environment, see also Turner, 1986.
54.   Cited in Ferry, 1992, p. 90.
55.   Singer, 1997 (1993), p. 53.
56.   Singer, 1997 (1993), p. 63.
57.   Cavalieri-Singer, 1993.
58.   Cavalieri-Kymlicka, 1996/8, p. 5.
59.   *Ibid.*, p. 11.
60.   Singer, 1997 (1993), p. 49.
61.   *Ibid.*, p. 34.
62.   *Ibid.*, p. 80.
63.   This is the position that Élisabeth de Fontenay clearly expresses in Fontenay, 2000. With regard to this topic, she resumes the thinking of Joel Feinberg, who argues for the extension of claim-rights to animals, but not freedom-rights, which belong to humans alone.
64.   I discussed these conceptions especially in Schnapper, 1998, pp. 422-6.
65.   Roy, 2000, p. 368.
66.   Roy, 2000, p. 368.
67.   Roy, 2000, p. 408.

3

The Aspiration to Autonomy

If political limits or barriers make democratic people impatient, what then can be said about their material living conditions? As has been shown, the link between the citizenship of an individual and his economic conditions characterizes modern citizenship. Economic autonomy is the condition underlying the political autonomy of citizen-individuals, which in turn founds the legitimacy of providential intervention. The sovereign citizen has the right to lead a "normal" existence, according to society's notions of normality; at the same time, the efficiency of economic production has increased collective wealth: in the name of democratic values, economic misery and ignorance are considered intolerable. "The State almost exclusively undertakes to supply bread to the hungry, assistance and shelter to the sick, work to the idle, and to act as the sole reliever of all kinds of misery. Education, as well as charity, has become in most countries at the present day a national concern. The State receives, and often takes, the child from the arms of the mother to hand it over to official agents. . ."[1] The Providence State takes it upon itself to alleviate "all kinds of misery," to provide "education" and "charity." Human beings are not only producers but also citizens. "Any human being who is unable to work because of his age, his physical or mental state, or his economic situation, has the right to obtain suitable living conditions from the collectivity. The nation proclaims the solidarity and the equality of all French people when faced with costs and responsibilities resulting from national calamities."[2] The institutions of the Providence State are in keeping with the logic of democratic inclusion and the social bond.

The Welfare State has ensured the autonomy of the individual with respect to his family and the economic market; it has correspondingly increased his dependence on the State.[3] An individual's retirement benefits do not depend on those of his spouse or on his family's income, but rather on the rights that he has personally acquired through his own work or handicap. Social affairs specialists vigorously criticize French legislation measures that have remained favorable to the family, and their recurrent criticism reveals the individualistic logic of providential society. One can concur with Gosta Esping-Andersen when he argues that the Providence State constitutes the most powerful "societal mechanism" for understanding modern society and for predicting its evolution in the future, because it reveals the characteristics of employment, social conflicts, and political forms adopted. In fact, the Providence State has contributed to the transformation of all social bonds.

Of the impact of the Intervention State on democratic society, I will retain here two crucial dimensions: the birth of *providential society* and the *trivialization of social relationships*. Both are linked to the aspiration to individual autonomy and to the search for a real equality of all citizen-individuals, whatever differences may exist among them in terms of competence, social condition, or age.

Providential Society

The Social State has contributed to the development of new kinds of jobs, to the transformation of the ways in which traditional trades and professions are exercised and to the reorganization of hierarchies and social inequalities. Professional identities, the social-status hierarchy, and the ways of experiencing diverse social conditions have been modified. Having become one of the essential sources of the social fabric, the Intervention State has generated a social world that can be called "social-democratic." If governments have trouble reforming such a world, this is because they are faced with reforming the national society that the Intervention State has created.

The "Embourgeoisement" or "Gentrification" of Salaried Employees, and the Limits Thereof

The Providence State has affected all professions by extending the salaried-employee class and the rights associated with it. Ever since the stabilization of the salaried-employee society, social protection has been linked to employment. It is through the intermediary of employment—present, past, or future—that individuals have also obtained the greatest protection. We have seen that a salary has become something very different from a simple remuneration for work performed; it has given birth to a series of obligations and rights as well as founded a genuine social status. It is in this sense that all jobs, trades, and professions, even those most directly linked to production, have been modified by the Intervention State. One can speak of an "embourgeoisement," or "gentrification," which is linked to the salaried-employee society; in other words, the tendency of salaried employees to rise into the middle class.[4]

This gentrification is relative and does not exclude inequalities. However, it has integrated all salaried employees into a unique system implying equal social rights. It has provided them with what were long the typical features of "bourgeois" security: the rights to retirement, leisure, medical care for oneself and one's family; to financial transfers compensating for family expenditures or for income loss resulting from illness or unemployment. The political rights born of social protection have guaranteed all salaried employees the equivalent of a capital or a "transfer property," as Abram De Swaan has called it. These political rights have provided salaried employees with what capital gave the bourgeoisie in the nineteenth century: the possibility of not being directly vulnerable to the ups and downs of a present job, and being able to plan out a life's project. The salaried employee has become entitled to a *"rente"*—that is, a pension or an annuity of sorts—from the State. In fact, the Minister of Labor used this same argument when speaking to the Consultative Assembly of 5 July 1945: "The Social Security system is the guarantee given to each and everyone that, in all circumstances, they will possess the means necessary for ensuring their subsistence and that of their families, in decent conditions. Justified by an elementary concern for social justice, this system responds to the preoccupation that workers should not suffer from the uncertainties of tomorrow, uncertainties which create in them a feeling of inferiority and which form the real and deep basis of the class distinction between those who possess, and who can thereby be confident about themselves and their future, and workers who are ever burdened by the threat of misery."[5] Inequalities subsist, but they can henceforth be analyzed in terms of a continuum. This is how Robert Castel's so-called "neo-bourgeoisie without capital" was born.

Moreover, the economic crisis of the 1980-1990 period reinforced the continuum formed by all salaried employees holding down a job or possessing a status linked to employment (retired people, for instance). The crisis set apart salaried employees (in other words 88 percent of the active working population) who were integrated into a unique social protection system (even if it remained inegalitarian) from those who had temporarily or definitely left it, or who had never entered it, and thus who became marginals—the "excluded."[6] The gentrification of salaried employees has been accompanied by the marginalization, or exclusion, of people whose competence does not respond sufficiently well to the demands of production. This has created new forms of inequality.

However, this kind of gentrification does not exclude precariousness for some salaried employees who have a job. The overall amelioration of the material situation of all salaried employees has limits which sociologists have analyzed and which I will recall here briefly.[7] The protection provided by the Providence State has not compensated for the effects wrought by the individualization of tasks and economic-market constraints. The intense, relentless flow of work, as well as the necessity of adapting to market conditions, have increased the number of economic sectors in which both workers and managers, obliged to accomplish performances defined by others and submitted to heavy demands as regards the pace of their working days, experience daily stress and express their dissatisfaction with their jobs. Even those who work in the most modern sectors do not all escape from this discontent. Computer technology, for instance, has created its own proletariat made up of people who are condemned to perform repetitive tasks involving no inspiration, creativity, or ambition. Although physical force is generally less called upon than before, the human relationships that become primordial at work can be very strenuous psychologically—all the more so in that individuals must internalize business-firm or corporate goals and can no longer simply daydream while they are performing physical work. Books about work problems and about moral harassment in offices and factories would not be so successful if they did not relate situations experienced by their readers.

In the case of workers, the constraints of economic organization reinforce the consequences of the collapse of the Communist dream. Surveys conducted in the Peugeot factories in Sochaux-Montbéliard revealed the overall weakening of the population group that most resembled the definition of a "social class" united by commonly experienced living conditions and by an ideology giving its members a strong consciousness of their values and collective will.[8] What was formerly working-class culture is henceforth shaken at its very foundation; workers no longer adhere to the ideology that, for decades, had inspired a project capable of mobilizing them. The end of the Communist dream has weakened their traditional values: solidarity, devotion, virility, a grasp of concrete, down-to-earth realities. These values appear "outmoded" in an age when certain techniques can be performed "at a distance" and when the organization of work is elaborated in offices; in an age marked by individualism and by the individualization of work tasks; and in an age when an employee is given the responsibility of fulfilling his mission. Autonomy in the organization of work and individualization in the performance of tasks have introduced competition among workers. The workplace solidarity that long characterized workers has declined and one observes them competing with each other in modern factories. Moreover, the future is uncertain and hopes of professional advancement and social climbing have vanished: workers find themselves "blocked" in the factory. Furthermore, the longer schooling of their children shows itself up to be an illusion: high-school graduates (with their French *baccalauréats*) are incapable of obtaining university diplomas in an academic social milieu which remains foreign to them; ultimately they end up in the factory, with little if any professional education behind them; they inevitably nurture a sentiment of failure and bitterness. They have not chosen to work in a factory; they have been forced to do so. Being a worker has become synonymous with social failure. Now called "operators" instead of "workers," they no longer possess an ideological system enabling them to view themselves as representatives of a revolutionary political project, and giving meaning to their living conditions and working-class condition. The integrated and mutually supportive "working-class society" that enabled workers to live among their peers by means of a rigid and self-protective culture—as it was described by Richard Hoggart—no longer exists.[9]

Although living conditions have objectively improved ever since the first social laws were passed, workers have lost—with the end of working-class and Communist ideology—the culture and symbolic resources that gave them honor and self-esteem. "There is a working-class sadness," wrote a former worker in 1945, "that can be cured only by participating in a political movement."[10] Moreover, the current stagnation of salaries and the increasing number of precarious and temporary kinds of employment since the years of economic crisis have been experienced as setbacks and humiliation. Comparing salaries and working conditions with those enjoyed by office employees and civil servants gives rise to bitterness. In an apparently paradoxical manner, a worker becomes more humiliated by his overall condition as he becomes objectively more integrated, which thus shows that he compares himself to all the other kinds of employees making up the salaried-employee society. The reduction of objective inequalities gives rise to feelings of humiliation, and encourages revolt against persistent inequalities.

The situation of all salaried employees evolves in an erratic manner, in their relationships to both work (*"travail"*) and employment (*"emploi"*), a distinction that Serge Paugam rightly makes.[11] In all sectors and at all levels, salaried employees are more autonomous in their jobs. This transformation of the relationship to work offers new opportunities, to the most competent employees, for displaying their skills and abilities. On the other hand, less competitive employees risk being marginalized or excluded, and feeling humiliated by increasingly demanding work conditions. Many salaried employees are equally worried about the future of their jobs: given the overall job-market situation, many firms, factories, and companies belong to declining economic sectors threatened by economic transformations or even by governmental, administrative decisions. All salaried employees are well aware that the number of precarious jobs is increasing. Yet aspirations to holding down a steady job have not diminished: a job with a contract of indefinite duration remains the social norm. If salaried employees who experience dissatisfaction with their jobs are taken into account, as well as those who sense that they suffer from the instability of the job market and who fear for their future, then "one can consider that 58 percent of all salaried employees experience professional difficulties today."[12] The highest social categories are not exempt from this situation: 25 percent of those belonging to the managerial class experience one of the forms of precariousness. Often submitted to ferocious competition among themselves, the latter experience daily the necessity of proving themselves; their competence is never definitely acknowledged; their professional duties and responsibilities ever increase. The only salaried employees who declare themselves happy are those who sense that their competence is evaluated fairly, both financially and symbolically, and who benefit from a job security enabling them to manage their career and project themselves into the future.[13]

Indeed, the positive identity of *homo democraticus* is more and more linked to his acknowledged competence. Everyone's aspirations have increased: because we live in a democracy, everyone has the right to have his or her qualities acknowledged. Is it not true that one finds, in the lowest socio-economic categories, what studies of welfare-assisted or poor people had already revealed, namely that the poor in a providential democracy are objectively less poor than poor people in the past, but that they feel more humiliated, to the extent that each person is responsible for his own destiny? Salaried employees with precarious jobs are also objectively in a less precarious situation than salaried employees in the past, but they risk feeling more humiliated. This explains why weak professional integration is closely associated with difficulties inside family relationships, with a reduced social life, and with weak participation in all forms of political life. Social protection does not eliminate the humiliation, stemming from professional failure, which marginalizes and excludes individuals.

Professions in the Intervention State

Some salaried jobs are direct products of State intervention. In the fields of both social services and education, the State has increased the number of what economists call personal services professions. The State creates new professions to prevent, or compensate for, different kinds of poverty or illness; it organizes the education of the population by means of the "republican" system of education, the spreading of "cultural democracy," and the encouragement of sports. In fact, the kinds of jobs represented by those who work, on the one hand, in health and social fields, and, on the other hand, in education and culture, have increased in number and have been professionalized. This development of providential professions has benefited from the massive arrival of women in the job market. As newcomers, they have taken on professional activities that extend, in another mode, their traditional family role.

However, the aforementioned INSEE socio-professional categories, which were originally modeled upon the industrial world—high-level management, middle-level management, employees, a structure that had in turn been inspired by military organization—do not sufficiently take this phenomenon into account. Education, as well as health and mental care for children and the elderly, were duties that were long undertaken free of charge—by obligation or vocation—by women, in the framework of the family. They have now turned into Welfare-State professions. A symbolic example of this evolution is the progressive disappearance of nuns who gave free health care to hospital patients; today they are replaced by male and female nurses with diplomas. One can also mention the case of women who hand their children over to childcare providers, or to daycare-center or nursery-school teachers, so that they themselves can exercise a professional activity, sometimes indeed as childcare providers or daycare-center teachers. The increased intervention of the Providential State in areas that once traditionally belonged to the family sphere is illustrated by the increasing number of "social" professions.[14]

The *increasing number* of different Providence State professions can be measured by diverse indicators, but especially by the increasing number of civil servants working for the Ministries of Education and Culture, as well as for the Junior Ministry of Sports; by the increasing number of social workers and employees of the public hospital system; and by the continuous creation of even more professions.

Let us examine the case of social workers. During the years 1970-90, the number of social workers increased threefold.[15] As their number grew, the kinds of social-services jobs diversified. The three oldest and so-called "basic" kinds of social-services professions are the social worker (*"assistante sociale"*), the specialized educator (*"éducateur spécialisé"*), and the socio-cultural activities organizer (*"animateur socioculturel"*). These three professions all existed before the economic crisis. During the years of crisis (the 1980s and the 1990s), a new series of professions was added. These included "specialized technical educators," "monitor-educators," "family workers," "medical-psychological assistants," "educators of young children," "counselors for social and family economic matters" (the modernized form of what was formerly called a "domestic education monitor"), and "representatives for legal guardians." In 1974, the then Prime Minister, Jacques Chirac, created a Junior Ministry for Social Aid, whose very existence confirmed the growing importance of social work, and its sundry institutions, in governmental policy. Ever since the beginning of the 1990s, in regard to the increasing number of population groups threatened by marginalization and exclusion, so-called "insertion"—as the French say—or inclusion policies have been adopted and policies especially aimed at big cities have been implemented. This has led to even more new professions: "local insertion agents," "minimum insertion income (RMI) mission representatives," "development agents," and so on. Among the jobs created by "individualized" or "social" employment contracts ("Jobs Useful for the Collectivity" [TUC], "Training Sessions for an Initiation into Professional Life" [SIVP], "Employment-Solidarity Contracts" [CES], etc.), many were devoted to social intervention, augmenting in the process the number of professions directly created by Welfare-State policies. The Youth Employment Contracts have induced such professions as "social emergency intervention agents," "socio-athletic mediators," and "coordinators for the readaptation of persons under medical care." This profession-engendering process is ongoing. A new law, the "personalized autonomy allowance," which was adopted in 2001, provides for the professionalization of at-home assistance (*"aide à domicile"*), by creating modernization funds designed to educate those who take care of dependent elderly persons at home. A Minister for the Family has envisioned organizing a "parental education program," for which specialized instructors will themselves have to be trained. All these professions participate in the growing intervention of the State in family life. The most marginalized families are directly taken care of by social workers; some families even complain that they no longer enjoy family privacy.

The same observations can be made about intervention policies in culture and sports; the two fields are indeed sometimes combined. The number of "cultural" jobs has increased spectacularly. From the diverse varieties of "cultural engineering"—a neologism that reflects a newly created profession—all the way to jobs stemming from the Youth Employment Contracts (such as "cultural heritage valorization and promotion agents" or "local cultural accompaniment agents"[16]), professions have developed at the same time as the Cultural Ministry budget has increased and its intervention has become more frequent. Cultural "mediators" and "diffusers" (agents, promoters, and the like) were given the responsibility of democratizing the various art markets and of reflecting, then acting upon, the spontaneous or more studied artistic practices of the population. As has been shown, the intervention policy of the Ministry of Culture has developed a social milieu made up of artists (whose number has increased, even as a socio-professional status for creative artists has been constituted), as well as administrators, cultural mediators and activities organizers—the sundry "cultural engineers"—who are linked to their "clients"—the creative artists—in an intricate network of interpersonal relations and mutual favor-trading. As it were, the Ministry of Culture has become the Ministry of Creative Artists and All Culture Professionals; in other words, of all mediators whose existence is linked to cultural intervention policy. In total, the number of "cultural mediators" has increased fourfold in twenty years, while the number of social workers has increased threefold.[17] The number of administrators and "socio-athletic activities organizers" (*"animateurs sociosportifs"*) has inflated similarly.[18] The same phenomenon has occurred in Australia, where multi-cultural policies have given birth to Ethnic Providence-State professions such as ethnic health workers, migrant health education officers, ethnic aged workers, in addition to all the "ethnic" cultural agents: translators, teachers, educators, journalists, and the like.[19]

The appearance of these new professions has been accompanied by a process of *professionalization* demanded by all employees working in these fields. They insist upon official recognition of their know-how and professional identities. This represents an additional factor that has induced bureaucratization. In such demands are blended a desire to corner off employment for oneself and a need to have one's competence—and thus dignity—acknowledged. Access to such professions depends henceforth on a specific form of education or training, officialized by a diploma—such as the one required for becoming a "local cultural accompaniment agent"—that in turn opens the door to salaried employment. The profession is exercised in accordance with a series of rights and duties, obtained by union action, and defined and guaranteed by legislation, especially after collective bargaining. Everyone who exercises a Providence-State profession in the fields of health, social assistance, or education must respect this logic. They have demanded, and obtained, the progressive professionalization of their specific activity. They participate in the extension of the salaried-employee class and increased bureaucratization, both of which are characteristic of the Intervention State. Their profession must be exercised in accordance with regulations developed by the Welfare State. In order to supervise the education of athletics managers and diminish the risks of accidents during athletic activities, the number of regulations in the sports world has increased spectacularly. Providence-State agents must respect bureaucratic logic, which inevitably classifies individuals into categories and applies formal regulations to them. Moreover, like all salaried employees, they defend their material and statutory rights. In

France (with its long tradition of a strong centralized State), education, titles, mandates, and employment are all defined by the State.
Below, we will examine the discontent nourished by this increased
professionalization and felt by salaried employees who, while demanding the advantages associated with professionalization, also
desire to define their profession with non-economic values: solidarity among human beings, artistic or intellectual creativity, the handing on of truth and beauty.

The Providence State has not only created new professions, such
as are represented by the multivarious mediators now intervening in
social, cultural, or athletic life. It has also transformed the social
conditions in which traditional trades and professions are exercised.
Let us remain in the cultural world and take the extreme case of a
"profession" defined precisely as not being a profession: the social
condition of "*artistes plasticiens*"—that is artists, sculptors, conceptual artists, and so on—has become closely associated with the protection provided by the Ministry of Culture, despite the fact that it
also depends on the art market. However, more than other professionals, artists proclaim that their activity is a vocation. They claim
to possess an absolute originality, upon which their ideology of rupture with all forms of tradition is based. Among all the intellectual
and creative professions, it is artists who formulate the purest vocational ideology. According to them, art cannot be taught and talent is
an innate gift: they adhere to a "charismatic ideology that recognizes no tribunal other than their own artistic conscience."[20] In their
discourse, they conspicuously refuse the legitimacy of both academic
and art-market recognition. At the same time, as much as or even
more than others, they have managed to benefit from the Cultural
Intervention State. In 1975, they demanded, and obtained, social-
security protection—the primary symbol of the rights linked to the
salaried-employee class—as well as privileges as regards social and
fiscal law. Ever since the 1980s, the State has accorded artists employment, financial resources, and—through commissioned works
and corresponding forms of recognition—a "capital" in regard to
their artistic reputation. During that decade, "the Delegate to the Plastic
Arts organized a series of meetings with the artists' inter-union organization. These meetings dealt with the social protection of artists,
with the granting of artists' work studios, with artistic property law,
with public purchasing of art, with commissioned works of art, with
professional status, and with the French law "of 1 percent" (whereby

new buildings must devote one percent of the total building costs to the commissioning of a work of art that will be placed inside or just outside the building)."[21] Because artists cannot enroll at the National Employment Agency (ANPE) to compensate for the deficiencies of the art market, the Ministry of Culture provides subsidies for setting up artist's studios, grants emergency allocations, awards individual creative-artist scholarships, allocates travel and research grants, commissions works of art, as well as helps artists find employment in art schools. According to a former high-level functionary in the Ministry of Culture, artists have become "cultural workers": henceforth, "a new social image of the artist is spreading. He is no longer an *artiste maudit* or a mandarin, a social deviant or an academician; like an architect or engineer, he is one of those who imagine the framework of daily life. In this respect, he naturally enters into the system of remunerations and social and juridical benefits of the other socio-professional categories. It is more and more acknowledged, in this day and age of mass production and consumption, that even solitary or anti-establishment artistic work is useful to our new kind of society."[22]

Career strategies and discourses are redefined by these objective conditions. The sense of artists' professional experiences has been transformed. State intervention has redefined the condition of artists, who can invoke the radical character of their absolute vocation all the while demanding, and obtaining, protection at least comparable to that enjoyed by salaried employees. Artists develop a charismatic ideology and, at the same time, participate in an organized collective activity that guarantees protective State intervention. Artists have acquired the right to define their own profession and to benefit from social protection without being required to "pay the price borne by other professional categories,"[23] that is the obligations of salaried employees who work in private business firms or public administration.

To take another example relating to the Cultural Providence State, the social condition of actors, like that of artists, is not independent of State intervention, even though the job market naturally continues to play an essential role in their career.[24] Like artists, they fluctuate between their claimed vocation of being free individuals—freer in fact than all other human beings—and the dream of belonging to ranks of civil servants and of seeing the rules of a meritocracy respected. On the one hand, they evoke their autonomy, the necessity of surpassing themselves, of being called into question with every new play and indeed with every performance, of being fully responsible for their destiny, of being at once themselves and someone else (the character), as well as their experience—thanks to a profession which is "unlike any other"—of self-fulfillment and creative liberty. At the same time, because they experience "the harshness of a milieu in which one needs to rebuild one's life every day,"[25] they aspire to the security provided by the institutionalized professions whose recruiting and specific field of activity depends on diplomas and titles. They muse about ways of organizing the acting profession so that everyone would have a full-time job.

In their case, the Providence State intervenes through unemployment benefits. The management of actors' job contracts is based on Unemployment Benefits Office (ASSEDIC) regulations which, in accordance with a specific benefit plan applied by a specific Social Security branch office, grant unemployment benefits to actors whenever they have worked at least 507 hours during the twelve-month period preceding the unemployment period. Obtaining the "507 hours" clause in a job contract has thus become a form of professional recognition, at once financial and symbolic; it is the "first signal of professionalism, in the eyes of both artists and technical personnel."[26] Similarly, studies of unemployed young people have shown that being signed up at the National Employment Agency (ANPE) had a positive connotation, to the extent that enrollment signified that a social status linked to employment had been obtained, even if the status was a negative one: because the young people were recognized as unemployed people, they could define their social status with respect to the job market.[27] The "507 hours" regulation guarantees a minimum of security to actors, whose lives necessarily fluctuate between an inspired creative vocation and the necessity of limiting the risks associated with a profession that is inevitably intermittent. This legislation can be objectively analyzed as an indirect subsidy to the theatrical world, a means of adding to the financing directly granted to theater groups by local and national governments: it is one of the tools used by the Cultural Intervention State in the theater world. But it also contributes to the symbolic recognition of professional identity; it gives meaning to the experiences of actors, to their techniques, to their professional identity, and to the relationship that they entertain with their professional activity.

The increasing number of "new" professions in a society which is aimed at the future, and which celebrates newness for its own sake, tends to belittle traditional jobs, trades, and professions. In order to appease suffering, priests are replaced by psychologists and social workers. We will see that the specific fields of competence and intervention traditionally reserved for medical doctors have likewise been reduced by the competing activities of diverse health professionals, on the one hand, and by various kinds of medical technicians, on the other. Intellectual professions are now split up into creative people, technical people who assist in the management of firms, and intermediaries involved in diffusion and promotion. The professions involved in cultural diffusion and promotion are favored with respect to those involved with creativity. The value given to diffusion and promotion is narrowly linked to democratic values: quantity becomes the more respected indicator of the value of intellectual production. The rhythm of artistic or intellectual work does not correspond to the rhythm of democratic life, in which "almost everyone acts" and in which "men are generally led to attach an excessive value to the rapid bursts and superficial conceptions of the intellect, and on the other hand to undervalue unduly its slower and deeper labors."[28]

The group made up of all those exercising professions created by the development of the Providence State is often designated by the terms "salaried middle classes" or "central constellation," which Henri Mendras views as characteristic of our society.[29] More than those who participate in the competitive economic market, members of these salaried middle classes claim to possess what are called "post-materialistic values."[30] In fact, this term also reveals the value system of sociologists who themselves belong to the world of the Providence State and who implicitly criticize the "materialistic" values of the economic world. These salaried middle classes actively participated in the "new social movements" of the 1970s, which were led by students, women, ecologists, regionalists, or pacifists, and which were theorized by Alain Touraine.[31] The members of these movements were massively recruited among those who exercised Providence State professions: teachers, research scientists, civil servants working in cultural fields, social workers, and health professionals. The forms of their group action obviously departed from the traditions of working-class union activities, in that they gave much importance to symbolic actions that could be reported on through the communications medias. The same categories of the population were in fact found, in 1997, among the demonstrators against the Debré Law (which was designed to control illegal migrant workers).[32] Moreover, it is among the same social classes that Buddhism has become fashionable in France. Lacking dogmatic references, this religion gives prime importance to individual experience, independent of any outside authority; it responds to the needs of *homo democraticus* for responsibility and to his dreams of roots—so much so that the reference to Buddhism is fueled by a "third-world" sensibility and by indignation against the Chinese policy in Tibet.

The Trivialization of Social Relations

The Intervention State contributes to the standardization of human relationships into a unique model, which is inspired by the world of production. From this viewpoint, the Intervention State actually reinforces the impact of the pre-eminence of economic activity on collective life. By intervening in human relationships through labor legislation, social protection, and the organizing of education and culture, it tends to trivialize relationships; that is, to make them more business-like, perfunctory, commonplace, ordinary, banal. Social bonds lose their specificity and conform to the models of commercial or bureaucratic relationships. One tends to question, or even protest against, the specific competence of certain individuals. In turn, this attitude maintains an oft-uncritical form of credence in the sagacity of "experts."

In a providential society, one's vocation is less acknowledged, and the number of professions increases. Here, it is necessary to recall Max Weber's distinction between vocation and profession (*Beruf*), with respect to the vocation of the scholar and the profession of the professor. The vocation of the scholar is characterized by "passion."[34] The "métier" or profession of teaching is defined by the concrete conditions involved: the way in which teachers are recruited, the steps in a teaching career, a teacher's rights and obligations, the remuneration associated with each career step, and the relation between a teacher and the pursuit of "pure science" (which corresponds to the scholar's vocation). Because professions replace vocations, all those who once defined their work in terms of "vocation" and therefore hoped to escape from the logic of bureaucracy or economics, now declare that their profession is in crisis.

The Crisis of the Inspired Professions

The evolution towards *"Beruf"* (Weber)—or, in the vocabulary of modern sociology, "professionalization"—is particularly striking in the case of professions which were formerly, in one way or another, linked to a form of the sacred. Today, doctors, lawyers, and priests increasingly conform to the model of a contract between equal parties. More generally, this same evolution can be observed in all people—such as teachers or social workers—who by defining their profession in terms of a "mission," "vocation," or "creative oeuvre," claim to participate in a social relationship of a specific kind, unlike all other relationships. For them, their profession is not exclusively "mercantile." They speak of and experience it in terms of a personal calling or commitment involving moral and humanist values. Choosing to practice that particular profession cannot exclusively be reduced to the desire or need for material gains. If one adopts Hannah Arendt's opposition between labor and work, such people belong to the work side of the equation: they belong to the world of intellectual inspiration.[35] They refuse to reduce their profession to simple professional competence and look down on the world of competitive production.

Caught between the poles of vocation and profession—and experiencing the corresponding tension, even contradiction, of the opposition—people who exercise one of the Social and Cultural Providence State professions express their personal discontent and willingly point to the crisis of their professions. They remain divided between references to charity or, more often, to "solidarity," to "special dialogues" like those bringing together doctors and patients (and to the "inexpressible" nature of this relationship), to their cultural or political "mission," or to their "creative oeuvre," and the realities of a profession which, like that of any salaried employee, is exercised in accordance with labor legislation.

The professions in the social-work field are a telling example of this tension. More than others, social workers (in the broadest sense) are caught between the pole of vocation, which transfigures their daily activities into a mission of "solidarity" (the secular version of the term "charity"), and the pole of "profession," as for any salaried employee. Most social workers enter the service of the Providence State because of their "prophetic calling" or their "inspired desire to volunteer."[36] They claim to have a "profession unlike any other"[37] and do everything so as not to be classified with ordinary employees or bureaucrats. The vocabulary of vocation, of witness and calling, which is derived from Catholic charity work, is now often made fun of in the professional social workers' milieu itself—but has not the style of discourse changed in all social milieus? In reality, "down-to-earth professional practices remain in many cases greatly influenced by the ideals which have marked the successive origins of the various professions and which refer as often to Christian humanism as to the secular morals of egalitarian democracy."[38]

Henceforth, social workers respond to this contradiction between vocation and profession by two kinds of attitudes and behavior, as is revealed by the analysis of their experiences. Some take refuge in the strict and scrupulous application of legislation, by limiting their role to the exercise of a bureaucratic profession. They resolve to respect all regulations and yield to the "temptation of sticking to office work and keeping files in order."[39] They take recourse in statutory norms in order to protect themselves from a feeling of failure. To the extent that they sense that their initial vocation has not been able to blossom amidst the bureaucratic constraints in which they exercise their profession, this falling back on a strict application of regulations constitutes a defense strategy. Those who adopt the second attitude, on the contrary, continue to refer to their "mission" and invoke the "sentiment of presence and the inexpressible in their relationships with others."[40] Their behavior more or less symbolically, more or less aggressively, departs from bureaucratic rules. For them, it is a way of remaining "effective," that is of remaining faithful to the idea that they have of their mission or vocation. Displaying their rupture from bureaucratization can take on various forms. In the following remarks, for example, a "street educator" ostentatiously describes his non-bureaucratic practices and legitimizes them in theoretical terms: "And it is only once they (the "institutionals," the judges and the functionaries) acknowledge my identity outside of the institution that I represent, that is when emotions are aroused and when a relationship is created outside the institutional process, that my work can really become effective."[41] The street educator can thus maintain his reference to a genuine vocation or mission. By adopting this attitude, he reveals his refusal to exercise the profession of a routine "low-level civil servant" or "pen-pusher." In the name of his calling, he condemns the ineffectiveness, lethargy, and formalism of bureaucratic practices, experienced as being even more intolerable in that social work—perhaps even an emergency—is concerned: his mission is to socialize and integrate children of socially modest backgrounds or to save teenage drug users.

Social workers attempt to enhance the value of their mission by contrasting it negatively to the idea of police control. Hence their sentiment of unease when sociologists, during the 1970s, exhibited social workers' objective complicity, even if involuntary, with law and order advocates, by showing that their intervention actually divided the working class and dampened its revolutionary ardor. Social workers could interpret this analysis only as a denunciation that struck at the very heart of their professional identity.

The same analysis can be applied to primary- and secondary-school teachers who define their profession as one of handing down knowledge and educating pupils and students. Given this position, it is not absurd that a French junior high school teacher, who is a civil servant by statute, should define his profession above all by a refusal to be a civil servant: "I think that these demands for a better life, which are made in all professions, as well as this desire for recognition, well I've seen social workers asking for the same things, the desire above all to be considered useful, and not just people with any old kind of job, I mean like low-level civil servants. . . . I don't want to be a functionary. I don't want to count the hours that I spend at work, no not at all. . . . Maybe a teacher who is functionary feels good at his job, precisely because he doesn't have to ask himself such questions. . . . Indeed some people ask themselves a lot of questions. But a teacher who really wants to be a teacher and an educator. . . ."[42] This woman demonstrates to the field worker, as well as to herself probably, that she continues to pursue her original project, despite difficulties and setbacks, of being a genuine "educator."

Like social workers (in the broadest sense of the profession), teachers find themselves caught between the reinterpretation of their job as a "profession" (or "*Beruf*" in Weber's vocabulary)—with corresponding demands for salary raises, better time schedules, and better working conditions that are put forth by teachers' unions—and as a "mission" (or "vocation"), namely that of handing down knowledge acquired during one's university schooling as well as that of participating in the directly political project of keeping alive the "republican mystique" inherited from the golden age of Third Republic primary school teachers, at least insofar as this mystique is nostalgically recalled: the goals of "building the nation," ensuring "republi-

can integration," "educating children of the poor," "integrating immigrant children." An indication of this situation is given when Lise
Demailly evokes the "mourning period" during which secondary
school teachers progressively give up the mission of handing down
knowledge acquired at universities and simply try to "keep their
classes under control." Teachers thereby find themselves reduced to
the role of social workers or cultural activities organizers.[43]

In France, the teaching crisis at the university level takes on specific forms because professors are functionaries who also must call
their vocation into question, faced as they have been by the mass
arrival of young people in universities. Universities were created as
places where new knowledge was developed and handed on to students or, in modern terms, places where *both* research and teaching
would be carried out.[44] The organization of universities is based on
a definition that Eliot Freidson sums up in these terms: "Universities
are remarkable social inventions for subsidizing work that does not
have immediate commercial value." The elaboration of knowledge
or, to cite once again Weber's expression, "pure" science or erudition, does not procure employment in the job market; it does not
have "immediate commercial value."[45] University professors formerly lived on their salaries as teachers—a profession that has commercial value—and not as research scientists devoting themselves
to "pure" science. Remunerated as teachers, they could also devote
themselves to scientific studies or "pure" erudition.

Democratic societies favor diffusion, at the expense of creativity.
The conception of universities as places where a profession—teaching—was carried out allowed professors to produce new knowledge
at the same time as they handed it on to students; yet this conception
has become contradictory with the demands and requirements of
democratic universities. The former balance between teaching and
research, on which universities were founded at the end of the nineteenth century, has been called into question. Teaching has been
dissociated from research, which is now conducted in specialized
institutions, and universities have been oriented towards the mere
diffusion or transmission of knowledge. Even this function is sometimes diminished: in specialized schools for public administration
management, for example, the transmission of knowledge from
teacher to student is now more often replaced by students self-pro-
ducing their own knowledge by researching and writing assigned
reports and the like. At best, universities have become places where

knowledge is still handed on; they are no longer places where new knowledge is produced and intellectual disciplines are renewed. In fact, all reports concerning universities regularly advise this. The modifications gradually introduced in the statutory obligations of academic teachers give impetus to this evolution. The profitability, and thus the quality, of universities is evaluated with respect to the number of students who graduate every year. This tendency bears down heavily on, and indeed becomes a constraint for, democratic society, which assigns itself the goal of ensuring that all its members enjoy a prolonged presence in the educational system and, for many of them, at the university level.[46] The burdens of "mass" education at the university level henceforth risk preventing professors from simultaneously devoting themselves to "pure" science. The number of university teachers has increased, as well as the number of those who do not maintain a personal vocation for research or erudition; they above all enhance their role as spreaders of knowledge and celebrate the virtues of pedagogy.[47]

Today, this evolution underlies the discontent felt by university professors; it is even more important than the relative decrease in their incomes and prestige. Professors who continue to refer to the traditional representation of the teachers' profession feel "reduced" to transmitting knowledge, rather than developing it as well. This explains why those who manage to reinterpret their professional activity still in vocational terms, or as the production of a personal oeuvre of scholarly work, do not experience the same discontent as those who reduce their profession to a mere means of earning their livelihood and who correspondingly adopt various compensation strategies, such as celebrating the virtues of pedagogy (which, they underscore, is not to be confused with knowledge), seeking out power within the academic institution (through university elections or union activity), or, as they grow older, by collecting academic honors, by aspiring to be elected to the Institut de France, or by accepting the award of a doctorate *honoris causa* from a foreign university.

The social role of university professors is no longer clear. They are directly useful neither for the management of business firms and corporations, nor for cultural democracy. Indeed, they are subjected to two kinds of competition: from technically apt individuals, on the one hand, and, on the other, from cultural "diffusers" and various cultural intermediaries and moderators. The former—who are experts in technical, financial, juridical, or commercial management, or who are "communication" specialists—belong to the competitive world. They are considered to be indispensable to the functioning of business firms and corporations, in which "human resources" people, capable of working at a high technical level, are required. Their social usefulness is immediately obvious. The latter—who range from well-known intellectuals who appear often in mass-media cultural broadcasts, to journalists and sundry cultural intermediaries and moderators (such as television book-chat hosts, moderators of radio debates, and the like)—are legitimized by the practices of cultural and political democracy. Journalists participate directly in political life, and the various kinds of cultural "diffusers" respond to the cultural aspirations of *homo democraticus*. The competition of the "cultural" world set up by the Cultural Intervention State and the mass-media "diffusion" market contributes to the objective fragility and social depreciation of the professorial milieu, which often subsequently adopts a defense posture, namely that of defending the "last privileges" of job security and long vacations. If one defines university professors as those who justify their vocation by devoting themselves to "pure" science (as, once again, Weber put it) or to "slow and profound work" (as Tocqueville phrased it)—which of course does not imply that professors always and really acted in this manner, but rather that it was the idea and ideal upon which universities were created and upon which university professors justified their vocation and professional status—then one can argue that the democratization of education, as well as the competition with experts, with "diffusers," and, in countries with a Cultural Providence State, with various cultural intermediaries and moderators, is transforming the academic teachers' profession, which had been redefined, at the end of the nineteenth century, as one linking the production and transmission of knowledge.

Similar analyses apply to the transformation of the museum curator's profession. This profession has always had two dimensions: the preservation of, and gathering knowledge about, works of art, which is the connoisseur's aim; and the presentation of works of art to the public. With the democratization and development of "cultural needs," nourished by the frequency of school-class visits and the spreading of democratic values, the second function now takes on the higher priority. "No longer can we simply be researchers and connoisseurs," remarks one museum curator, "we also have to be cultural activities organizers, corporation presidents, and intellectuals."[48] The effectiveness of museum curators now tends to be measured by statistics concerning the number of visitors to their museum or exhibit. Curators who above all conceived their role as that of a researcher or connoisseur view as heavy chores the material tasks and managerial organizational work that results from the growing number of people visiting museums; these chores limit, or even make impossible, their former activities as producers of knowledge. Other curators, who are closer to democratic values, essentially devote themselves to administrative work, to the organization of cultural activities, and to the commercial aspects of museums.

These analyses can also be applied to the demise of "small farmers" ("*paysans*," in French), who have been transformed into modern farmers or large-scale cultivators ("*agriculteurs*"). According to Henri Mendras, no characteristic of small-farmer society ("*la société paysanne*")[49] gives an accurate picture of the evolution of modern farmers, who now follow production management schemes and take part in worldwide agricultural markets. The majority of farms are now agricultural companies ("*entreprises agricoles*") and are the property of an officially registered business company or corporation ("*société civile*"), not of a single family; most family members exercise a professional activity outside of the agricultural world. Agricultural production is industrialized—techniques replacing know-how handed down from one generation to the next—and even sometimes relocated to a different part of the country or to a foreign country. This evolution induces the discontent of the agricultural world. Farmers remain nostalgic for the bygone days when they were called upon to make "a great mobilizing objective" come true, that of "feeding the nation better, more copiously and more cheaply. . . . The rupture is as serious and moral as the overall economic uncertainty."[50] Once they have become businessmen like other businessmen, farmers feel deprived of the mission that once gave meaning to their activity of "feeding mankind."

Professions dealing with knowledge are more valued than those involving social work, and the latter are more valued than those whose function is to maintain law and order. As it is experienced, the hierarchy of Welfare State jobs, between the poles of profession and mission, and between those of social control and moral inspiration, conditions the significance of professional experiences. This hierarchy is not officially formulated as such, but it is intensely experienced. Among all the professions directly linked to the Intervention State, the greatest "misery" is felt by those who sense that they are "reduced" to a function that is inferior to the one that they originally imagined: the university professor whose considers him or herself "reduced" to being a mere teacher and no longer the creator, through devotion to "pure" science, of new knowledge; the junior high school teacher who becomes aware that his or her function is no longer to hand on knowledge, but rather that it has been "reduced" to that of a social worker or monitor[51]; the social worker who can no longer help people threatened by marginalization, exclusion, or impoverishment, and who feels "reduced" to merely filling out and keeping administrative files or to being the involuntary (in sociological terms, "objective") collaborator of police forces; the prison guard who realizes that it has become impossible for him to fulfill his missions of protecting society and helping convicts to re-insert themselves back into society, both of which were associated with the more valued work of social workers, and who thereby feels "reduced" to the single function of maintaining order inside the prison.[52]

The "crisis" experienced by a profession and the reinterpretation of professional identities take on different forms, depending on the relations that the profession entertains with the Intervention State. In France, professors and numerous doctors are functionaries; artists benefit from cultural intervention, although they are exclusively subjected to the laws of the economic market in other countries. It is therefore necessary to take into account the institutional history of a profession, which can belong to the public sector or depend, partly or totally, on the economic market. It is also necessary to take into account the specificity of each profession. There is a more "natural" demand for health care, but no spontaneous demand for culture; the latter demand results from a process of learning and from acquired cultural knowledge. However, one finds similar forms of professional identity crises in all professions more or less directly dependent on the Intervention State. In all cases, one questions the evolution of the profession and the sense of exercising it in a society in which the impact of democratization ensured by the Providence State is combined, throughout society, with the preeminence of technical efficiency, competition, and mercantile relationships.

Public services—in other words, the tools of an action that is supposed to be specifically political and to escape, by its very nature, from economic logic—also tend to adopt the model of business firms or corporations. Primary school teachers no longer feel that they are

"Hussars of the Republic" invested with the mission of conveying and promoting the mystique of the nation and the Republic. Magistrates sense that are treated as if they were ordinary functionaries, whose mission—handing down justice—is no longer acknowledged in all its grandeur. The national postal system must also take profit making into account. In France, the resistance movement that has roused public services functionaries into action should not prevent us from seeing that it is rearguard fighting. Other countries have limited the role of public services and have subjected them to efficiency studies. English civil servants, for example, are now reduced to their regalian role. The positivism of the economy influences that of the Providence State.

Ideal Medical Practice

The trivialization of social relationships can be illustrated by examining the most prestigious professions—namely those of law and medicine. Both lawyers and physicians claimed, more than other professionals, to establish literally "extraordinary" relationships with their clients and patients. For doctors the Providence State, and for lawyers the economic market, have respectively introduced models of bureaucratic or competitive relationships into the type of relationship that was formerly entertained.

The evolution of medical practice especially reveals how traditional professions now follow a trivialized model of social relationships. Doctors have always been a favorite example for theoreticians of professions, in the sense of American sociology. In this case, "profession" is not to be taken in Weber's sense, but rather in the sense of what we call, in French, the "liberal professions" (*"professions libérales"*). Liberal professions were derived from medieval trades or professions; their right to organize themselves and their intervention monopoly was acknowledged and officialized by the modern State. Only medical-school graduates have the right to use the title "doctor"; only doctors have the right to provide cures for patients; only doctors have the right to recruit new doctors—their peers—and to make a ruling about the practice of their profession.[53] This intervention monopoly is guaranteed by a special high-level diploma, which is awarded in a university but given by peers, "thus making these trades vocations worthy of bourgeois aspirations and linking them to high culture."[54]

During the period in which this specific liberal profession was the best organized and most widely held in esteem, approximately 1890-1960, both the intervention monopoly and the self-regulating features of the profession were justified by the ideology of the singular and inexpressible dialogue that is established between a doctor and his patient; and by the idea, reinforced by the profession but acknowledged by all people, that medical practice was of a sacred order. Because doctors, like priests, deal with life and death, they share the privilege, not of exercising a profession, but rather of entertaining a charismatic relationship—the clinical relationship—with their patients. Doctors of course did not neglect to perform the rituals that reinforced this charismatic relationship. The absolute respect of medical secrets—a secular transfer of the role of confessional secrets for a Catholic priest—symbolizes this. The obvious pleasure with which doctors belonging to the generation who practiced between 1930 and 1980 would refuse, in the name of medical secrecy, to give out the most anodyne news about their closest friends only more graphically epitomized this sacred dimension of their activity—sacred, in that this behavior differed radically from daily forms of social relationships. One finds echoes of this position in remarks made by retired doctors who practiced medicine during this period: "I practiced, and believe in, a *liberal* profession. I like human contacts. I like to follow through on my own responsibilities. I am free to prescribe whatever medicine or medical acts that I think are best and finally—but for how much longer?—I can confront the force of public law with my right to professional secrecy."[55] In discourse concerning the profession, religious connotations in fact crop up frequently, such as in the saying "On entre en médecine comme on entre en religion" ("One enters the medical profession in the same way that one takes religious orders"). Other telltale phrases like "*amour du prochain*" ("love of one's neighbor"), "*aventure spirituelle*" ("spiritual adventure"), "*sacerdoce*" ("devotion to duty," literally "priestly calling"), "*sagesse*" ("wisdom"), "*sens de l'existence*" ("meaning of existence"), or "*confession des malades*" ("patients' confession") are regularly used by physicians who enjoyed happy professional lives, equivalent in their minds to the "most beautiful profession in the world." The preponderance of doctors in various ethical committees is a heritage of this conception.

The rigorous norms governing relationships among medical colleagues or, in French, "*confrères*" (a significant term, with its emphasis on "brothers"), were another sign of the extraordinary character of this profession: they demonstrated that professional relationships among physicians remained aloof from the habitual competition that takes place between social individuals. The high incomes enjoyed by some doctors, until recently, was merely the consequence of the practice of a profession that was not experienced as a professional activity subjected to competition, but rather as a status linked to the individual person, thus allowing a quasi-religious relationship to be established between doctor and patient.

The instituting of the Intervention State has changed these relationships. The logic behind the medical establishment's autonomy and intervention monopoly had always given a contradictory character to the relationships between physicians and the State.[56] The ideology formulated by medical doctors had always insisted on autonomy, whereas the practice of medicine depended on the State, which guaranteed that autonomy. The medical profession had developed its own definitions and its own market, all the while appealing to the State so as to be protected by law. It is the State that guaranteed the medical intervention monopoly; it is against State power that the institutions representing the medical profession asserted and established themselves. The Providence State has introduced a new stage in the relationship between the State and the medical establishment. By widely opening up access to health care, it has transformed the objective conditions of the practice of medicine by increasing the number of patients—that is, clients—for doctors. Yet it has also called into question the sense of a vocation whose very nature justified the demand for, and the practice of, professional autonomy.

The Providence State is not the only reason for these changes. The development of medical techniques has modified clinical relations, as well as the relationships among the different professions that work together in the practice of medicine.[57] In the singular dialogue between physician and patient, all sorts of other medical professionals now intervene: specialists, laboratory biologists, simple medical technicians. Doctors now rarely practice their "art" without requesting that acts be performed by others, ranging from simple blood samplings to the various forms of medical imagery. The specific—clinical—relationship between doctor and patient is now limited by such techniques. When a physician needs to collaborate with colleagues[58] who are more competent than he is with respect to certain techniques, or with members of one of the regularly increasing

number of paramedical professions, he enters—like any professional—into a rationalized organization of work. He collaborates or
competes with medical technicians and, as regards his "human" relationships with patients, with all the other health professions: nurses,
midwives, physical therapists, psychologists, and so on.[59] The "art" of
medicine has become ever more a collective professional practice.

As for the social protection system, it also contributes to the transformation of doctor-patient relationships. The State is no longer
merely the guarantor of the doctor's autonomy. The Social Security
claims offices of the Intervention State, as well as private insurance
companies, directly intervene in the singular dialogue. Doctors increasingly become direct salaried employees (in hospitals) or indirect salaried employees (through the reimbursement—for medical
acts—that they receive from the Social Security system and private
insurance companies). Henceforth, as a former doctor laments, "certain physicians practice medicine like shopkeepers. . . . The vocation of being a doctor hardly exists anymore."[60]

A more complete analysis of this evolution would need to take
into account the modification of the "social" demand for medicine.
Computer programs and Internet resources enable doctors to become informed about medical progress all over the world; yet at the
same time, they limit his autonomy and charisma because a patient
now also has access to the same information. The increasing number of health magazines, special television programs, and pharma-
ceutical guides create specific demands in patients—is not health
the primary value of a democratic society?—and a sort of familiarity
with, if not competence in, the world of health. This is all the more
true in that average educational levels have risen. It has become
difficult for doctors to totally ignore his patients' demands, because
they are also his clients.[61] His medical competence no longer com-
pels respect for its own sake.

To the extent that the profession, in the sense of American sociology, constituted a normative and regulatory model that was established in a general way, its gradual disappearance lies at the heart of
what is experienced by physicians as the crisis of their profession.
The relative decrease in income that is experienced by the majority
of doctors is of course a crucial dimension of this crisis. However,
beyond this strictly economic aspect of the crisis, their discontent
first and foremost derives from the fact that physicians—after having taken advantage of the enormous development of their activity

thanks to the Social Security system and the imperative mass demand, in a democratic society, for health care, as Claudine Herzlich puts it—now find themselves, and their professional activities, obligatorily subjected to the control of institutions outside of the medical establishment per se, namely the claims offices of the Social Security system. Physicians are increasingly losing grasp of the sovereign privilege of taking care of their own affairs, even if, in France, the governing board of the official medical doctors' association (the "Conseil de l'Ordre des Médecins") still effectively resists this development. But for how much longer? The computerized management of both medical acts and the reimbursement of prescribed medicines, as well as the inevitable auditing of health expenditures (which have become public expenditures), can only contribute to the gradual dissolution of the rules of medical secrecy and the "inexpressible" relationship that doctors claim to maintain with their patients. Protest by doctors against controls and, more generally, against all the obligations resulting from the administrative management of the medical profession—little matter if the protest is formulated with respect to medical practice in public hospitals or in private doctors' offices—is linked to the questioning of liberal professions in general and to the difficulties of maintaining an idealized reference to a profession experienced as a vocation. Physicians evoke the crisis of medicine, and the end of professional autonomy, which used to be the guarantor of the singular relation between doctor and patient.[62] Yet the democratization of health care and State intervention are gradually making professional autonomy obsolete. The liberal profession model, which is still given great value and continues to dominate representations, is probably nothing but a relic.

From "Classical Law" to "Corporate Law"

The practice of law provides an example of a profession which, while continuing to invoke the singularity of its "mission," has—for an increasing number of lawyers—reconverted itself and entered the competitive economic marketplace, thus relinquishing the specificity of an original relationship. The fluctuation between practicing a liberal profession linked to defending individuals—a political vocation, a mission associated with human rights—and participating in the competitive economic sector explains how the world of lawyers has divided. Some lawyers continue to refer to the "classical bar" (the *"barreau classique"*) and to its vocation, while others now refer to the "corporate law bar" (the *"barreau d'affaires"*).[63]

The former, who are still more numerous in France, conform to norms inherited from the "liberal" law profession of the past, even if this heritage has been "noticeably altered"; they reject the idea of exercising an ordinary profession subjected to the logic of competition. They continue to invoke their political vocation (and the services that they provide to individuals), their defense of human rights, and their respect for fundamental freedoms. They thereby underscore the originality of a relationship based on mutual confidence between two human beings. This relationship recalls the singular dialogue between a doctor and his patient: the service provided integrates two human beings into a personal and political exchange in which commercial notions are secondary. This ideology of a political vocation is inscribed, symbolically speaking, in a great tradition going back to Ancient Greece, including for instance Antigone's defense against Creon's demands and the reason of State. For lawyers, it is a conception inherited from a glorious tradition that "is maintained as an almost natural predisposition, handed down from one generation to the next, and always ready to be reactivated."[64] According to this model, the laws governing a lawyer's professional relationships with his fellow lawyers—as in the case of medical doctors—fortify and symbolize the non-mercantile nature of a lawyer's relationships with both his clients and his colleagues. The French national bar association—the "Ordre des Avocats"—attempted to keep this vocation alive, until the Law of 1990.

This law henceforth authorizes another model of legal practice, that of the "corporate law bar." The expected consequences of the economic liberalization associated with the Treaty of Rome revealed the crisis of the liberal profession—the "classical bar"—of law practice. It became necessary to help all French legal professions face up to international competition, in France as abroad. Indeed, French lawyers were faced with the dual competition of Anglo-American law offices—which had fully adopted the transformation of the profession—and auditing and accounting firms that were directly working for business firms and corporations. The Law of 1990 offered a compromise. It attempted to limit the consequences of the economic market and competition, and to maintain the great tradition of law practice, all the while giving lawyers the means to enter the world of business firms and corporations.[65] The law marked the end of a purely liberal profession, but it also limited the transformation of the practice of law into a capitalist enterprise. The law concluded a long period of crisis whose ferocity was consistent with the stakes: a questioning of the identity of the various legal professions, the sense of the legal profession, its purview, and its claim to an intervention monopoly. The law took note of the transformation of the profession, which had moved from offering services exclusively to individuals—its political vocation—to providing services to business firms and thereby collaborating with economic production. All the while, the law attempted to protect the "liberal" features of the profession. It confirmed and validated the split in the legal milieu, one part of which intended to maintain the traditional sense of the liberal profession, while the other part devoted itself to the competitive sector. Like all laws based on compromises, is this one destined to last?

In any event, it has enabled corporate law to develop, characterized by relationships of a mercantile and competitive kind. The relationship between a lawyer and his client has become strictly commercial, and is regimented by a contract. Lawyers following this model of legal practice underscore its modernity; they express their indifference to the national bar association, the Ordre des Avocats, and adopt the logic of competitiveness; they adhere to the ideology of economic liberalism and prize financial success. They have adapted themselves to the world of business firms and the economic market. In that they directly participate in economic life, they have become economic agents like any other such agents. For them, fellow lawyers are no longer colleagues, *"confrères"*—implying the idea of non-commercial relationships—but rather rival competitors. Although they still represent a minority in France, this kind of lawyer is increasing in number, especially among the younger generation. Their corresponding way of practicing law tends to eliminate the specificity and the political horizon of law practiced as a liberal profession. Yet an individual lawyer can in fact follow, according to the case at hand, either model and thus combine the two kinds of legal activity. Conceivably, the experiences of many lawyers, divided between the ideology of their traditional mission and vocation and the willingness to adapt the legal profession to the logic of capitalist enterprise and the economic market, fluctuate between these two conceptions, and each time according to different configurations.

Public law about liberal professions has gradually confirmed and validated this evolution. At the present time, liberal professions are subjected to civil law, not commercial or corporate law. They are not considered to be "ordinary" business firms acting in a market: they exercise activities in which altruism plays its role; relationships with clients are absolutely personal; and talent is the primary value. But law is now in the process of 'trivializing' liberal professions by considering them to be economic agents like any other such agents."[66] French and European governmental authorities have applied commercial law to liberal professions. A clientele can be "sold," for example. In a ruling of the First Civil Chamber dated 7 November 2000, the Court of Cassation ("Cour de Cassation") recognized the notion of a *"fonds d'exercice libéral,"* that is non-tangible property that had resulted from the exercise of a liberal profession; up to then, only shopkeepers possessed a law concerning the selling of their non-tangible commercial property (*"fonds de commerce"*). The Court ruled that it was "not illicit to sell a medical clientele when a liberal profession was constituting or ceding its non-tangible property."[67] In the practice of a profession, once a clientele is at stake, as in the case of commercial firms, all prerogatives—and in particular professional secrecy—lose their validity. In fact, professional secrecy is already in decline.[68] It is already the case that non-liberal professions cannot plead professional secrecy in front of a judge. Bankers are even required to alert the authorities whenever they notice suspicious money transfers in bank accounts. Some wish to extend this system to lawyers, because more and more lawyers practice corporate law. The latter still claim that their relationship with clients is of a special kind, and point out that they are the guardians of freedom against repression, even against the repression stemming from the application of the penal code. The Law of 7 April 1997 effectively gives a lawyer the right to refuse to hand over a secret to an authority requesting it. But in a ruling dated 2 July 1999, the Criminal Chamber of the Court of Cassation limited this right to cases solely concerning the defense of individuals, and thus did not extend the right to cases in which lawyers collaborated in commercial activities—thereby juridically validating the existence not only in general of a dual model for the exercise of the profession, but also specifically that of the "corporate law bar." A new amendment to a projected law on economic regulations obliges lawyers exercising legal counsel to reveal to judicial authorities any potentially fraudulent practices, as is already the case with bankers. If this amendment is adopted, it would represent a new stage in the trivialization of liberal professions, ever more obliged to fall in line with characteristic commercial and economic practices.[69]

The relationships between physician and patient, lawyer and client, priest and parishioner, professor and student, and social worker and "assisted" citizen increasingly conform to the model of contractual relationships between equal individuals (or equal parties); that is, to a fundamentally egalitarian relationship model that is established between a provider of services and his client. *Homo democraticus* becomes impatient whenever faced with competence, including that of a physician or lawyer. Competence calls into question his own sovereignty. Relationships that he maintains with others lose their political or metaphysical horizons. All professional practices tend to become trivialized in this sense. The term "user" (*"usager,"* in French) henceforth designates all sorts of relationships, effacing the specificity of each relationship with respect to all others.[70] Doctors are gradually becoming salaried employees of the Social Security system; priests are becoming social workers and providers of sacraments. Corporate lawyers who work with firms are gradually replacing lawyers who conceived of their profession as that of defending individual liberty. Despite their professional job tenure, judges are increasingly becoming functionaries like other civil servants. Professors are supposed to produce university graduates, museum curators to collect visitors. Although they would not dream of giving up the material security and social standing that are provided by the Providence State, teachers, judges, doctors, and social workers—all of whom are directly or indirectly functionaries of the Social State—deplore the fact that the State insufficiently acknowledges the absolute originality of their vocation. This is because the sacred dimension—made up of religious belief, situations of life and death, humanist or political values—is diminishing. The professions that gave an even indirect or modest shape to collective values, and thereby instituted them, are affected by the erosion of collective transcendence, be it religious or political.

That no economic liberal (in the French sense) still questions the legitimacy of the Providence State illustrates well the dynamics of democracy, and the obviousness now attached to the extension of social and economic rights, considered in their broadest sense. These rights now appear natural rights. Taking note of the pertinence of Marxist criticism and the existence of the Providence State, no one today dreams of denying the significance of the social and economic rights that give a concrete, daily meaning to the idea of citizenship. Material survival in conditions ensuring the dignity of each and every person appears to be a citizen right that democratic society, following the principles upon which its legitimacy is based, is required to satisfy. The 1948 Universal Declaration of Human Rights includes both the political rights of the French Revolution of 1789—or freedom-rights—and the social and economic rights defended by socialist thinkers—or claim-rights. This may well have resulted from the necessity of obtaining the votes of the Soviet block so that the Declaration could be passed with a large majority. Yet beyond these political circumstances, the Declaration represents a broader agreement about the necessity of not exclusively appealing to freedom-rights and of taking into account the real conditions underlying the exercise of these rights. The debate is now only about their nature, as was seen in the preceding chapter concerning social and economic citizenship. Should one conclude that they have become the genuine political rights? Or should one retain the idea, expressed by economic-liberal thinkers (in the French sense of the term), that they indeed represent the conditions underlying the exercise of political rights, yet are nonetheless of a different order?

Whatever answer is given to this question, which remains open, the very principle of the Social State is no longer discussed. Even more tellingly, it appears today that claim-rights are not antagonistic to freedom-rights; that they are inscribed in their own history and logic; that they deploy the virtualities or the consequences of the sovereignty of the citizen-individual. Thinkers reputed to be economic liberals, like Raymond Aron or John Rawls, have both analyzed claim-rights as a political project susceptible of resolving the tension—perceptible as early as 1789—between the proclaimed equality of all citizens and the inequalities of real, living individuals; they each proposed democratic theories based on the integration or synthesis of freedom-rights and claim-rights.[71] Even if one continues to study the tension, indeed the contradiction, between the individualism of modern societies and the socialization of wealth that is organized by the Intervention State[72], and even if one still examines the limits that need to be established for redistribution so that it does not slow down production, it is clear that no one calls the principle of redistribution into question. The debates are about the means and the limits of intervention, about the possibilities and the means of attaining financial equilibrium when needs are undefined, and about the timeliness of changing from an equality principle to an equity principle as regards the management of the wealth transfer system.

At the same time, in public life, one constantly invokes the crisis, failure, or even the end of the Welfare State. Criticism of globalization is willingly accompanied by an invocation of the end of the national Providence State. It is thought that social protection will become ineffective when confronted with decisions made by transnational business corporations and conglomerates that can avoid applying the social regulations of providential nation-states. Jürgen Habermas, for example, considers that it is an obvious fact that the Intervention State is retreating, that the flexibility developing in the economic world with respect to the management of human resources is relentlessly destroying social protection. Is globalization really causing the withdrawal? This is not the place to discuss such a question. One can only point out that this is not the case if one examines redistribution statistics; despite the clearly-stated aims of the governments of Ronald Reagan and Margaret Thatcher, the redistribution percentages have remained stable ever since the mid-1970s.[73] Yet it is also true that the political significance of the Providence State has become less clear and that it no longer constitutes, in the same way as in the past, a genuine political project opposed to the communist project. Moreover, some analysts even think that it is no longer adapted to the demands of the new economy, that the "institutions of the Providence State, inherited from the cold war and from the Keynesian era, appear to be in growing contradiction with the functioning of an open economy"—and that this is particularly true for "corporatist-state"[74] political systems. In any case, what is significant for the dynamics of democracy is the ever-present and ever-renewable feeling that the Intervention State is both insufficient—whereas it redistributes in France more than half of the gross domestic product—and threatened—whereas all attempts to profoundly reform it, up to now, have failed.

Notes

1.   Tocqueville, 3, IV, 5, edition of 1868, p. 499. English translation: II, p. 323.
2.   Preamble of the 1946 Constitution, paragraphs 11 and 12.
3.   Whence, for example, the current debates about the recuperation of sums resulting from the succession (or estate) of deceased persons who had benefited from various social minima. Should the ultimate providential logic be applied, whereby the State would take care of these persons and then recuperate from their succession whatever sums had been allocated during their lifetimes, or should what remains of familial solidarity (implying the obligation to nourish) be preserved, the State thereby not recuperating from the succession the sums that had been allocated? In this debate, one sees the opposition between the traditional logic of the family and that of

the autonomy of the individual, which has culminated at the moment in incoherent measures implying the recuperation of certain, but not all, social minima from the succession of deceased persons. After a long parliamentary debate and an amendment to the governmental project, the new personalized autonomy allocation measure does not imply recuperation from the succession.

4. This is one of the essential topics in Castel, 1995.
5. Cited by Marc Lazar, "La République à l'épreuve du social," in Sadoun, 2000, vol. 2, p. 356.
6. Paugam, 1996.
7. A bibliography about workers can be found in Beaud-Pialoux, 1999. On the recent transformations of capitalism, see Boltanski-Chiapello, 1999.
8. Beaud-Pialoux, 1999, from whom I borrow these quick observations.
9. Hoggart, 1970 (1957).
10. Cited by Beaud-Pialoux, 1999, p. 424.
11. Paugam, 2000.
12. Paugam, 2000, p. 366.
13. Paugam, 2000, *passim.*
14. See the first chapter above.
15. On 1 January 1998, 800,000 social workers "having a status recognized as such," 350,000 nurses in 1997, 330,000 nurse's aids in 1999. Cf. *Études et résultats de la DREES*, Ministère de l'Emploi et de la Solidarité, No. 79, September 2000, No. 12, March 1999, and No. 54, March 2000.
16. An example of the recent creation of a new profession. According to the *Lettre d'information du ministère de la Culture et de la Communication* of 23 April 2001 (No. 81): "In 1999, in partnership with the Cultural Affairs Directors for Local Collectivities in the Paris suburbs, the Prevention Association of the Villette Science Museum and Music Museum Site (APSV, "Association de prévention du site de la Villette") conceived and put into action the first training of local cultural accompaniment agents. This professional qualification is inscribed in the field of cultural mediation. It articulates the tasks that establish relationships between the public and an artistic heritage, and enhances the cultural expression of population groups. Ten young people were recruited for this special training, which is validated by a State diploma entitled "Technician-Organizer for Popular Education and Youth (BEATEP, "Brevet d'État d'animateur technicien de l'éducation populaire et de la jeunesse"). The diploma then enables the graduate to enter public competitions for territorial civil service jobs. The training includes a qualification stage in the framework of a Youth Employment Contract in a municipality. An APSV project, overseen by the Ministry of Culture and Communication—specifically by the Delegation for Plastic Arts, the Funds for the Encouragement of Creativity, the Delegation for Development and Territorial Action, the Direction of Architecture and Cultural Heritage—as well as the Ministry of Youth and Sports and the Inter-ministerial Delegation for Cities, then finalizes the training."
17. It is well known that the budget of the Ministry of Culture aims to represent 1 percent of the entire State budget, and that of the Ministry of Sports to represent 0.5 percent. But it is necessary to add the contributions of local collectivities. 22,000 "cultural" agents worked for the Ministry of Culture and local collectivities on 1 January 1999. The credits of the Ministry have been multiplied by 70 since 1959. Cf. Saint-Pulgent, 1999, pp. 42 ff. The credits devoted to creation in the field of plastic arts was multiplied tenfold between 1981 and 1982, and doubled between 1982 and 1983. According to other estimations, the number of jobs linked to cultural and audiovisual development is approximately 415,000. In order to have an idea of all the civil servants working in the fields of education, culture, and sports, it is

necessary to add to these figures the number of functionaries in the Ministry of National Education—over one million.

18.   At the beginning of the 2000s, 44 "manager-agreements" ("*accords-cadres*") had been signed in the Ministries of Employment and Solidarity, of Youth and Sports, as well as by prefects, which should result in the creation of 20,000 Youth Employment Contracts devoted to athletic management and organization. Cf. Lionel Arnaud and Jean-Pierre Arnaud, "L'État et le sport: construction et transformation d'un service public," in Arnaud, 2000, p. 71.

19.   Pons, 1996, p. 266.

20.   Moulin, 1992, p. 249.

21.   Moulin, 1992, pp. 117-9. In the following pages, one will find a description of all the measures taken for ensuring the social protection of artists.

22.   Augustin Girard, article "Création (politique publique de la)," in Waresquiel, 2001.

23.   Moulin, 1992, p. 255. In non-sociological terms, one Minister of Culture termed this "having the begging bowl in one hand, and a Molotov cocktail in the other."

24.   Menger, 1997; Paradeise, 1998.

25.   Paradeise, 1998, p. 209.

26.   Menger, 1997, p. 310.

27.   Schnapper, 1994 (1981).

28.   Tocqueville, 3, I, 10, edition of 1868, p. 69. English translation: II, p. 44.

29.   Mendras, 1988.

30.   Inglehart, 1997.

31.   See the work of Alain Touraine and his collaborators: Touraine et al., 1981; Touraine *et al.*, 1980; Touraine et al., 1984.

32.   Kaltenbach, 2001, p. 154.

33.   That is "the medical and paramedical professions, social workers, teachers, artistic professions, cultural intermediaries." Cf. Hervieu-Léger, 2001, p. 89.

34.   Weber, 1963 (1919), p. 63.

35.   Boltanski-Thévenot, 1991.

36.   Bourdieu, 1993, p. 231.

37.   Ion-Tricart, 1992 (3rd edition), p. 4.

38.   Ion-Tricart, 1992 (3rd edition), p. 62.

39.   Ion-Tricart, 1992 (3rd edition), p. 72. Corinne Rostaign has produced a similar analysis with respect to the relations of prison guards to their profession. Cf. Rostaign, 1997.

40.   Ion-Tricart, 1992 (3rd edition), p. 58.

41.   Excerpted from an interview cited in Bourdieu, 1993, p. 256.

42.   Excerpted from an interview cited in Bourdieu, 1993, pp. 659 and 656.

43.   Demailly, 1991.

44.   Renaut, 1995.

45.   Freidson, 1986, p. 436.

46.   The number of students, in France, was 60,000 in 1953; 300,000 in 1968; 1,500,000 in 1998; and more than 2,000,000 at the beginning of the academic year 2001-2.

47.   This is the origin of the recurrent "great debate" opposing, in various medias, those who favor research and knowledge, and those who favor pedagogy.

48.   Cited by Octobre, 1999, p. 357, who outlines the objective conditions of the carrying-out of this profession.

49.   "1. The relative autonomy of farmer ('paysan') collectivities with respect to the surrounding society, which dominates them yet which tolerates their originality. 2. The structural importance of the domestic group in the organization of economic life and the social life of the collectivity. 3. An economic system of relative autarchy,

which does not distinguish consumption and production, and which entertains relationships with the surrounding economy. 4. A local collectivity characterized by tightly knit inner relationships and by weak relationships with surrounding collectivities. 5. The decisive function of the mediation roles performed by authorities between farmer collectivities and the surrounding society." Cf. Mendras, 1995, pp. 14-5.

50.   Hervieu, 1993, pp. 79 and 84.

51.   Rosine Christin, in Bourdieu, 1993, p. 654.

52.   For the special problems experienced by professions devoted to maintaining law and order in a society with "lax" values, it is necessary to consult Dominique Montjardet's work on the various police corps. Especially pertinent to the analyses that I am outlining here is Montjardet, 1988.

53.   In France, the Law of 30 November 1892 ensured the status of the profession. The Law of August 1940 instituted the Ordre des Médecins, which guaranteed the autonomy of the profession.

54.   Freidson, 1986, p. 433.

55.   Excerpted from an interview cited in Herzlich et al., 1993, p. 236.

56.   Hassenteufel, 1997.

57.   Schweyer-Binst, 1995.

58.   Medical doctors and teachers belong to professions that use the terms of "*confrères*" and "*collègues*" (both mean "colleagues") in order to show that the relationships established between members of the profession are not of a competitive nature.

59.   For this topic, see Aïach-Fassin, 1994.

60.   Cited in Herzlich et al., 1993, p. 236.

61.   In the vocabulary used by doctors, the term "client" is gradually replacing "patient."

62.   In the United States, where social protection is less developed, the intervention of private insurance companies as well as that of lawyers and judges into the relationship between doctors and patients has similarly transformed the meaning of this singular dialogue.

63.   Everything concerning lawyers is borrowed from Karpik, 1995, *passim*, and especially pp. 452 ff.

64.   Karpik, 1995, p. 455.

65.   The law combines the monopoly of juridical activity, reserved to lawyers ("*avocats*"), appellate court lawyers ("*avoués près les cours d'appel*"), notaries public ("*notaires*"), bailiffs ("*huissiers de justice*"), certified auctioneers ("*commissaires-priseurs*"), judiciary administrators ("*administrateurs judiciaires*") and official liquidators ("*mandataires liquidateurs*"); the fusion of lawyers and juridical councils ("*conseils juridiques*") with the creation of an option of working as a salaried employee; an organization associating a national council and the distinct orders; and the creation of "liberal profession" firms more than half of whose capital must be held by lawyers belonging to the firm, the rest belonging to members of the juridical and judiciary "family." By favoring lawyers, the law regulated the most bitter conflict: the one opposing lawyers and certified accountants. Accountants who worked directly for business firms and corporations continued to see their competence restricted, by law, to their main activity.

66.   Marie Anne Frison-Roche, "Les professions libérales, des entreprises presque comme les autres," *Le Monde*, 23 January 2001.

67.   Ibid.

68.   The diminishing of professional secrecy does not concern only liberal professions; it is a more widespread tendency, for secrecy is contradictory with the publicity and public openness that characterize democracy. This was recently illustrated when the

Bishop of Bayeux, who had not denounced a priest who had practiced pedophilia, was himself convicted.

69.   Similarly, architects have constituted only an incomplete liberal profession, to the extent that they have never obtained an intervention monopoly. Many architects have decided not to practice their profession as a liberal profession. As early as thirty years ago, the profession of architect already appeared to be a "pre-modern version of a profession that is inadapted to the modernization of construction processes." Some architects have become agents of the Cultural Providence State, functionaries of the State or local collectivities who counsel, administrate or teach (such as architects who work on French monuments, urban counselors, or architecture school professors). Others directly participate in production by working as salaried employees in real estate promotion agencies, in construction firms, or as entrepreneurs. Ever since the beginning of the 1970s, the "mission" of building for human beings the ideal house or city essentially exists as a myth nostalgically maintained by the profession. Cf. Moulin et al., 1973.

70.   Demailly, 2000. See also the entire issue of *Lien social et politiques—RIAC* (Montreal), devoted to *Relation de service et métiers relationnels*, No. 40, Autumn 1998.

71.   This observation is made by Mesure-Renaut, 1999, p. 206.

72.   See for example *État-providence*, 1996.

73.   De Swaan, 1995 (1988), p. 304.

74.   Baverez, 2001, p. 801.

4

The Dialectics of Equality and Authenticity

The dynamics of democracy extend into the current debate about the appropriateness of recognizing "cultural rights." This term does not mean the rights to education and culture, to which respond, as has been seen, various kinds of Providence State intervention carried out by the Ministries of National Education, Culture, and Social Affairs. The term "cultural rights" here means, to cite Sylvie Mesure and Alain Renaut's definition, "the rights of an individual to possess and develop, possibly in conjunction with other individuals in a group defined by shared values and traditions, his own cultural life, which corresponds to a cultural identity distinct from that of other individuals or groups."[1]

During the past twenty years, in English-speaking countries, debate about the public acknowledgment of such rights has been developing among political philosophers. The echoes have been rather slow in reaching France. Yet one can surmise that the debate will eventually reach this side of the Atlantic because of an oft observed law pertaining to the spread of culture. If the force of the so-called French "republican" tradition has up to now constituted an obstacle to the extension of the debate, sensitivity to "multi-culturalism," however ambiguous the term is—or indeed because of its ambiguity—is increasing. Because this sort of sensitivity is inscribed in the very continuity of the dynamics of democracy, one may deduce that it will continue to increase and that it will more often be expressed, through various kinds of State intervention.

The current debate takes off from scratch, as it were, or—alternatively—recycles in the name of democratic values the critique of traditional citizenship that was formulated as early as 1790 by Edmund Burke, then developed by several romantic and counter-revolutionary writers who were hostile to the individualistic and voluntarist inspiration of citizenship. Let us recall that these thinkers criticized,

131

from various angles, the abstraction of the notion of citizen, which tore the individual from his tangible historical and religious roots; they denounced the will to create an artificial society based on the individual and not on a collective body that would give meaning to an individual's destiny; they underscored the perverse consequences that would result from the ambition to build up a rational political order which would violate the hierarchical nature of societies and deny the historical heritage informing them. According to this viewpoint, societies should remain within the framework of the institutions inherited from the past, especially those ensuring the exercise of real, concrete freedoms. Today, those who advocate public acknowledgment of cultural rights or the constituting of a multicultural society are, in no wise, supporters of counter-revolutionary thought; they do not oppose the value and meaning of traditional "community" to modern citizenship and modern "society" (to take up the classic vocabulary of the sociological tradition). They formulate their criticism by appealing to the notion of "genuine" or "real" democracy, and invoke its development in the future. In English terms, this is what can be called the *liberal* critique of *liberalism*. In this sense, the critique parallels that of Marxist thinkers, who likewise desired to establish real democracy in the future, even as they criticized the limits and the insufficient qualities of formal citizenship.

The Acknowledgment of Dignity

Nation-Building and Democracy: The Classic Solution

Within a national society, as a rule, the various extant historical collectivities[2] and the political organization of the society do not coincide. Nations have always brought together historical collectivities and diverse peoples, even though the principle of nationalism originally asserted the legitimate right of any one collectivity or people (included in the nation) to form an independent political entity. Even those nations most resembling the idea of a nation-state— that is, where the historical collectivity, or the people, overlap with the political organization—have always been heterogeneous. A democratic society thus had to manage the ethnic or ethnico-religious diversity of the population groups gathered within the same political entity, all the while maintaining the necessary unity of the public realm. The democratic society had to establish institutions likely to ensure at once the equality of all citizens and the various expressions of the "authenticity" of individuals who referred to particular religious and historical traditions. Citizenship is also a tool for managing diversity.

Democratic nations have thus always been "multicultural" by definition, to use the modern term, in that they were made up of population groups that differed, among themselves, with respect to their religious practices or references, their regional or national origins, or their social conditions. In accordance with the principles of citizenship, French "republicans" intended to manage this diversity, not by means of "the denial of one part"[3] of an individual, as one readily says today, but rather by means of the principle of the separation of the public and the private realms. To the private realm were relegated the diversity of cultures, that is the freedom of individuals to maintain and nurture particular historical or religious attachments and loyalties, thanks to the respect of public freedoms such as are guaranteed by the freedom of assembly, the right to practice freely one's religion, and the right to use one's native language in the private realm. In the public realm, the ways and means of collective life were unified and organized by the political institutions of citizenship. This is the theory on which American *liberalism* is based; in this case, one speaks of "liberal orthodoxy" or "procedural" liberalism. In France, these are the principles of "republican integration." By distinguishing the public and private realms, French republicans and American *liberals*—who are otherwise different yet who nevertheless concur as regards the means of managing diversity[4]—have endeavored to combine the civil and political equality of citizens with respect to their particular religious and historical attachments, and to ensure at once the unity of society by means of common citizenship and the freedom of individuals to make existential choices. The various expressions of particular loyalties were accepted as long as they did not contradict the principle of the freedom of each individual and the equality of all. *Liberalism*—or citizenship—is a *principle* of tolerance, even if it was sometimes, and even often, applied without any tolerance whatsoever during the period of nation-building and nationalist feeling, and even if some of those who proclaim themselves to be "republicans" in France today are not distinguished by their excessive tolerance.

According to this so-called "classic" conception, multiculturalism is a right, because the separation of the public and private realms is the principle upon which the political order is founded. Multiculturalism is inscribed in the very principles of modern democracy and of an *État de droit*, in other words a State based on and bound by law. The principle underlying social organization is that of integrating population groups by means of the unity, the equality, and the universalism of the public domain, which is the common ground where citizenship is taught and exercised.[5] This principle implies that individuals must conform to constraints that are imposed by this shared public realm. The multiculturalism of the society must be controlled, and expressions of multiculturalism must be submitted to the norms and values of the public realm. If the cultural specificities of particular groups are compatible with the demands of collective life and its values—the freedom and equality of all persons—then nationals and aliens legally settled in the national territory have the right to cultivate their particularities in their personal life as well as in their social life, as long as the rules of the public realm are respected. Yet these specificities should not be used to establish a particular political identity that is recognized as such within the public realm, which must remain the shared common ground where citizenship—its practices and its language—is exercised.

The Critique of Liberalism or Genuine Democracy

This classic solution is henceforth considered obsolete by theoreticians of a communitarian persuasion. It is criticized for having primarily aimed at ensuring the equality of individuals at the expense of the authenticity of their religious and historical roots. Moreover, argue such thinkers, the population groups gathered into the same political society have become more multifarious than in the past; many such groups wish to preserve the traits of a singular culture—different from the national majority culture—through which they can give meaning to their lives. It follows that a democratic society should open itself up to this aspiration.

Here, I do not intend to summarize the thinking of such writers, who differ in their specific inspiration and theories but who nonetheless share a communitarian inspiration, without actually forming a strict school of thought. Instead, I would like to draw out the sociological sense of this intellectual movement and show how it illustrates the dynamics of democracy. The movement indeed reflects a sensibility that has spread throughout the majority of the population and is summarized by the ambiguous term of "multiculturalism." Ever since the 1970s and 1980s, multiculturalism has become the object of widespread reflection, as well as of political demands and militancy, in all Western democracies. It is widely asserted that the multiculturalism of social and religious life has increased through the effects of the great population migrations toward Europe since the end of Second World War. However, it has not been proven that the objective diversity of societies is actually greater today than it was in the past. How, in fact, can the diversity of societies be measured? During periods of nationalism, societies were not culturally homogenous, either; it was nationalists who proclaimed the existence of a united and homogenous people in order to legitimate their demands for the independence of the people. This being said, the significance given to diversity has changed. Today, diversity *per se* and the individual's right to authenticity have become values shared by the majority. In all countries, "assimilation" or "integration" policies are contested. In the United States, criticism of the national ideal and its underlying realities, the discovery of the existence and the value of *ethnicity*, as well as acknowledgment of the right of long-persecuted minorities to obtain compensation, have called into question the legitimacy of both the *liberal* solution and the national policy of integrating, or assimilating, immigrant population groups.

More generally, it is true that the political order based on relations among nation-states is weakening. Transnational phenomena—and transnationality in general—are developing. Examples include the number and activity of non-governmental or supranational organizations, the size of the uprooted population groups that such organizations directly take under their wing, and the directly political role played by international associations such as Amnesty International and Greenpeace. Problems concerning the environment, transportation, demography, population migration, and economic development now need to be dealt with by various organizations at a supranational level. One moreover observes a growing dissociation of political society, identity references, and economic practices. Economic and political realms do not coincide and the number of population groups that maintain particular loyalties or allegiances (relating to identity) beyond the national society in which they have settled is increasing. As we saw in the second chapter, when modern societies open themselves up to more diverse population groups, then the question of the traditional relation between nationality and citizenship is raised. Finally, with the spreading of modernism and post-modern thought, the change in collective values contributes to the undermining of the classic solution of *liberalism. Homo democraticus* is reluctant to let particularisms be transcended by means of politics; he gives precedence to the value of particularisms *per se,* as well as to the primary rights of an individual to be himself.

According to communitarian thinkers, genuine equality should include decent economic living conditions for individuals—all the more so in that the Providence State seems to have attained its limits. In their view, genuine equality also implies that the dignity of each individual should be secured by public recognition of the dignity of his culture, in both the intellectual and anthropological senses of the term. Canadian philosophers such as Charles Taylor and Will Kymlicka cite their own country as an example. Canada was founded on the idea of two peoples, one English, one French. Yet even if French-speakers possess the same economic conditions as the English-speakers, can they really experience genuinely equal conditions if they cannot use their language in public social life, if they are forced to express themselves in the language of the majority, which is not theirs, while the inverse is not true? Despite the myth that Canada was shaped by two "founding peoples," the English-speakers—because they are in the majority—do not have to learn the language of the French-speakers. This is why the dignity of each individual, a democratic value *par excellence*, cannot depend on decent material living conditions alone; it must also depend on the acknowledgment of his authenticity; in other words, on culture, which by definition is shared with others: it is this culture that gives meaning to an individual's existence. As is stated in an official text of the Quebecois government that justifies the implementation of a multicultural policy, "without equality among the various collective cultural heritages, equality among individuals can only be formal."[6]

Today, all writers of a communitarian persuasion concur in their criticism of the false neutrality of the State when it asserts that it abstains from intervening in the field of culture as it does in that of religion. In fact, whether linked to a nation or a particular "societal culture"[7], the National State is never neutral. The practices and values of the public realm impose themselves on particular historical collectivities, whose customs and values are gradually marginalized, then eliminated. In the past, the process of national integration compelled minorities to use the national language, in other words that of the majority, by eliminating from the public realm all other languages spoken by immigrants, or by regional or national minorities (such as autochthonous population groups). Reduced to private use, such languages eventually vanished. The calendar, the national holidays, and all majority customs were imposed on everyone, majority and minority members alike. The Christian holiday of Christmas is celebrated by Jews, Muslims, atheists, Buddhists, and animists. The educational system and public institutions instill the norms and values of the majority. By adopting immigration and naturalization policies favoring those who seemed the most likely to participate in the dominant "societal culture," the Canadian nation built itself up, all the while destroying minority cultures. Members of minorities were the victims of this process. This kind of analysis is obviously particularly persuasive in the case of autochthonous population groups. Yet little matter whether national policies were imposed by violence or in indirect ways, they transformed the language, social practices, values, heroes, symbols, and holidays of the majority into the language, social practices, values, heroes, symbols, and holidays of the entire population. Moreover, the electoral system was organized in such a way as to make minority representation improbable. *Liberalism*—or the "republican" management of diversity—was unable to acknowledge cultural pluralism and adapt itself to it. From this standpoint, it follows that it is necessary to break with such policies and recognize rights that have always been denied. It is necessary to reconsider the problem of rights for minority groups that have been victims of historical injustice in order to establish, at last, genuine democracy.

The classical management of diversity is thus shown up to be inoperative or, at best, insufficient for ensuring a democracy worthy of the name. It is considered to be no longer responsive to the need of human beings to have their dignity acknowledged, not only as abstract citizens, but also as real, living individuals who possess a singular history and culture. This is even truer in that the objective solidarity imposed by the Intervention State through obligatory tax levies remains abstract and bureaucratic; it does not foster a sentiment of genuine, tangible, down-to-earth solidarity among individuals and does not induce direct exchanges among them. The very conception of an autonomous citizen who freely participates in political sovereignty implies that he can enjoy self-development within his culture and, consequently, that his culture is fully recognized in all its historical dignity. The acknowledgment of individual participation in a culture is hitherto the very condition underlying the exercise of citizenship. Granting rights to minorities is a condition determining, as well as a means for encouraging, the autonomy of citizens and their ability to make "good decisions in good lifetimes." Charles Taylor subsequently develops the idea that it is necessary to adopt a policy of public "recognition" of particular cultures so that genuine democracy can be established. For him, one's identity is partly shaped by recognition, or by its absence, or indeed by the faulty perception of one's identity by others. In this perspective, lack of recognition represents more than a neglect of the respect normally due to another person. Recognition is not just a form of politeness that one offers people: it is a vital human need.[8] The breaking down of bonds among individuals and the overall "de-bonding" of liberal society thus need to be compensated for by lively and active intermediary corps or groups whose very existence at once presupposes community sentiments and allows individuals and groups to be acknowledged. This would respond to the unease and discontent of Western democratic societies: when identities are no longer stable and each individual is responsible for constructing his own identity (which is bound to be unstable and uncertain), the recognition of this identity becomes the essential social concern and cannot be separated from the individual's culture.

According to Michael Walzer, it is now necessary to shift from Liberalism 1 to Liberalism 2, in other words from an organization of society that is based on State abstention and the defense of individual rights (Liberalism 1), to an organization in which communities would be recognized publicly, on the condition that fundamental individual rights are respected (Liberalism 2). The State would be committed to the survival and prosperity of a nation, a particular culture, or a specific religion, or even a limited number of nations, cultures and religions, provided that fundamental rights of citizens who have other commitments (or no commitments at all) are protected.[9] In this way, Walzer reasons, social bonds can be reinforced and strengthened. Similarly, Will Kymlicka's thought has moved in the direction of instituting differentiated kinds of citizenship, on the condition that they are not contrary to human rights.[10]

The debate between *liberals* and communitarians reveals the tension between the two great democratic values that were conceived in the eighteenth century, namely the—by definition abstract—equality of all individuals and the authenticity of individuals and groups, which implies priority being given to the right to be oneself, even at the expense of constraints deriving from the collective order. In their concern to liberate human beings from the throne and the altar, Enlightenment thinkers and revolutionaries had called for human rights in general, that is those pertaining to abstract individuals and a community of citizens based on the "equality of free and reasonable human beings."[11] However, the rise of nations during the nineteenth century then induced a celebration of "the spirit of the people" or "the spirit" of each nation, defined by a specific culture and "genius." This is one of the constitutive tensions of democratic nations, torn between the universality of citizenship and the reality of the historical and religious attachments of real, living individuals.

In the name of democratic demands and an individual's primary right to authentic self-expression, communitarian thinkers criticize the individuality and abstraction of the concept of "citizen." By demanding various forms of public recognition of cultural singularities, they invoke the significance and the value of a fusion with Sameness, of down-to-earth experience, of the tangible bonds established among human beings. They point out that human beings ever desire to be united with their fellow man and to see their dignity fully acknowledged. They celebrate the immediacy of a sensitive "community" that bonds human beings to each other and gives them a sense of identity. They criticize the rational utopia of the republic and the establishment of a public realm formed by political institutions and by only officially acknowledged relationships among citizen-individuals. Their claims reveal the dissatisfaction and reluctance of *homo democraticus* when faced with the transcendence of republican politics.

An "Ethnic" Intervention State?[12]

The Significance of Institutions

The theoreticians and advocates of multiculturalism thus call for the acknowledgment of "cultural rights"; in other words, as has been described above, "the rights of an individual to possess and develop, possibly in conjunction with other individuals in a group defined by shared values and traditions, his own cultural life, which corresponds to a cultural identity distinct from that of other individuals or groups." It is clear that the very idea of "cultural rights" is connoted positively in democracies. "Culture" is an ambiguous term, which is associated at once with the generally recognized value of cultural relativism and with various kinds of action undertaken by the Ministry of Culture in favor of artists and the spreading of culture, and with the intention of resolving the philosophical and economic crisis experienced by democracies. Advocates of cultural rights cleverly, or unconsciously, take advantage of the ambiguity of the term. Not everyone can have in mind the distinction, honed by Sylvie Mesure and Alain Renaut, between the epithet "cultural" when related to the homonymous ministry, and "cultural" when "cultural rights" are invoked symbolically and in the sense given to these rights in identity politics, the legitimacy of which is theorized by thinkers of a communitarian persuasion. Who would contest the idea of granting "cultural rights" when in fact all individual rights—in political, social and cultural fields—as well as cultural diversity and tolerance have become the democratic values *par excellence*?

For the clarity of our analysis, it nonetheless seems justifiable to qualify these rights as "ethnic" and raise a question: Is it necessary to constitute an "ethnic" equivalent of the Social and Economic Intervention State? The term "ethnic" is deprecated in the French social realm; in both daily parlance and much academic research, "ethnic" is opposed to "civic." Yet it is possible to use the term in neutral fashion, as I have been doing (following upon Ernest Gellner and Anthony Smith), by showing that societies shaped and structured by citizenship were inevitably caught up in tension between "ethnic" bonds among individuals—in other words, resulting from the fact that they share the same (more or less real or invented) history, the same culture, and the same language[13]—and the rationality of the principle governing the political and juridical transcendence of citizenship.

By qualifying as "ethnic," rights that are generally termed "cultural," I clearly expose myself to criticism imputing that I am hostile to the public recognition of such rights. Yet using the term "ethnic" has two advantages. First, it avoids the ambiguity and haziness of the word "cultural." It is no coincidence that both Alain Touraine and the theoreticians of Cultural Ministry policy use the expression "cultural democracy"[14]—though in different senses. The latter mean Cultural Ministry policy; the former, a desirable evolution envisioned for the republic. Second, the term "ethnic" enables one to formulate an essential question that is too often neglected by advocates of cultural rights: to what extent can the rights of specific historical collectivities be recognized in the national public realm, without calling into question the common values and practices permitting the formation of a democratic society based on negotiation and compromise? The infra-national communities that are called "ethnic"—the historical collectivities—can obviously enjoy the freedom of maintaining a language, a culture, and a specific collective memory, provided that they are not contrary to common values. But to what extent can the common realm of citizenship be multiple and diverse? How can individual freedom and equality for all citizens—a principle that *liberal* philosophers and moderate communitarian thinkers do not call into question—be reconciled with public acknowledgment of distinct cultural "values" and "traditions," which are collective because they are "shared"—to cite once again the terms used in Sylvie Mesure and Alain Renaut's definition? How can one publicly recognize today—that is, through public measures implying the use of public funds—that cultural rights are an integral part of those individual rights that a democratic society, given its values, is required to guarantee?

In other words, can the Welfare State be extended to "culture," in the senses given to this term historically and in identity politics? The development of the Providence State had "responded" to the first criticism leveled against citizenship, namely the denunciation of the gap between proclaimed civic equality and the reality of social and economic inequalities among individuals and groups. Is it now necessary to "respond" to the second criticism, which attacked the abstract nature of the citizen-individual, by proclaiming the recognition of cultural rights? If both modern *liberalism* and the republic managed to act upon, thanks to the Providence State, the claims—considered legitimate—of the workers' movement and to ensure that all citizens and legally settled aliens benefited from the same social and economic rights, then how can—or should—the new demand for public acknowledgment of cultural rights be taken into account? Should not *liberal* society endeavor to accept the truthful elements in the critique formulated by communitarian thinkers, as it formerly did with respect to Marxist-inspired criticism, without abandoning the absolute preeminence of individual rights, which lie at the heart of its political project? In this case, a new stage in the history of citizenship, and the critical reflection necessarily accompanying it, would be ushered in.[15]

However, is the parallel between the demands for social and economic rights—which led to the Social Intervention State—and the demands for cultural rights, upon which this debate is based, entirely convincing? It does not seem self-evident that the critique of citizenship that was carried out in the name of economic rights can be transposed to the cultural domain. The world of economics is "concrete," real, tangible, down-to-earth; it is constituted of social practices. In this respect, the world of "culture" is not a reality of the same nature. Democratic societies abstain from defining the good. They do not directly organize, *through institutions*, the meaning that human beings give to their acts and existence, nor the ways by which they construct meaning in order to explain evil and unhappiness. Democratic societies acknowledge citizens' right to participate in *social practices* through which this meaning is formulated. A democratic State does not recognize a belief in God, but rather the right of individuals to establish places where specific religious rites and ceremonies can be carried out; it also acknowledges the right of individuals to have such practices (as are related to their beliefs) respected—on the condition that they conform to the imperatives of the public realm and do not contradict common values. This freedom depends on the religious freedom of individuals, not on collective rights. Even in the most secular countries, a series of legal measures and practices regulate the relations among the State, institutionalized religions, and various other religious groups. Yet today, if "religious" practices can be independent of political practices, can the same be said of "cultural" practices, which take place on the political and identity level? Kymlicka comments that the inclusion of workers and migrants is not of the same nature[16]: economic inequalities are not of the same order as political and identity differences. The exclusive defense of identities, which risks being fostered by the acknowledgment of particular communities defined in terms of national or religious origin, is not always compatible with democratic dialogue and compromises, and with the acceptance of the common rules established by the public realm.

The significance of institutions has not disappeared with the evolution of national and industrial societies. It is true that institutions have changed in form and that individuals increasingly contest them. Neither institutions nor the value of tradition are accepted as such. Yet collective life cannot be carried on without certain kinds of relationships which are established among individuals, and which are inherited from the past and crystalized by law. Similarly, collective life cannot be perpetuated without certain habits which are handed down from one generation to the next, and which form as many limits to individual autonomy as conditions governing the exercise of individual liberty. The sociology of the Subject does not imply that each individual, having become the creator of his own existence, can in turn give birth to social life without appealing to existing institutions—even to the extent of reinterpreting or transforming them. The sociology of the Subject implies that a subject retains a certain mastery of his destiny, within limits which he has defined for himself.

Hence, it is necessary to think in terms of institutions. Otherwise, one's analysis of the problem risks getting bogged down in attempts to come up with syntheses, which blur the contradictions and the costs, both financial and political, of the various policies. Because we ourselves have all been deeply fashioned by democracy, we spontaneously or naturally espouse the causes of values that are in fact caught up in tension: freedom and equality, the equality of citizens and the freedom of individuals to remain loyal to a real or invented collective past. Yet all public policies have an economic, social, and political cost; none imposes itself absolutely. Each policy is inscribed in a specific national history. Communitarian thinkers should indeed be the last to believe that a national "solution" viable in one country would necessarily be a solution for a different country.

Multicultural Policies

Because reflection on these matters should be based on historical experience, it is now important to examine the consequences of the multicultural policies that have been implemented, especially in Canada and Australia. Yet it is equally important not to forget that, despite differences between these policies, they both differ from European historical experience in two essential ways: New World countries recognize that their population was formed through immigration; the value of historical diversity is inscribed in their national political project; they have maintained religious bonds in social and even political practices, despite institutional secularization.

The goal of multicultural policies has been to ensure real equality of diverse population groups. This situates such policies within the democratic aspirations of individuals and within the dynamics of the Providence State. In the United States, it was a question of integrating Afro-Americans into mainstream American culture and collective life; in Canada, that of ensuring equality among the two founding peoples, the immigrants, and the autochthonous peoples, as well as encouraging everyone to participate in Canadian society; in Australia, that of recognizing and favoring the contribution of non-British immigrants and aborigines to collective life. The policy of multiculturalism was officially established in Canada in 1971, before it became that of Sweden in the following years. Australia officially adopted the policy of multiculturalism in 1982.

Until 1971, both English- and French-speaking Canadians espoused a "nativist" ideology. They were hostile to the arrival of new immigrants not belonging to the two founding peoples of the country. Both desired to maintain "their order of hierarchical ethnic differentiation, constitutive of the 'Canadian vertical mosaic.'"[17] The institutions of the immigrant communities—their churches, schools, newspapers, and associations—had been created by the immigrants themselves; at first, the State did not intervene in "ethnic" life. The policy changes began in 1962, when immigration restrictions based on the country of origin were abolished; only economic and socioeconomic criteria were retained as conditions governing immigration. A Canadian Declaration of Human Rights, which broke with the English tradition, was proclaimed in 1960. In the following decades, the demands put forth by the Quebecois in their "quiet revolution," alongside those emanating from organized ethnic communities (notably the Ukrainians, the Poles, and the Germans), provoked a change in policy.

Multicultural policy was applied at the levels of the Federal State and the member-states of the Federation. The federal authorities responsible for the 1971 policy sought to promote the preservation and sharing of cultural heritages, facilitate mutual appreciation and comprehension among all Canadians, permit the sociocultural integration of immigrants and increase their social and political participation. This policy aimed at creating a Canadian identity through the acknowledgment of diversity and to favor the integration of diverse population groups into the national society.[18] The policy was accompanied by a rejection of all forms of collective rights. As Trudeau stated when introducing the law, "Canadian identity will not be undermined by multiculturalism. Indeed we believe that cultural pluralism is the very essence of Canadian identity. A policy of multiculturalism must be a policy for all Canadians." Subsidies were granted for the support and development of specific cultures, essentially in schools and the communications media. Measures were taken to revise history and literature educational curricula, so that the contributions of minorities would be acknowledged; holidays of minority religions were accepted as legal; specific clothing (such as the Sikh turban or the Jewish kippa) were accepted; anti-racist educational programs were adopted; regulations were established in schools and business firms to prevent racist and sexist language; public funds were allocated to ethnic study programs and festivals; public services conducted in native languages were provided in governmental agencies; bilingual education programs were set up in primary schools.[19] Translators of the main immigrant languages allowed immigrants to express themselves in certain public agencies, such as social service departments and hospitals. However, the folkloric nature of these cultural preservation programs was rapidly criticized. The cultural vocation of the 1971 policy subsequently weakened. Instead, programs designed to fight against racism and discrimination, as well as the management of interethnic or interracial relations, became increasingly favored. Of the two goals of multicultural policy, the preservation of ancestral cultures and the equal participation of immigrants in Canadian institutions, the latter became increasingly important. The federal government emphasized "the idea that Canadian citizenship implied inconvertible common values."[20] In 1985, the policy was redefined; "Heritage Promotion" represented only a part of the policy, the two other parts being "Institutional Adaptation" and "Integration." In 1988, a Secretary of State of Multiculturalism confirmed this evolution. The ambition of preserving original cultures was subordinated to the goal of favoring intercultural relations and the integration of minorities, especially "visible minorities." Federal funds were no longer allocated to "monoethnic" cultural communities, but instead to organisms encouraging citizenship and tightening social bonds, and to those fighting against racism and discrimination. It henceforth appeared that "there are limits to tolerance and diversity."[21] In 1991, the Secretary of State of Multiculturalism added "Citizenship" to its official title. Henceforth, it became a question of "favoring the expression of common values within a pluralist society," of encouraging the civic participation of everyone and of mobilizing energy for creating social bonds. The policy of acknowledging communities and subsidizing their activities above all became one of the tools of this policy.

Multicultural policy has given birth to an Ethnic Providence State that aims, through the symbolic recognition of specific cultures and their contribution to the Canadian nation, at favoring access for all members of society to official jobs and public life, and at resolving social tension among groups; such had formerly been the goals of the Social Providence State. The Ethnic Providence State has created its own civil servants, organizers, and administrators. However, English continues to be the language used in public life and in all political and administrative institutions. English is the mother language of all children who are born of immigrants and who go to school in the English-speaking parts of Canada. In all of North America, English is the language of social success and upward mobility. Multiculturalism has become an integration policy that is more flexible than traditional "assimilation," which is adapted to an immigration society which possesses a strong liberal tradition and which has not experienced violent forms of separatist claims. Quebecois nationalists have not become terrorists. Whatever criteria are used to measure immigrant integration, it continues; the tolerance of diversity is subjected to the respect of common values and to the integration objectives of Canadian society. This policy also allows the different problems raised by different kinds of claims to be avoided; in other words, the demands emanating from French-speakers, from immigrants, and from national minorities, the first group demanding a form of political autonomy; the second group, associations and subsidized communications media; the third group, "historical" compensation.

Because Quebec is engaged in a process of national construction based on the most traditional arguments (those pertaining to a common language and culture, and to the collective will to preserve them in an English-speaking world), it is striking that the dynamics of democracy induced Quebec to adopt a multicultural policy in 1981. This specific policy is more ambiguous than that promulgated by the Federal State, for it includes the desire to assimilate all the population of Quebec, especially the new immigrants, to the language and culture of the French-speakers. This has not prevented the establishment of an Ethnic Providence State. The Ministry of Cultural Communities and Immigration, created in 1981, is responsible for "the coordination and the establishing of the Quebec government action plan with respect to 'cultural communities' (CC)."[22] The typical style of Providence State administrative prose shines forth here. The policy includes forms of symbolic recognition, programs for fighting against racism and discrimination, and subsidies for preserving and renewing traditional languages and cultures in schools and in the communications media. Yet the use of original languages in the public realm is restricted by Law 101, which imposes French as the public language and limits the freedom of Quebecois to attend English-speaking schools.

The policy in Australia is of the same kind.[23] For a long time, Australians defined themselves through assimilation with the mother country, which indeed led them to fight on all the battlefields of the two World Wars. It was only in 1948 that Australians became Australian citizens, a status replacing that of British subjects. In 1971, the nationality law was reformed and extended to non-British population groups (knowledge of English ceased to be a requirement). Until then, Australian policy had remained ferociously loyal to the British, or "Anglo-Celtic," tradition, that is to *common law* and to the so-called "Westminster" system of political organization. When multicultural policy was introduced in 1982, it broke symbolically with this tradition, which had been opposed, ever since the 1960s, by recent immigrants from Europe (especially Italy and Greece) as well as Asia. According to its advocates, it was important to avoid "the social dangers inherent in any policy whose goal is to repress cultural diversity and impose integration."[24] In Australia, the same kinds of measures can be found as in Canada, some designed to combat discrimination and racism (the Law of 1975), others to recognize, through practical and symbolic measures, the diverse origins of the national population. The State finances radio broadcasts in more than sixty foreign languages that are spoken in the population at large, and provides a Special Broadcasting Service (SBS) for the television network. In schools, classes are given in some of the immigrant languages, although all pupils learn and speak English. "Ethnic" social workers take into account the particular needs of migrant population groups. Yet while multicultural policy is aimed at immigrants, it has not provided a solution to the predicament of the aborigines. They obtained the right to vote only in 1962, and were included in the national census only in 1967. Today, they can choose to retain their special status or, instead, to integrate themselves into Australian society like other citizens. Yet multicultural policy affects them only in secondary ways, which reveals the insufficiencies of the policy.

Australian sociologists, some of whom were the direct inspirers of multicultural policy, now point to its limitations. They note that the language, as well as the political and juridical system, remain those of the British tradition. The Ethnic Welfare State has developed a world of professionals specialized in public and especially social services, the communications media, and schooling. Yet despite innovations in linguistic policy, institutions responsible for responding to ethnic difference, and the growing presence of the most recent immigrants in parliament and government, the *Westminster system* and *common law* continue to shape and structure collective life. Specific cultures continue to be subjected to collective values: for example, excision practiced by communities originating from Ethiopia, Erytrea, Sudan, and Somalia is still liable to criminal prosecution.[25] In conformity with the British tradition, Australia has not signed the Declaration of Human Rights. Australian multicultural policy has not questioned political traditions or induced the assimilation of political and juridical conceptions brought along by European (especially Italian and Greek) immigrants.[26] The policy has probably attenuated the tensions of a society continuing to consider itself purely British, even though the population has become increasingly diverse. Even the most ardent advocates of multicultural policy point out the risk of ethnic loyalties taking precedence over participation in Australian society.

In Canada as in Australia, State intervention in ethnic matters has created a corps of educators of "ethnic" origin, as well as teachers specialized in a new academic discipline called "intercultural education"—not to mention translators, journalists who work in various media, association organizers, public services employees, and social workers specialized in programs for immigrant or "ethnic" population groups. An ambiguous intercultural ideology has developed even more widely in that it is in harmony with post-modern discourse, which celebrates freedom, particularism, the right of every individual to be himself, "diversity"—a term especially employed in the United States to justify *affirmative action*—and fragmentation. Multiculturalism has affinities with democratic values. Yet the constraints of collective life limit, in reality, the diversity of the public realm. The Ethnic Providence State, with its social and cultural dimension—which sums up multicultural policy—is a means of symbolically recognizing diverse population groups; and symbolism has a role to play in politics. As long as a common language and common political institutions regulate public life according to the norms of a State organized by law, multicultural policy will remain inscribed in the logic of the Intervention State, whose potentialities it indeed deploys. Adapted to democratic values and inscribed in the very dynamics of democracy, such a policy can be defined as a flexible *liberalism* as well, as a tolerant republicanism, or as an Ethnic Providence State. It represents one of the dimensions of providential democracy.[27]

Indirect Policies

In France, "republican" reluctance persistently curbs or slows down evolution toward an Ethnic Providence State, whereas the Cultural and Sports Intervention State is particularly active. France is the only European country in which the Minister of Culture claims to have finally obtained, in 2001, a budget equal to 1% of the national budget and in which the Secretary of State for Sports has the ambition of reaching 0.5% (to which must be added the contributions of local collectivities). At the same time, anything contributing to an acknowledgment of ethnic identities is rejected in principle. In accordance with the tradition of national integration, the public existence of specific groups within the population is not recognized. It is individuals who are to be integrated, not specific communities.[28] The sense of this political attitude is established by Article 1 of the Constitution, which asserts the principle of the indivisibility of the Republic and states that France "ensures the equality of all citizens before the law, without distinction of origin, race, or religion." These principles have again been confirmed by decisions made by the Constitutional Council. "The Constitution recognizes only one French people, composed of all French citizens, without distinction of origin, race, or religion."[29] The Constitution is thus opposed to "recognizing collective rights for any group whatsoever that is defined by a community formed by a common origin, culture, language, or belief."[30]

This is why the recent evolution of French policy is all the more striking. The forcible dynamics of democracy nonetheless gradually impose themselves through various arguments and disguises.

For example, it is in the name of geographical inequalities that the State Council (Conseil d'État) advocates adopting equity rather than equality measures, by asserting that "numerous questions revolving around the equality principle concern its spatial element: should population groups living in mountainous and coastal regions be dealt with in the same ways, and similarly for those living in rural diversification zones and increasingly populated urban agglomerations, in small little-populated counties ("communes") and big cities, in areas affected by the industrial crisis and regions with a strong tourist industry potential, in underprivileged suburbs and prosperous towns, etc." Problems that are termed "ethnic" in Canada or Australia are introduced in France by the expression "underprivileged suburbs." Henceforth, the criterion of situational differences, which enables an administrative or constitutional judge to adapt the equality principle[31], can be applied: "The equality principle is applied with flexibility as regards geography."[32] Statutory law has taken a similar turn. For instance, according to the Law of 4 February 1995, whose advocates highlight its goal of "ensuring equal opportunity, for each citizen, throughout the national territory," "the policy of territorial planning and development corrects the inequalities in the living conditions of citizens tied to a specific geographical situation. . . . It aims to compensate for territorial handicaps. It establishes dispensatory measures modulating the financial burdens imposed on individuals."[33] In order to accomplish this, the law provides fiscal advantages, and exemptions as regards employer's contributions to the Social Security system, for firms, corporations, or factories who agree to set up their business in various areas or districts legally defined as Territory Planning Zones ("Zones d'Aménagements du Territoire"), Rural Priority Development Territories ("Territoires Ruraux de Développement Prioritaire"), and Sensitive Urban Zones ("Zones Urbaines Sensibles"). Because correctives to so-called "republican" citizen equality are introduced by these policies, limits are specified and it is stipulated that the measures are temporary. Obviously, speaking of "territorial handicaps" or "territorial discrimination" is a way of masking the fact that a form of affirmative action is introduced in favor, not of territories, but rather of people who have a link with the territory and are socially defined by that link.[34]

The proclaimed refusal to take into account any "ethnic" dimension is thus circumvented by the use of social and territorial criteria. Big city policies have also "targeted" (to use the vocabulary of the various protagonists involved) "sensitive quarters," which are defined in territorial and socioeconomic terms, so as to avoid the "ethnic" stigmatization of the population groups living there. For example, measures were successively adopted to define Business Zones ("Zones d'Entreprises") in 1986; Sensitive Urban Zones ("Zones Urbaines Sensibles") in 1991; Urban Redynamization Zones ("Zones de Redynamisation Urbaine," ZRU) in 1995; Urban Free Zones ("Zones Franches Urbaines," ZFU) in 1996. In all cases, attempts are made to favor the creation of jobs by granting tax deductions, and exemptions as regards employer's contributions to the Social Security system, to firms, corporations, or factories that set up business in such defined areas and recruit their employees from among the local inhabitants. It is clear that these measures were aimed at population groups which, given the geographical concentration of the economically weakest immigrant population, would have been called "ethnic" in Canada or Australia. Moreover, the very term "quarter" ("quartier") has come to mean, in colloquial French, "urban areas or districts mostly inhabited by economically weak population groups stemming from immigration." Although the policies are based on socioeconomic, not ethnic, criteria, they are indeed most often understood in ethnic or racial terms by the various social actors involved. This is also the case for policy concerning the Priority Education Zones ("Zones d'Éducation Prioritaires," ZEP), established in 1993, which increase the subsidies and means furnished to schools in socially underprivileged quarters—such as bigger teaching budgets and strict limits as to the number of pupils per class. Classifying schools in a Priority Education Zone takes social criteria into account: the number of pupils repeating grades, the proportion of slow learners, the number of drop-outs who leave the school without a diploma, the average family income, but also the proportion of foreign pupils and average number of children per family. In reality, these social criteria are tightly linked to "ethnic" categories because of the geographical concentration of economically weak immigrant population groups. Despite this fact, the official policy is still to provide—according to the Law of 1989—"specific educational care" to "school population groups stemming from underprivileged social categories," and thus not to take into account particular origins or identities. Similarly, the activity of social workers also becomes de facto "ethnic" work when it is aimed at population groups defined by social and economic criteria. The development of athletic policies in "sensitive quarters" has the objective of controlling the behavior of "young people." Sports stars from immigrant population groups are asked to return to their former urban or suburban low-cost housing districts (called "cités" in French), show how their success is due to hard work, and encourage similar vocations among "ethnic" population groups.

Sometimes, policy measures are more direct. In the name of both universal and "cultural" values (in the sense ascribed to the latter adjective by the Ministry of Culture), local collectivities grant subsidies to Jewish or Armenian libraries or cultural associations, because these communities represent a specific historical heritage or "memory." In the name of the mission of social work, some religious charitable organizations, specialized in aiding immigrant population groups, are subsidized by public authorities. In the name of the religious freedoms ensured by the rules of secularism ("laïcité") in public life, associations that could be called "ethnic" are recognized as religious and benefit in this respect from a status guaranteed by the Law of 1905 (governing non-profit organizations and associations). This might seem paradoxical in a State where secularism is asserted so vigorously. Thanks to budgets allocated by various big city policies, local authorities financially help "cultural" associations, although some of the beneficiaries illustrate a willingness to express more "ethnic" than "cultural" references.[35]

This apparent hypocrisy has a purely political significance. Words wield weight in democracies. They not only give names to objects and phenomena, but they also contribute to the creation of social realities. The social sciences themselves, which emanate from society and are applied to a specific society, also contribute to shaping society. This is why official studies and surveys conducted by administative departments of the French State refused, for decades, to take into account the "ethnic" origin of population groups. In official statistics, a French citizen had neither religion nor national origin (stemming from the period before he or she acquired French nationality). This willful ignorance of ethnic origins was creative; it was a tool in the policy long called "assimilation." The reassertion of universal principles, even if by vocabulary alone, was considered to be not without impact on the symbolic, and thus political, level. Today, it is thereby all the more striking that this tradition has been swept away by the dynamics of democracy. The republican vocabulary is increasingly denounced as hypocritical and ineffective. Sociologists increasingly demand the "truth" about integration processes and about the varieties of racial discrimination because they have a direct professional interest in disclosing such realities. In the struggle against forms of discrimination, it is first important to learn about them, and thus to introduce ethnic and racial categories into the most official sociological research.[36]

In fact, this policy has recently changed. Criteria concerning an individual's national or "ethnic" origin are increasingly taken into direct account, even if such expressions as "young people from sensitive quarters," or "young people from an immigrant background" remain coded names enabling one to avoid using directly "ethnic" or "racial" terms that might lead to difficulties. In France, it is not officially possible to refer straightforwardly to the categories of social life, such as "Arabs," "Muslims," "North Africans," "Blacks," and so on—who in most cases would be French citizens. Yet policemen and social workers who themselves originate from underprivileged suburban areas are assigned to the same kinds of areas because they are thereby considered to be "closer to" those whom they are supposed to assist or control; similarly, the Police and the Paris Metro System (RATP) recruit—as a part of the youth employment contract program—"big brothers" who are responsible for controlling their "little brothers."[37] These are the first examples of official "ethnic professions." The famous Paris-based university specialized in political science, the Institut d'Études Politiques, has established de facto quotas for admitting students from "sensitive quarters," among whom one expects to find young people of "immigrant backgrounds." The government henceforth aims to fight against racial discrimination, by adopting the model of English-speaking countries. On 16 July 1998, the Ministry of Justice distributed a circular letter to general public prosecutors ("procureurs généraux") and State prosecutors ("procureurs de la République"), with the title: "The Fight Against Racism and Xenophobia." In February 1999, the Ministry of the Interior created, for each administrative "department," a Departmental Commission on the Access to Citizenship ("Commission départementale d'accès à la citoyennété," CODAC). According to the minister's own terms, these commissions are designed to "detect" and "track down phenomena of discrimination, and, first of all, discrimination in everything that involves employment, including access to the competitive written and oral examinations for civil service jobs, and to the preparatory education necessary for passing them."[38] In April 1999, the Ministry of Employment and Solidarity created a new organism, the Discrimination Study Group ("Groupe d'étude des discriminations," GED). The latter elaborated a declaration, called the "Déclaration de Grenelle," for combatting racial discrimination in the world of labor; on 11 May 1999, it was adopted by the State and by union and management officials. Finally, on 2 May 2000, a circular letter from the Prime Minister proposed new measures for fighting against racism; attempting to coordinate the action of three ministries in the framework of a law submitted to the Parliament in June 2000, the letter concerned access to citizenship and anti-discrimination measures. In recent French political history, the Minister of the Interior who best embodied the most rigorous republican tradition was Jean-Pierre Chevènement. Yet in a speech given on 15 February 1999 to a meeting of prefects, he asserted "that the National Police should reflect the population." Stating that "it was not a question of quotas," he asked prefects to "diversify recruitment" and "enable young people of immigrant backgrounds to find employment in the police."[39] A communication from the Prefecture of Police noted that "young people of immigrant backgrounds" could be found among local social "mediation agents."[40]

"One can only be struck by the lightning speed with which *affirmative action* discourse and policies have found a home in France."[41] It is the powerful dynamics of democracy that are revealed by this policy shift in the country which, because of its traditional republican ideology, has the most strongly resisted the multiculturalist model and which tends to view the American integration model in negative terms, even to extremes of caricature. Intervention from an Ethnic Providence State seems to have become as ineluctable and irreversible as that of the Social Intervention State. Public authorities increasingly take into account each population group's singularities. This tendency is encouraged by specialized institutions, social workers, and sociologists directly committed to the fight against racism and discrimination; moreover, in accordance with their proclaimed values, the media are also sensitive to the phenomena. How, then, will it ever be possible to reverse this trend?

By reading the report presented on 4 March 1999 to the Parliament by Claude Bartolone, at the time the Delegate Minister for Cities, one becomes aware of the impossibilities of a reversal. The Minister summed up the Pact for Relaunching Cities ("Pacte de relance pour la ville") that had been adopted by the Law of 14 November 1996. He revealed the perverse consequences of the program: the relocation of firms, corporations, and factories; situations in which businesses seeking financial benefits would set up shop for a while, take advantage of the encouraging conditions, then disappear; real estate speculation, and so on. He noted that "in a general way, measures such as the Urban Free Zones (ZFU) and Urban Redynamization Zones (ZRU) had only a limited impact on economic activity and employment in 1997, which represented the first year of the programs," and that, more generally, "the cost of the measure thus seems rather high, in comparison with the results in terms of net job creation; on the whole, its effectiveness remains limited, in 1997." He nevertheless concluded: "No scheme provides for the pure and simple suppression of the measure. The seriousness of the problem of unemployment in districts experiencing difficulties justifies maintaining, and accentuating, the efforts of the State. The government does not want to call into question the commitments made by the State as regards the entitled business firms and the local collectivities, which have in some cases made big investments to enhance the value of their Urban Free Zones. However, the government deems it necessary to limit the perverse effects in the future and to reinforce social effectiveness."[42] Once they have acquired them, all parties "entitled to rights" ("ayants droit," as the Minister put it in French)—whether they be business firms, local collectivities, or individuals—retain those rights in regard to the Providence State.

The discourse of *affirmative action* has spread all the more quickly in that it responds to a social situation that social workers and sociologists increasingly term "ethnic." With its local dimension, "ethnic" or "community" consciousness grows with the sentiment inhabiting population groups in the so-called "sensitive" suburban areas—the coded French term used for designating suburban districts where young people of immigrant backgrounds are numerous—that they are marginals, outcasts. In many studies carried out during the 1980s, children of immigrant parents long identified with a specific locality. To a question such as "Do you feel more French or Algerian (or Tunisian, etc.)?"—a question implying the abstraction of a national identity and possibly also that of citizenship—they would assert their identity by replying "I am from Marseilles," "I am from the '4000' Housing Development," and so on. However, ever since the end of the 1990s, an attitude of radical protest seems to be spreading. A calling into question of all intellectual competence can be observed, as applied to an elite defined as "technocratic" and a culture termed "bookish"; both are considered to be aristocratic with respect to the genuinely democratic nature of cell phones and roller skates, accessible to everyone. It is thought that these technical tools enable one to enter into "resistance" against the society of political representation and competence.[43] The interpretation of current world conflicts, in which a fundamental opposition between Muslims and the Western world is often invoked, reinforces the consciousness of groups living together in the same, generally underprivileged, social realm. Already observed during the 1980s[44], antisemitism is spreading among suburban Muslim population groups who are fueled by echoes of the Middle-East conflict and by a proclaimed solidarity with the Palestinians. In Sarcelles, since the end of the 1980s, Jews have themselves broken with their traditional policy of discretion, which was linked to the privatization of religion; the public realm is now "ethnicized": traditional dresses for women, kippas for men and boys, the increasing number of Jewish shops, the central role played by synagogues in collective life, even pilgrimages imported from Jewish customs in Tunisia and Morocco. In the evening, at the end of the Sabbath, young Jewish people fill the streets. Encouraged by the municipal government, charitable institutions support the solidarity of the "Jewish community."[45] National institutions have nonetheless curbed extreme forms of identity demands.

Cultural Democracy or a European Public Realm?

The sense of today's debate about European citizenship is inscribed in this evolution of democracy. Both the weakening of the idea of political transcendence and what can be called the gradual "ethnization" of social life have encouraged various positions. For some observers, European citizenship is in the process of taking note of the transformation of society, of recognizing the value of multiculturalism, and of constructing a new, genuinely democratic, citizenship that eschews the political transcendence characterizing a republican citizenship inherited from a national history. In this regard, European citizenship recognizes democratic liberty or, to use Alain Touraine's terms, "cultural democracy." Other observers, who are more loyal to a political conception of citizenship, reflect on the construction of a European public realm and on the ways that political citizenship can be reconciled with the cultural rights of nations within Europe. Jürgen Habermas represents this position.

For advocates of cultural democracy, the multiculturalism characterizing modern democracies is confirmed and validated by the development of European citizenship. "In our societies," remarks Alain Touraine, "it is no longer possible to consider oneself 'democratic' without accepting the idea of a multicultural society. However, many men and women still reject such a society and remain attached to the ideal of a society based on an individualist-universitalist conception of rights. . . . France established a political democracy before most other countries, but it was very late in constructing a social democracy. Does France not risk falling, today, even farther behind in regard to the elaboration of a cultural democracy? Is France not locking itself into a model too specific and too authoritarian to be understood and adopted by other countries?"[46] For Alain Touraine, "cultural democracy" is more a "democracy oriented toward the defence of political, social, and cultural rights of individuals than a republic defined by institutions and sovereignty . . . . A social and cultural conception should replace the State-like conception of a nation. A nation is no longer defined by the creation of a unified realm of citizenship which hovers above social and cultural diversity, but rather, on the contrary, by the search for intercultural communication and social solidarity: a united society which diminishes distances and lowers barriers, but which also is oriented toward dialogue."[47] By organizing the collective life of diverse peoples and by instituting this "social solidarity" through the development of solidarity schemes established by the European Providence State, the construction of European democracy would respond to this evolution toward "cultural democracy." The point is not to construct European citizenship in accordance with the model of national citizenship, for we are faced with the "necessity of giving new meanings to sub-national, national, and supranational institutions as well as to . . . cultural orientations, social conflicts, and the construction of social identities."[48] Conceived in this way, Europe would validate the de-politicization—in the classic political sense—of modern society and the end of republican transcendence.

Alain Touraine's conception resembles that of other writers who, in different terms, invoke the coming of "plural democracy." They wish to reconsider left-wing politics in terms of a "radicalization of democracy," as defined by the "extension of the principles of equality and freedom to a growing number of social relationships," for "the specificity of modern democracy lies in the acknowledgment of pluralism."[49] In this regard, democratic pluralism should therefore supplant *liberalism*. Alain Touraine also echoes Michael Walzer's "democratic socialism." Walzer advocates the development of a grassroots movement made up of associations in which even the socio-economically weakest categories would participate, whereas

for the time being such movements are dominated by the middle-
level and higher social categories. For Walzer, the "most decisive
test of any kind of socialism is its capacity to make society itself the
continual creation of ordinary men and women." This pluralism
should, moreover, surpass the classic theories of Robert Dahl[50] or
Raymond Aron[51], who both considered the coexistence of several
different powers to be one of the characteristics of democracy, as
opposed to the single power structure of communist societies. The
question is no longer that of acknowledging diverse "spheres of justice," in other words the various dimensions of social life, each organized by different values, but rather that of fully recognizing the
diversity of historical identities within the same national society.
According to this position, it is only in this way that genuine democracy can be established. The importance liberally granted to differences will prevent explosions of hate. The problem of nation and
nationality demands a *liberal* solution. Michael Walzer, especially,
seeks thereby to recuperate the active principle of civic republicanism and to constitute a public sphere beyond communities.

These theoreticians of cultural democracy stand opposed to writers adhering to a political conception: according to the latter, European citizenship should acknowledge the existence of particularisms,
but retain the political significance of citizenship and convey the
values common to European democracies as they are expressed
through the espousal of human rights. Such writers note not only
that the sovereignty of national law is demolished by European law,
but also by population mobility, which has increased the number of
individuals with more than one nationality. They also take into account the fact that many population groups of foreign origin now
desire to be "citizens in another way," that is by remaining loyal to
an original culture or nationality, all the while participating in the
society in which they have settled. The construction of a united political Europe and the presence of permanently settled aliens call for
a dissociation of the historical links between nationality—considered as a community of culture inherited from the age of nations—
and citizenship, which is an exclusively political practice.

Because such writers wish to ensure that this dissociation threat-
ens neither social cohesion nor democratic practices, and that social
integration does not become purely "functional" (in this respect, they
are opposed to the theoreticians of the "new social and economic
citizenship"[52]), they argue that it should be accompanied by what

Jacqueline Costa-Lascoux calls a genuine "contract of citizenship." Citizenship rights would be granted to aliens, yet on the condition that they make a commitment "in favor of conforming to democratic values" and that they respect national legislation as regards human rights. They would otherwise be free to remain attached to a particular culture—yet on the condition that social practices stemming from that culture are not incompatible with the supranational principles of human rights.[53] More specifically, these practices should involve "respecting the fundamental rights of persons (notably the rights of children, and non-discrimination with respect to race, sex, or religion, etc.), a reformulation of secular or non-religious qualities ("une laïcité reformulée" in French), and participation in the tax and social-protection systems."[54] The rights of population groups that desire to preserve their cultural rights and be "citizens in another way" can thus be combined with the exercise of a European citizenship based on common values.

Such analyses, which result from considering the participation of population groups of foreign origin in the life of European societies, join Jürgen Habermas's more philosophical reflections. He develops the concept of "constitutional patriotism." He suggests breaking the historical link between citizenship and nationality, all the while retaining the purely political sense of citizenship. He argues against "the conventional form of national identity" which links nationality and citizenship—and which can be called "classical citizenship"— and calls for the elaboration of a "constitutional patriotism" referring "no longer to the real, concrete totality of a nation but rather, on the contrary, to abstract processes and principles."[55] In consequence, he continues, it is necessary to dissociate the levels of patriotism and citizenship, that is dissociate the "nation" (like France and Germany), which would remain the "locus of affectivity," from the "State," which would become merely the "locus of law." In this way, national identity, with all its cultural or ethnic dimensions (the sharing of a common language, history, collective memory, and culture), could be separated from civic and political participation, which would be based on reason, on the respect of a State founded on law, and on human rights at the European level. National cultures would thereby be fully maintained and organized alongside a kind of civic practice that itself would be detached from national belonging. Patriotic sentiment, which is the very expression of a "culture," would therefore no longer be linked to a particular historical and cultural nation, but rather to the very principle of a State founded on law. Constitutional patriotism would allow the practice of citizenship through European political institutions, while the nation would remain the locus of cultural and identity allegiances. In this manner, "cultural rights" inherited from a particular culture and history would, at the same time, be dissociated and respected, and the exercise of citizenship would be founded on the principles of an *État de droit*—a State based on law—which are common to all European countries.[56]

Jean-Marc Ferry has pursued this train of thought and universalized it, by developing the idea of post-national identity. It, too, would exclusively refer to the "principles of universality, autonomy, and responsibility that underlie the conceptions of democracy and of a State based on law (*État de droit*)."[57] Citizenship would hitherto be founded on a "reflexive moral identity whose principle is, moreover, inscribed in the French Declaration of the Rights of Man and the Citizen, with the right (for individuals) and the duty (for citizens) to rise up against tyranny."[58] Individuals would adhere to the principles of a State based on law (*État de droit*) and to the republican idea (excluding all references to a territory and a particular, concrete, cultural and historical community). This could in fact be the very project of a united political Europe, which would become the place where democracy was practiced beyond national feeling and fervor, beyond the traditional form of the nation-state, henceforth a thing of the past. A united Europe would thereby represent an "opportunity to be grasped, for it could lead to the political rearrangement of those same democracies that national States no longer allow to be organized in ways enabling them to meet the challenges of globalization."[59] A united political Europe would not be a bigger nation-state, nor a federal State modeled on federal States such as exist today. The European State would not possess sovereignty in the same sense that national States do. Its purpose would be purely ethical. It would carry out "civic education." The European people would not be comparable to the peoples of nation-states. It would thus be important to highlight the political culture common to all European nations, that is beyond the particular cultures and histories of specific nations, and to continue to de-nationalize history by encouraging all nationals to critically "reflect upon their relationship to their own history."[60] In such a way, a "moral community" susceptible of legitimating the "legal community" forged in Brussels could be developed. A new entity combining civic principles and multifarious cultural loyalties could be created; in other words, an entity that would be the most privileged form of modern democracy.

These debates about the possible future of Europe reveal a search for a new way of combining the principles of citizenship and the acknowledgment of the multifariousness of nations and collective identities, and of avoiding the demands of a national republic all the while maintaining the essential values on which the republican ideal is based: freedom and equality.

The logic of the Intervention State operates at this "ethnic" level, for the State is induced to diversify, and to increase the number of, its interventions in order to ensure the equality and the dignity of all. Because *homo democraticus* is impatient when faced with any kind of limit or barrier, the State is induced to intervene ever more often in social, economic, and family life, as well as to recognize ethnic particularisms more or less symbolically, more or less directly. This even applies to a country with a unitary tradition like France, where multicultural policy and "communitarism" are officially rejected and often passionately contested. Political rights, social and economic rights, the rights to education and to professional training, and the rights to cultural and athletic practices, have all been claimed by individuals, have been acknowledged as legitimate demands, and, up to a certain point, have been obtained because of the development of the Providence State in its various dimensions. Public recognition of "cultural," "identity," or "ethnic" rights increasingly appears to be an imperative prerequisite of real equality. Indeed, the Providence State increasingly becomes responsible for these rights. Providential democracy tends to favor particularisms.

The growing intervention of the State in all fields of social life tends to make ever less perceptible the distinction between the public and private realms, a distinction upon which the principles of both *liberalism* and French republicanism were founded. This new fluidity—to whose spread feminist research has contributed by emphasizing the political significance of relationships even within the family, the "private" realm *par excellence*—has made it increasingly difficult to base political decisions on the idea of a border between public and private spheres. The new fluidity is inscribed in the even vaster evolution of social life, in which the boundaries between categories of social action are ever more blurred: political, religious, ethnic, and social realms are no longer clearly distinct. What can be called the growing "ethnization" of social life is inscribed in the dynamics of democracy. The claiming of real rights for individuals is a growing phenomenon. It responds to each democratic individual's aspiration to a full acknowledgment of his or her singularity, and to the weakening of all collective transcendence, whether religious or political.

Notes

1. Mesure-Renaut, 1999, p. 261. Will Kymlicka speaks of the acknowledgement of the "distinct identities and needs of ethnocultural groups." Cf. Kymlicka, 2000, p. 141.
2. I have shown elsewhere why this concept seems useful for designating what are generally called "ethnic groups" or "radical groups" (in American sociological literature) or "peoples" (in nationalist literature). Cf. Schnapper, 1998, p. 75.
3. Mesure-Renaut, 1999, p. 201.
4. Catherine Audard, "Political Liberalism, Secular Republicanism: Two Answers to the Challenges of Pluralism," in Anchard, 1996, pp. 163-175.
5. Schnapper, 1991.
6. Declaration of the Quebec government, as quoted by Danièle Juteau: "L'État et les immigrés: de l'immigration aux communautés culturelles," in Guillaume *et al.*, 1986, p. 44. Reproduced in Juteau, 1999, pp. 61-75.
7. According to Will Kymlicka, from whom I borrow this summary of the common points shared by communitarian theoriticians. See Kymlicka, 2000.
8. Taylor, 1994 (1992).
9. Walzer, 1997 (1992).
10. Kymlicka, 1995.
11. Weil, 1971, p. 35.
12. I had finished writing this text when I discovered that Danièle Juteau had already used the same expression. She characterizes the Ethnic Providence State thus: "Distributing choice pieces to some, crumbs to others, so that the regulation of ethnic social relationships is ensured.". Cf. Juteau, 1986.
13. Obviously, this definition excludes any biological dimension.
14. See below.
15. This is the topic of Mesure-Renaut, 1999.
16. Kymlicka, 2000, p. 179.
17. Juteau, 1986, p. 42.
18. This is borrowed from Helly, 1999, and Houle, 1999.
19. Kymlicka, 1995. Most of these measures indeed represent a "moderate" or "tolerant" liberalism, and depend on universal values. However, can one really believe that the most recent multicultural policy measure (cited by Kymlicka), which creates schools reserved for Black children who cannot bear integrated schooling, actually favors their integration?
20. Houle, 1999, p. 109.
21. Houle, 1999, p. 119.
22. In order to accomplish these objectives, that is "maintaining and developing cultural communities ('communautés culturelles,' CC), making Quebecois French-speakers sensitive to the CC, and favoring their integration," three organisms were created: a committee for implementing the action plan aimed at cultural communities ("le comité d'implantation du plan d'action à l'intention des communautés culturelles," CIPACC), a mixed interministerial committee for the general coordination of the

action plan ("le comité interministériel mixte de coordination générale du plan d'action"), and a committee for equal employment in civil service of the cultural communities ("le comité d'égalité en emploi dans la fonction publique des communautés culturelles, CIPACC). Cf. Juteau, 1986, p. 46.

23. Pons, 1996, and Davidson, 1997 a and b.

24. Pons, 1996, p. 115.

25. As Richard Harding put it: "Our multiculturalism will implode if we tolerate a barbaric practice only because it is traditional in the victim's (or victim's parents') native country." Cf. Pons, 1996, p. 298.

26. Davidson, 1997 a and b. See also Pons, 1996, pp. 292-3.

27. For Sweden's multicultural policies and their effects, one may consult Schierup, 1989 and Alund-Schierup, 1991. A more complete analysis should obviously take into account American policy, but this is beyond the scope of the present study. A good introduction may be found in Lacorne, 1997.

28. This was the topic of the first report of the High Council on Integration ("Haut Conseil à l'intégration"), in 1991. See also Noiriel, 1988, and Schnapper, 1991.

29. Decision 91-290 of 9 May 1991 (status of Corsica).

30. Decision 99-412 of 15 June 1999 (European Charter for Regional or Minority Languages).

31. "Considering that the equality principle is not opposed to law solving different situations in different ways, nor to law sometimes ruling against equality because of the general interest, provided that, in both cases, the resulting difference in treatment is in direct relationship with the object of the law that establishes it." In the United States, the "diversity" objective justifies, in the name of certain social justice goals, decisions that are contrary to the equality of rights of individuals. Cf. Oudghiri-Sabbagh, 1999.

32. Conseil d'État (Council of State), 1997, p. 95.

33. Cited in Calvès, 1999, p. 17.

34. Inversely, "geographical diversity" was also used by the Ivy League universities to restrain the number of Jewish students, who often came from the Northeastern part of the United States. Equity policies always run the risk of inducing formal inequalities. Cf. Oudghiri-Sabbagh, 1999, p. 448.

35. The way local collectivities divert the "ethnic" dimension is the topic of Milena Doytcheva's doctoral thesis (in preparation).

36. This argument led to the decision to introduce, into the English Census of 1991, the following categories: "Whites," "Caribbean Blacks," "Black Africans," "Other Blacks (specify), "Indians," "Pakistanis," "Bangladeshis," "Chinese," "Other Ethnic Groups."

37. 80% of the "accompaniment agents" in the buses of the Lyons suburbs are, for example, of North African origin.

38. Cited in Calvès, 1999, p. 69.

39. *Ibid.*

40. *Le Monde,* 21 September 1999.

41. Calvès, 2000, p. 78.

42. Cited in Calvès, 1999, pp. 20-1.

43. This information has been provided by Jacqueline Costa-Lascoux (oral communication).

44. Leveau-Schnapper, 1987.

45. For this topic, see Laurence Podselver's work, especially Podselver, 1996.

46. Touraine, 1997, p. 242.

47. Touraine, pp. 278-9.

48.   Touraine, 2001, p. 37.
49.   Mouffe, 1992, pp. 125-6.
50.   Dahl, 1965.
51.   Aron, 1965.
52.   See Chapter 2 above.
53.   Costa-Lascoux, 1992.
54.   Jacqueline Costa-Lascoux, "Vers une Europe des citoyens," in Costa-Lascoux-Weil, 1992, p. 292.
55.   Habermas, 1990 (1985-90), p. 238.
56.   I have discussed Habermas's conception, especially in Schnapper, 1994, pp. 181-2. See the special issue of *Cahiers de l'URMIS*, No. 7, June 2001.
57.   Ferry, 1991, p. 194.
58.   Ferry, 1991, p. 195.
59.   Ferry, 2001, p. 35.
60.   Ferry, 2001, p. 286.

5

The End of the "Republic by Divine Right"?

The erosion of political transcendence that can be observed, in various forms, in all providential democracies is probably more advanced in France than elsewhere; and it is also in France that the tension between an ever increasing amount of Providence State intervention and the proclaimed principles of the unity and the universality of the Republic is more obvious. In France, more than elsewhere, a willingness to build up a Republic against an Ancien Régime was at the heart of the political project. Finally, in France more than elsewhere, revolutionaries desired to establish a political system which would embody the general will as it transcends each individual will and conforms to universal reason. Yet today, what is left of this republican project to create another form of transcendence—that of the Nation and the Republic—and direct it against religious and monarchical transcendence, each of which, in close association with each other, had for centuries shaped and structured the construction of France?

The Sacred Republic

Before the end of the Ancien Régime, the idea of "nation" had gradually supplanted that of royal sovereignty, even in the discourse of eighteenth-century Jansenists. Yet this idea was still informed by the doctrine of the two bodies of the king, whereby a mystical royal body was distinct from the king's natural body: "The king is dead, long live the king!" Even if the republic established another principle of legitimacy, it inherited this abstract idea of a royalty—that is, of a "corps politique" or, literally, "body politic"—whose existence transcends the natural body of the king. Republicans were indeed following this tradition when they elaborated "the Two Bodies of the Republic."[1] Like the king, the republic managed to survive its successive incarnations.

The Religious Model

During the century that followed the French Revolution, republicans sought to replace dynastic and religious transcendence by political transcendence as a manner of organizing collective life and the relationships among human beings. Throughout the conflict between traditional France and revolutionary France which marked the history of the nineteenth century, these two Frances opposed each other, each of them claiming to represent the "true" France. The conflict between the Revolution and the monarchical and religious Ancien Régime actually lasted until after the Second World War. The very basis of political legitimacy was at stake. By carrying on tasks that resembled the secular work of the Catholic Church, as well as by working against it, republicans conscientiously strove to "imprint the republic in hearts and souls," as Jules Michelet put it.

In order to carry out this ambition, it was important to develop new collective symbols and new rituals. It is well known how hard revolutionaries tried to inscribe their action in a new collective "era" born with the Revolution and designed to replace Time as defined by Christianity. With this universal aim, the revolutionary calendar instituted a ten-day week—as a universal basis—and borrowed the names of days and months no longer from the Christian tradition, but rather from Nature: "Nivôse," "Ventôse," "Pluviôse," "Fructidor," etc. A new era was thus proclaimed—Year I of the Republic—which was to replace the Christian era. Revolutionary first names, borrowed from either Nature or a revolutionary mythology likely to be accepted by everyone, were supposed to gradually supplant the names of saints. The invention of new holidays had the same purpose. By creating a feast day for the Supreme Being (the "fête de l'Etre suprême"), the desire to proclaim an entirely new era was symbolically established, one which was also supposed to create a new Human Being. The construction of a social realm that was at once revolutionary and universal, with the country administratively divided into *départements* of equal size, also contributed to the founding of this new world.

This is why even today, as a remote heritage of this same intention, republican holidays tend to "duplicate" religious holidays. "Every religious holiday has its secular double."[2] Exuberant New Year's Day festivities thus "respond," element by element, to the religious and family gatherings that take place one week earlier, on Christmas

Day. The May 1st labor-day parade and the May 8th Second World War Victory Celebration similarly "respond" to the religious trilogy of Easter, Ascension, and Pentecost. The July 14th Bastille Day "responds" to the Assumption of the Virgin, on August 15th. On November 11th, the Republic commemorates those who died in the First World War, thereby "responding" in a national and patriotic manner to the dual religious holidays of All Saints' Day and All Souls' Day. The old May 1st revolutionary parades used to borrow their particular style from Catholic pilgrimages during the Easter liturgy; the street dancing and fireworks displays of the July 14th celebrations, from pilgrimages celebrating the Assumption of the Virgin. In this way, the traditions inherited respectively from a Catholic and monarchical past and from a republican and revolutionary mythology are both celebrated and blended—or continue to confront each other symbolically. As one holiday leads to the next, the two Frances are thus juxtaposed symbolically.

The educational model developed by the Catholic Church was directly and conscientiously adopted by the republicans. In the 1789 registers of grievances, in which people called for a Declaration of Human Rights, the expression "catechism of citizens" is frequently found. The expression is not without deeper significance, even if it probably also derives from the vocabulary of the period. Several "republican catechisms" were published during the Revolution. As late as 1863, Jules Ferry himself penned a *Petit Catéchisme électoral principalement destiné aux départements bretons* ("A Short Electoral Catechism Mainly Intended for the Départements of Brittany"). In many cases, the question-and-answer educational method employed in these manuals resembled that of traditional catechisms. In the Pantheon, the "grateful fatherland" (as the frontispiece of the monument phrases it) gathers in its "great men" so as to consecrate them as its saints; in other words, as intermediaries between the people and the Republic. Primary-school teachers at the end of the nineteenth century, who were nicknamed the "Hussars of the Republic," were responsible for spreading the cause of reason and patriotism— values which had miraculously been brought together by the Revolution. Primary-school teachers thereby formed the lower clergy of the Republic, taking daily care of the people and guiding them down the path of republican virtue. Similarly, even as the Catholic Church possessed its sacred tongue, Latin, the language of the Republic, French, was supposed to impose itself upon everyone, eliminating in the process all regional languages, dialects, and patois which could not be common to all citizens. As Talleyrand remarked when presenting his report on public education, only "an ever increasing amount of daily education" would be able to imprint "new sentiments, new mores, and new habits," on the souls of citizens.[3] In 1794, the *Rapport sur la nécessité et les moyens d'anéantir les patois et d'universaliser l'usage de la langue française* ("Report on the Necessity and the Means of Annihilating All Patois and of Universalizing the Usage of the French Language"), presented to the Convention by the *abbé* Henri Grégoire after he had finished his investigation of patois usage, had the aim of "knitting together the national community within the bosom of the Revolution."[4] Still more generally, within a hundred years, as Charles Péguy had clearly perceived, the education instituted by republican teaching had secularized Christian morality by imposing, in the name of the Republic, values traditionally taught by the Catholic Church, such as maintaining a stable family and performing honest work. The morals professed in primary schools were aimed at teaching citizens to be good fathers, good spouses, as well as honest and hard-working; citizens would be rewarded, not by the promise of a heavenly paradise, but rather by a sense of duty that was accomplished within, and for, the Republic.

Recent studies have cast light on the role of so-called "republican theologians," the best example of whom is Charles Renouvier. He rose up against both the positivist determinism of Auguste Comte and the conception of the world as conveyed by the Catholic Church.[5] Republican transcendence opposed religious transcendence not because it adopted the positivist rejection of all forms of transcendence, but rather in order to construct its own form of transcendence. Although the Republican State was not religious, it represented a spiritual power. The Republic appealed to morals. The forms of daily life were subsequently supposed to bear the marks of these morals. The secular civil register, or "état civil," instituted direct competition with the Church for the consecration of rites of passage—births, weddings, funerals—and the official registration, in the name of the Republic, of the essential stages of an individual's lifetime. Revolutionaries also made an immoderate use of oaths—a new kind of sacrament, as it were. If oaths today seem obsolete or intolerable, this is partly because their use has been discredited by the memory of the one taken, by civil servants and magistrates, to obey Marshal Pétain during the German occupation of France; but it is especially because the very idea of a republican sacrament has lost its meaning. A sacrament bringing an individual into a relationship with the beyond—be it God, the Republic, or Morality—is hardly harmonious with the positivism of collective life and social relations in a providential democracy.

Similarly, "dying for one's fatherland" was designed to supplant the Christian martyr's supreme sacrifice. The war monuments to the dead, tens of thousands of which were erected in all counties and townships ("communes") of France, today recall the First World War of "14-18" (as the French say), because that war is commemorated every year by a ceremony on November 11th. Actually, war monuments were raised by the hundreds after the War of 1870-1. Even more significantly, beginning with that year, monuments were built to honor those who had died in wars from the revolutionary past, in other words those who, in 1792 or 1815, had died to defend "the fatherland in danger." "A blossoming of war monuments accompanies the arrival and the triumph of the Third Republic."[6] Upon war monuments to the dead is inscribed the fatherland's gratitude to its "children who have died for it." By highlighting and celebrating their sacrifice, war monuments impose the idea that the living can in turn be called upon to perform the same sacrifice.

The history of how voting has been specifically performed in France shows that it, too, has been inspired, with increasing similarity, by religious models.[7] Voting in France takes place on Sunday, the day of mass.[8] All citizens vote on, and during, the same single day. Voting thus becomes a manifestation of the unity of the Nation in actuality. Although during the mid-nineteenth century, voting often took place in churches, in courtrooms, or even in the private homes of the current mayor or of an important manor or chateau owner in the area, gradually voting came to be organized in recognizable public areas that were clearly distinct from all private property. Polling places were set up in public schools or town halls, which, in the smallest counties and townships ("communes"), often occupied the same building. Even if modest, these public polling places—called "bureaux de vote" in French—are the locus of the *res publica*, even as the church is the locus of divine presence. For many years, drumrolls announced the opening of the polls and then—a half-hour ahead of time—their imminent closing, just as church bells call the faithful to worship. In this way, the time devoted to the voting ritual was given a special consecrated significance and shown up to be different from secular time. The objects used during the voting ritual in France—the checking of national identity cards or driver's licences, the table upon which are aligned separate stacks of paper slips ("bulletins") upon which are printed each candidate's or party's name, the custom of picking up a slip for each candidate or party (by which the voter does not reveal his intention to the polling-place official sitting behind the table), the curtained voting booth or "isoloir" into which each voter then goes, the envelope into which he or she places just one of the slips of paper, the padlocked ballot box into which the voter then drops the envelope, concluding his or her vote by signing the registered voter list—, the way (before the polls are opened) by which the president of each polling place arranges the room and assigns the chairs where each official "member" of the polling place will sit and what he or she will do, the strictly codified rules that the president applies when the ballots are counted one by one after the closing of the polls, all contribute to giving a special rigorous definition to the time devoted to voting on election day. The slightest details of the proceedings of this "celebration" are provided for in the electoral code, which has been extended and refined over the years, and which indeed continues to be so through ever more precise directives promulgated by the Ministry of the Interior. These directives detail rules about the voting booth, the itinerary that each voter must follow within the polling place, the tables behind which the official members working at the polling place must sit, how the ballots will be counted, and how the election outcome will be made public and communicated to the Ministry of the Interior. Within a polling place, as in a church, one's behavior must be suitable, discrete, and respectful. A citizen exercising his citizen rights and duties should be honest and conscientious.

It is probably the modification of the ballot box, or "urne," standardized at the end of the nineteenth century, which is the most significant.[9] The Reform of July 1913, which codified most of the objects belonging to the electoral paraphernalia that we use today (the tables, envelopes, slips of paper, curtained booths, and ballot boxes), made the ballot box the center of the ritual performed within the polling place. The ballot box gradually became an almost sacred object worthy of respect. It now occupies the center of a genuine altar: the table on which are placed, in a specially predetermined arrangement, the various paraphernalia used for voting. In 1988, an additional statute required that the ballot box be transparent. The ballot box guarantees the anonymity of the procedure; it ensures the equality of the votes by giving a tangible sense to the expression "one man, one vote." Finally, it symbolizes the individualization of the electoral gesture. By voting in an election, an individual is magically transformed into a citizen; he reveals the general interest—a "substitute for violence," as Victor Hugo phrased it. Inside the ballot box, each individual's opinion is transformed into an expression of citizenship and the General Will. In the chalice, wine becomes the blood of Christ; in the paten, the eucharistic wafer or bread becomes the flesh of Christ.

It is revealing to compare voting in France and Great Britain. In the latter country, voting is done during the work week, usually on a Thursday. Voting usually takes place in public schools, but, depending on local needs and resources, polling places can also be set up in private schools, religious schools, churches, or social services centers. The ritualistic aspects are few, and they can vary from place to place. Voting is a commonplace, familiar gesture that possesses none of the solemnity associated with voting in the French Republic. Another conception of voter and voting is thereby revealed. In England, the electoral colleges inherited from the past are unified electoral bodies which retain a certain independence, and not fractions of a unique and homogeneous electorate, as is the case in France. If voting is less ritualized and possesses few quasi-sacred qualities, this is because the general interest coincides naturally with the sum of all private interests. One needs none of those magical elements which, during a French election, transform a private individual—with all his or her beliefs, allegiances, ruling passions, and interests—into a citizen. English democracy is older and also more familiar to its practitioners.

Republican rituals nevertheless possess intrinsic limits because they are not aimed at a beyond. A republican society is self-founded. A republican ritual remains relatively impoverished in the sense that it is self-referential and includes no mediation with any form of transcendence. The revolutionary calendar failed. People continued to give names of saints to their new-born children. The rites of passage, as celebrated in their secular forms—be they "republican baptisms" (which are legally possible yet rare), wedding ceremonies in town halls, or "republican" funerals organized by funeral homes, with flowers and a few speeches given by friends—only weakly convey the trials and strong emotions of human life, in comparison to the splendors of elaborate Catholic ceremonies with their hymns, organ music, sacraments, communion, sermon, and incense.[10] Religious holidays long continued to punctuate collective life. "Parish civilization," to quote Yves Lambert's expression, shaped and structured by religious practices controlled by the Catholic Church, was maintained until the Second World War in the most religious regions of France. The Pantheon, at which only secular, republican funerals have taken place ever since 1885, has always been an "empty" (as Mona Ozouf has pointed out), austere, and icy temple. The monumental, ten-ton, twenty-foot-high bronze statue made by the Morice brothers, which represents a Marianne with a Phrygian cap and which was inaugurated on 14 July 1883 at the Place de la République in Paris in celebration of the Republic, peace, and universal suffrage, "is like a shipwreck on the margins of history . . . . The silhouette of the Republic inspires neither hostility nor enthusiasm."[11]

The republicans indeed found themselves faced with a contradiction. They were endeavoring to construct rituals based on shared traditions and emotions—which can be called "ethnic"—whereas republican society draws its legitimacy from an abstract, rational civic principle. "An abstract notion cannot serve as a mooring post for experienced impressions, even if it was the notion itself that provoked the impressions. It is the sign that thereafter takes its place. . . ."[12] This is why this "faceless State," as Maurice Agulhon put it, took on a woman's face after the republican regime had come back into power at the end of the nineteenth century. At the time, the only official emblems of the French Republic were the "RF" initials and the three-colored flag. Yet beginning in the 1880s, it was Marianne, with her Phrygian cap, who came to embody the Republic and who replaced the images of the king in the public realm. Today, a bust representing her still presides over ceremonies that take place in French town halls; and sometimes another bust of her can be seen on the front of the building. Marianne has been depicted on urban monuments, stamps, and coins. Gradually this image of a Woman-Republic, all the more omnipresent in that she is polysemous, became that of France.[13]

More generally, the rituals and images of the Republic have always been closely associated with national patriotism. It is in the name of the Republic that nation-building was carried out in France;

and the lead was taken up elsewhere throughout Europe during the age of nationalism, though in these cases feeling and fervor incited by national identity, not by republican reason, were appealed to. It is well-known that all European countries, throughout the nineteenth century, followed the same model when constructing the tools and symbols of their national identity.[14] First, ancestors were created in accordance with the model of the mythical Ossian, who became the author of what was called the "Scottish *Iliad*." In France, the myth of "our ancestors, the Gauls" replaced the myth of two races; historians from Jules Michelet to Ernest Lavisse played a preponderant role in creating a national identity. Everywhere, a national language was invented or imposed: the use of the national language became a duty. Yet if national patriotism had to be mustered in France, this is because appealing to "autonomous individuals gifted with reason"— as implied by the republican idea—has always been insufficient for uniting human beings; they also need to share emotions if they are to "create a society"—except during the brief period of the French Revolution, which is probably one of the reasons why those years continue to fascinate historians and republicans.

The Republic even sought out support in local, more tangible, and immediate kinds of patriotism that would be more directly experienced by population groups. Through the compulsory, free, public primary schools that were created and structured by means of Jules Ferry's legislation, the republicans of 1880 imposed French as the common language. This was done at the expense of regional languages. At the same time, the republicans cultivated a sentiment of local attachments as an indispensable propaedeutic to a sentiment of national loyalty. The official Third Republic educational ideology, as formulated in the publications and directives of the Ministry of Public Instruction, was "unity in diversity." "Little fatherlands," or "petites patries," were systematically celebrated in the teaching of history, geography, and French, and local know-how was encouraged. Official national textbooks had special editions designed for specific *départements*, and special programs brought together primary-school teachers in each *département* to work on projects devoted to local patriotism—which now seemed to be the prerequisite to national patriotism. A child's attachments were meant to spread, by means of successive concentric circles, from his family to his school, then to his region, and finally to his fatherland. According to the national mythology, the "great voice of France . . . is made up of distinct voices that sing in unison." The ideology of the Vichy government during the German occupation of France—notably, the "return to the soil"—benefited from the solid regionalist tradition of the Third Republic.[15]

By attempting to stage the rationality and the abstraction of the Republic, republicans indeed found themselves up a dead end. As it turned out, the sacred qualities that they had tried to develop responded only imperfectly to the human needs of celebrating the rites of passage which punctuate individual lives, of giving meaning to hardship, and of seeking out answers to anguished questions about one's fate.

The Utopia of Representation

The problem of "representation" in the Republic draws on two conceptions inherited from political philosophy. The first is that obeying the law constitutes the supreme form of political freedom; that is, when citizens "personally or through their representatives"—as Articles 6 and 14 of the Declaration of the Rights of Man and the Citizen phrase it—have participated in the elaboration of the law. The second conception is that this participation is accomplished through the citizens' choice of those who govern them and through their subsequent judgments about the actions that have been taken by those whom they have elected: elections need to take place at regular intervals so that those who govern are regularly submitted to the judgment of citizens. Once an ordinary individual is elected, he or she is transformed into a representative of the general interest. The nation—one and indivisible—exists in and through the gathering of representatives elected by the entire citizen body.

The invention of the idea of representation, which is not a part of our ancient Greek heritage, was first justified by practical arguments. It was impossible to put direct democracy to work in vast monarchies: how would it be materially possible to bring together all the people within the confines of the agora? In the modern world, it was impossible to reconstitute the Greek *polis*, made up of a small number of citizens linked to each other by direct and personal relationships. Modern citizens could not materially and directly exercise power in political entities that were too vast and complex. Direct democracy was thus, in Carl Schmitt's terms, "impraticable."[16] Moreover, it was important to choose the most competent men to govern the country. This was especially Montesquieu's argument.

However, these arguments were not the only ones. It was not only because of practical or technical reasons that the idea of direct democracy was eliminated. It was not just a matter of citizens accepting that someone else speak and act in their stead during a predetermined period of time. An election *per se* established a form of transcendence based on the idea that an abstract political society was not to be confused with real, living individuals. In fact, this was the idea of the sacred which was developed by Émile Durkheim and upon which his own notion of republicanism was based. An election "purifies democracy"; it "filters the choices of the people" and can re-establish "the empire of superior virtue and talent which direct voting, full of popular passions, might have failed to recognize"; it is thereby important that "the results" of universal suffrage are "permanently corrected so that the legal will of the people, and the real will expressed by a people who in this sense becomes more real than the first, can be adjusted by means of this purification."[17] Representation was legitimated by the transfiguration of the elected individual through the very fact of his or her election. Elected individuals ceased to be individuals like other individuals; they thereafter embodied the general interest, which is not the same as the sum of the interests of the individuals and groups who make up the "people" in the political sense of the term. Elected individuals were no longer representatives of the fraction of the people who had elected them; they now represented the entire people. "Every deputy represents the entire nation," as Sieyès famously put it. The idea of representation implied that wise men, because they were competent and detached from their real, concrete, down-to-earth attachments, were more likely to formulate the general interest, which transcends the interests of each individual by its very nature. Representatives alone could convey the general will—itself an expression of universal reason—and the revolutionaries' faith in continuous, irreversible progress. According to Sieyès, this general will would take shape in the National Assembly because discussion, the exchange of ideas, and the confrontation of opinions would lead to enlightenment.[18] "Government through detachment," as he put it, was the only practicable way of constituting a government of the people by the people.

In England, it was by appealing to transcendence that the idea of "virtual," as opposed to "real," representation was developed. As early as 1774, Edmund Burke had asserted that the parliament was not "a *congress* of ambassadors from different and hostile interests, which interests each must maintain, as an agent and advocate, against other agents and advocates; but Parliament is a *deliberative* assembly of one nation, with one interest, that of the whole, where, not local purposes, nor local prejudices ought to guide, but the general good, resulting from the general reason of the whole.[19] When faced with the demands of American colonists during the conflict provoked by the Stamp Act of 1765, the lampoonists favorable to the British government competed with each other to satirize more vividly the theory of virtual representation. "None are actually, all are virtually represented; for every Member of Parliament sits in the House, not as Representative of his own Constituents, but as one of that august Assembly by which all the Commons of *Great Britain* are represented." Despite great degrees of rank and property, despite even the separation of some by three thousand miles of ocean, the English people were assumed to be an "essentially a unitary homogeneous order with a fundamental common interest. . . . All Englishmen were linked by their heritage, their liberties, and their institutions into a common people that possessed a single transcendent concern."[20] The notion of virtual representation was then used by the English to belittle the significance of elections and limit the voting rights of colonists. Because American colonists were hostile to a conception preventing them from being represented in the Westminster parliament and from participating in the decision to levy taxes, they obviously appealed to the idea of real representation.

Yet once the American colonists had won the War of Independence, they oscillated between the two conceptions and long debated their respective virtues. Virtual representation corresponded to their republicanism, but they had appealed to the idea of real representation in order to justify their rebellion against the home country. During the decade which followed the War of Independence—and which was marked by the elaboration of the forms of political organization through widespread debates and a series of experiments—Americans theorized and tested both conceptions. As a result, they ultimately invented, in actuality, the "modern" delegation. "No political conception was more important to Americans in the entire revolutionary era than representation."[21] Did those who were represented have a mere right to petition their representatives, so as to make themselves heard, or did they have the right to give them instructions? This was indeed the issue at the origin of modern democratic practices. What makes this period fascinating is that the debates (in which intellectual traditions ranging from Greco-Roman political philosophy and Christian theology to English liberal empiricism and Enlightenment rationalism clashed or converged) were immediately transposed into social forms. The confrontation of conceptions and institutions was immediate and constant.

However, after having been led to claim the rights of real representation in their struggle for independence, and after having been tempted to establish a republic resembling a real and direct democracy, the Americans began "voicing a broadening awareness of what excessive localism, binding instructions, and acutely actual representation signified for their assumptions about the nature of republican politics."[22] They then created the institutions based on representation which, still today, have essentially retained their original forms. The birth of the American nation was celebrated by contemporaries and historians alike. James Madison asserted that the American Republic was unique and without precedent: it had invented the idea of representation, notably "the delegation of the government to a small number of citizens elected by the rest." Madison was actually only formulating an opinion here that was simultaneously being expressed by numerous other contemporary journalists. During this great confrontation, which was as intellectual as it was political, an "entirely new conception of politics" was formulated, "a conception that took [Americans] out of an essentially classical and medieval world of political discussion into one that was recognizably modern."[23] After ten years of widespread discussion and political experimentation, the Americans had invented the idea of modern representation.

In contrast, the States General ("États généraux") of the old France were based on the idea of "imperative mandates." During the States General of 1321, for example, delegates from cities replied to questions raised by the king only after they had consulted with their mandators. The States General elections of 1789 had not clearly chosen between a traditional political mandate, which tightly bound the mandatary and the mandator into a genuine civil contract, and a modern political mandate; that is, between an organic conception of the body politic and the contractual and individualist conception which is associated with political modernity. However, beginning on 23 June 1789, the king "quashes and invalidates—as anti-constitutional, as contrary to official summons letters, and as opposed to the interest of the State—the restrictions of powers which inhibit the freedom of deputies who have been chosen."[24] In their opposition to the tradition of imperative mandates stemming from the Ancien Régime, the French revolutionaries imposed upon institutions the idea of the transcendence of the Nation. Article 2 of Title 3 asserts: "The Nation, from which alone all powers derive, can exercise power only through delegation. The French Constitution is representative. . . ." The revolutionaries vigorously attacked the imperative mandate, which submitted the elected mandatary to his electors by obliging him to vote in accordance with their instructions.[25] They were indignant that the elected mandatary was transformed into a simple "machine"—into a subordinate "commis-deputy"—and that decision-making thereby preceded deliberation. Representatives were henceforth granted the legitimacy and the freedom to draft and propose laws on matters that concerned the general interest. "Because the French nation is entirely and legitimately represented by the plurality of its deputies, neither imperative mandates, nor the voluntary absence of some members, nor the protest of the parlimentary minority can ever curtail its activity, alter its freedom, attenuate the force of its statutes, or restrain the limits of its legislative power in areas under its jurisdiction, which essentially extends over all parts of the Nation and all French possessions."[26]

"Most Constituents consider that their task is to build a representative political system, which they clearly oppose to democracy."[27] However, although the institutions of the Republic were based on representation, the very notion continued to be contested and applied with difficulty because of democratic values and the idea of the sovereignty of the people. "Representation has been the stumbling block of French democracy for two centuries."[28] In France, more than elsewhere, the practices of a republic based on representation have never excluded an aspiration to a sort of identification between electors and the elected—an identification stemming, at the same time, from Rousseau's philosophy and from the memory of the mystical union bringing together a sovereign and his subjects. The Revolution inherited this image as well. Appealing to the notion of the sovereignty of the people as an permanent and exclusive source of the General Will, Rousseau was opposed to the idea of representation. The idea of an imperative mandate was never totally eliminated; it became popular once again at the end of the Second Empire and in the first years of the Third Republic.[29] In this respect, several propositions for new laws were submitted to the Chamber of

Deputies during the 1880s, but the deputies refused to discuss them. During the political turmoil of the nineteenth century, in which two parliamentary monarchies, two empires, and three republics came successively into power, representative governmental systems were weak. Political institutions oscillated between regimes in which power was given to an assembly which embodied the idea of "absolute representation" and which handed over the monopoly of power to the representatives of the nation by eliminating the intermediary corps, and Bonapartist-like regimes in which identification between those governing and the governed was asserted. As Napoleon III put it, "the nature of democracy is to be personified in one man." For a long time in France, the parliamentary system did not eliminate "nostalgia for power embodied in a single man."[30]

The tension between real and virtual representation, or between a real people and a represented people, constituted the political modernity which developed at the end of the eighteenth century. But the historical conditions underlying the birth of the citizen have made this tension particularly acute in France. The debate about the compatibility between representation and democracy has never ended. To cite a single example, the legal philosopher Raymond Carré de Malberg, in his *Contribution à la théorie générale de l'État* ("Contribution to a General Theory of the State," 1920) distinguished "national sovereignty" and "popular sovereignty" by radically opposing "representation" (linked to the former) and "democracy" (linked to the latter).[31] It is true that an "ambivalent and complex relationship with abstraction" continues to be maintained.[32] Those who are nostalgic for the imperative mandate or direct democracy, and who are critical of institutions based on representation, are recruited among those who are reluctant to accept a certain autonomy for politics and to recognize the value of pluralism and the significance of distinctions among the various professional corps and hierarchies. To a certain extent, institutions based on representation find it difficult to be in harmony with the unitary or totalizing conception of "citizen" in the French sense, as it was conceived during the Revolution of 1789. Founded upon the idea of a separation between the State and civil society, and on the distinction between electors and the elected, the republic based on representation was criticized by those who, despite differences in their intellectual or political persuasion, all desired to re-establish a deep identification or fusion between the people and those who govern them. In the first stage, the criticism came from upholders of the Ancien Régime and from those nostalgic for a direct democracy ensuring the mystical union of the people. Subsequently, criticism was formulated not only by socialist and communist thinkers calling for a "social democracy" in which the producer would replace the citizen, but also by Gaullists who had inherited a Bonapartist inspiration and, finally, even by Christian Democrats. Beyond marked differences in political viewpoints, these kinds of criticism all shared the same hostility to the idea of representation, and the same aspiration to make the representative *be* the people. In their view, because representation was based on a fundamental asymmetry between a representative and those whom he represents, it kept the people away from political power. In this sense, representation was anti-democratic by definition.

The Weakening of a Republic Based on Representation

Today, it is the transmutation undergone by representation that has weakened. Those who govern continue to draw their legitimacy from institutions based on representation. But representation has ceased to be the instrument of political transcendence and has become the means by which the needs and identities of citizens are expressed.[33]

Homo democraticus has trouble tolerating the limits and the constraints imposed upon him by institutions; he claims the right to contest their legitimacy. Moreover, the distinction—established by an election—between a representative and those whom he represents seems to him contradictory with the principle of equality. Two centuries earlier, political modernity had replaced the inequality of birth by the inequalities of worth and virtue; it had preserved the idea of the ineluctable nature of inequality and had accepted its perpetuation. The distinction between representatives and those whom they represent is based on an inequality of competence: the former are considered to be superior in this regard. Today, the inequalities of worth and virtue, and even that of age, tend to be denounced in the name of democratic values. Inequality in general is increasingly considered to be unacceptable. The legitimacy of practices based on representation are accordingly weakened. The need for direct participation and for identification with politicians grows when every individual aspires to be a sovereign himself. *Homo democraticus* tends to think that he can be represented only by himself.

The End of the Utopia?

Indeed, in all aspects of public life, both the legitimacy of law—an invention of classical Greece—and representation—an invention of political modernity—are now called into question. This is above all true of politics, but it is also true of other realms of social life: political parties, labor unions, academic institutions, institutionalized religions, and, more generally, all institutions drawing their authority from tradition and even from law. In 1968, when all institutions were fundamentally challenged, forms of direct democracy reappeared: power was given to general meetings (and not to a small group of decision-makers); voting was conducted by raising hands; members of administrative or academic committees were chosen by drawing straws instead of by electing the most competent or active members.

The signs of a loss of faith in the practices of a republic based on representation are well known. Voter abstention is increasing in all countries.[34] Both voter registration and voting itself are decreasing, for all kinds of elections. Even when comparing the same kind of election, voter participation is decreasing everywhere, especially among younger, less educated, and economically weak voters. Voters consider that the stakes are low; that the various political parties espouse similar, if not identical, policies. Elections are increasingly less often "election battles" which draw out strong voter participation, and increasingly more often "elections of appeasement" to which voters not participating in the political milieu in the narrow sense of the term become increasingly indifferent. Even in France, where an opposition between "The Left" and "The Right" long shaped and structured partisan politics, the prospect of voting one or the other faction into power no longer suffices to create an "election battle."

Specialists have likewise discovered the "volatility" of voters: the same voter can successively vote for candidates belonging to different parties. These so-called "mobile voters" or "new voters"—in other words, those who vote for a right-wing candidate or a left-wing candidate depending on the election issues and the personality of the candidate—represented 10% of the electorate between 1986 and 1988. A study conducted after the presidential elections of 1995 showed that hardly more than a third of the voters had voted for the same political camp during the three preceding elections.[35] This is probably less a sign of de-politicization than a symptom of democratic individuals' desire to express personal choices, to appraise politicians' personalities, and to reject the terms of the "voting offer" that is tendered to them by political parties. A voter no longer accepts being enrolled in the institutions that traditionally organize representation. He no longer necessarily respects the voting recommendations of the party to which he feels closest. Similarly, the number of "undecided voters" is increasing; that is, those who are slow in making up their minds about their vote.[36] Some of these undecided voters hesitate among several candidates; they tend to be politicized voters whose educational level is high. Other undecided voters are not very politicized and less educated; their last-minute decision does not imply hesitation among several candidates. However, in all cases, voters make a personal choice. They can thus change their minds from one election to the next, as well as during a given political campaign, without taking political-party action into account.

It is above all the idea of "delegation" (to cite once again the eighteenth-century term) that is called into question; in other words, the idea of political transcendence. However, this is not the same thing as a lack of all interest in politics. During the 1990s, there was evidence showing that the percentage of permanent non-voters was less than 3%, that a third of all French voters participated in all elections, and that the other citizens voted or abstained from voting in accordance with their analysis of the election stakes.[37] The variations in voter participation reveal that French voters are likely to go to the polls when they sense that the issues are genuine. They always turn out in greater numbers for presidential or municipal elections—whose significance they understand—than for regional or European elections; many citizens even ignore the existence of the European parliament and the system of regional government. The behavior of young voters, who are the least numerous to vote, reflects that of the entire voting population: selective and precisely targeted voting, depending on the issues and the voter's specific interests, and irrespective of political-party recommendations.[38]

This calling into question of representation does not lead to a rejection of the fundamental rules of democracy, namely the idea that conflicts of interest and values should be regulated and controlled by the votes of citizens and the compromises among various social groups, all of whom should abide by common rules. The fact that one votes and accepts the results of an election reveals an agreement and a conviction: conflicts must be resolved by voting, not by violence. The French expression "élections, piège à cons" ("elections are traps for fools"), which was "rediscovered" in 1968, remained confined to student and intellectual milieus; the voting rate was particularly high in June 1968. The results of elections are never contested.[39] *Homo democraticus* regularly proclaims his belief in human rights, so strongly in fact that "human-rights-ism" has become a political ideology. Although young people's abstention rate is the highest in the population at large, they tend to admire great political figures who have lead at once universal and patriotic struggles: Nelson Mandela, Martin Luther King, Jean Moulin, or Charles de Gaulle.[40] Moreover, voting is constantly used to resolve differences of opinion or judgment in all aspects of social life. Voting is used in courts of law, in literary prize competitions, in French Academy elections, in committees when university professors are hired, and in meetings of strikers who are deciding whether to go back to work. Nor has the symbolic character of elections disappeared. A presidential election day especially creates collective expectation; during the day, before the results are announced in the evening, even the economically weakest citizens can have the feeling, or the illusion, that they hold the fate of the "great and mighty" in their hands. It is an ephemeral moment during which the community of citizens becomes self-aware, as it were. Universal suffrage authenticates the dignity of each and everyone in the ideal democratic utopia in which all free and equal citizens, through their vote, express the general will.

The increasing number of types of direct and immediate political action likewise reveals a growing reluctance with respect to all that is "legal" and "representative," which are respectively considered too abstract and too indirect. In France, the number of street demonstations has greatly risen. It is true that sometimes few people participate, that often few if any immediate results are obtained, and that their effectiveness can appear "illusory."[41] However, certain demonstrations have had undeniable political consequences. In June 1984, in Versailles, a street demonstration of nearly a million people in favor of private schools compelled a legitimate government (because it had been legitimately elected) to withdraw from the agenda of the National Assembly a project for a new education law which had been legitimately drawn up in accordance with the rules of a republic based on representation. Since then, examples of decisions forced upon the government by street demonstrations have not been rare: in 1986, the "Devaquet Law" project concerning higher education was withdrawn from the National Assembly; in 1994, a measure designed to establish a minimum wage for young people, called the "SMIC-Jeunes," was likewise withdrawn; in 1995, a project designed to align civil-servant retirement pension plans with legislation that the then prime minister, Alain Juppé, had developed for the private economic sector was abandoned; in 1999, Claude Allègre, at the time the Minister of National Education, was removed from office and replaced. The impact of opinion polls and the press on election campaigns seems more influential than the elaboration of a platform by political parties.

In the name of democratic values, the idea that an election leads to a difference between representatives and those whom they represent—upon which republican transcendence is based—is accepted reluctantly, if not rejected entirely. Although citizen-individuals considered, in a first phase, notable politicians, and in a second phase, political party officials and workers, to be their legitimate representatives, this is increasingly less often the case. "More than the replacement of one type of elite by another, it is the perpetuation, indeed perhaps even the widening, of the gap between the people and the political elite governing them that provokes a feeling of crisis."[42] This interpretation needs to be qualified. In the past, neither traditional notable politicians and elected officials whose competence was acknowledged, nor political-party officials and workers, were closer to their voters than politicians are today. It is not the objective "widening" of the "gap between the people and the political elite governing them" that is responsible for the "feeling of crisis," but rather an increasing demand for resemblance or identification between voter and elected official.[43] Power has become personalized, personified. A voter must have the sense that he can recognize himself in the politician who is supposed to represent him. Consequently, voters inevitably claim to be ill represented by politicians. The simple acknowledgment that a "specialized group of people" exists who are devoted to political activity—and whose existence is linked to the idea of representation—provokes indignation. French citizens henceforth consider it unacceptable that their elected officials belong to what appears to be a caste made up of former students of the École Nationale d'Administration, as well as of journalists, pollsters,

and "communications" specialists. The juridical measures protecting the presidency are criticized accordingly: "the President of the
Republic is a human being like any other." In the name of the real
equality of all individuals, the distinction between the political function—which is abstract—and the real, living person exercising it has
not found complete endorsement.

The constant demand for "transparency" likewise expresses a rejection of the distance, established by an election, between voters
and politicians. The demand that a government make its action public—the "reign of criticism," as Reinhard Koselleck puts it[44]—goes
back to the eighteenth century, when individuals began aspiring to
exercise a right to examine State affairs. This demand has increased
with the rise of providential democracy. Whereas secret balloting
appeared in the nineteenth century as the necessary prerequisite to a
voter's full freedom (since it protected him from the pressure of
neighbors or local authorities), the complete transparency of social
life today responds to the fully sovereign individual's demands and
to the idea, formulated as an ideal, for public openness in a democracy. Even in France, secrets and the "opacity" of political practices—inherited from a specific history of the French State, symbol-
ized by the expression "l'État, c'est moi" ("I am the State," as Louis
XIV is attributed to have declared)—which protected men in power
and which tended to blur the distinction between the monarch's personal wealth and the finances of the nation, are beginning to appear
outrageous and unacceptable. Now vigorously questioned are habits inherited from an age-old tradition which furnished those in power
with considerable public funds whose use was not at all scrutinized
in the same way as citizens' incomes and private financial resources.
However, at the same time, society is becoming more technical and
more difficult to understand; the desire for transparency runs up
against the constraints of complex societies. Who is capable of comprehending State finances or a balance sheet charting how wealth
has been redistributed among various social groups, in accordance
with the requirements of the social protection system? During the
autumn of 2000, the "cagnotte" episode (which involved the revela-
tion that a special "cash kitty" of public funds had been set aside by
the government and not been accounted for publicly) showed how
difficult, if not impossible, it is for a common citizen to understand
how his taxes are used. Voters now unanimously denounce corruption. More and more Americans think that the political class serves

specific interests and not the general interest; the French likewise view politicians as "rotten."[45] Corruption is all the more closely associated with the very idea of politics that, in providential democracies, tension has arisen between democratic demands and the growing complexity of the wealth redistribution system. On the other hand, does not any power associated, to a greater or lesser degree, with the sacred imply a certain use of secrecy?

Politicians respond to the expectations of voters by pointing to the daily actions they take for improving living conditions. Because politicians sense that voters are unwilling to listen to them, they rarely formulate grand projects giving meaning to the destiny of the collectivity beyond the immediate reactions of public opinion. On 30 June 1988, Michel Rocard, speaking about the general orientation of his political policy (he had just been appointed prime minister), dealt with the civil society at length and called for the birth of a "socialism of daily life." A few months later, he admitted that one could not govern against opinion polls. During his electoral campaign, Silvio Berlusconi promised to govern Italy in accordance with the model of private enterprise, and to do so with the success that he had experienced as a private entrepreneur. He was elected and became prime minister. All politicians point to the value of "proximity" and "local concerns," even when they are candidates for national positions. They mention their political-party partisanship only with great discretion.[46] A political party's effort to "parachute"—as one says in French—a candidate from Paris into a local provincial voting district ("circonscription") in which he or she has never been active politically increasingly results in an election defeat for the parachuted candidate. In fact, within political parties, local party officials have difficulties applying decisions made by the national party leaders, even in left-wing parties, which have inherited the transcendental value of the Party. A new law submitted to the Parliament during the year 2001 called for the development of "proximity democracy," to respond to voters' aspirations.[47] Above all, voters now want good administrators. The importance given to daily life, both in fact and speech, reveals that politics increasingly tends to manage everyday relationships among human beings and not to put into action an overall project—underwritten by common values—which would attempt to make viable a way of living together. Institutionalized religions and political parties, which respectively organize forms of religious or political transcendence on the collective level, so as to produce meanings that can be used to explain social injustice, as well as individual and collective hardship, have indeed modified their discourse and practices. Both the catechism of the Catholic Church and the instructions given to the candidates of the best organized and most "governmental" political parties—the Socialist Party (PS) and the right-wing Rassemblement pour la République (RPR), now rechristened the Union pour un Mouvement Populaire (UMP)—first take into account down-to-earth everyday problems. In France, democratic individuals use the familiar second-person-personal "tu"-form when speaking to each other, in the name of their fundamental equality, and even believers use "tu" when praying to God. The Communist Party, with its idea of "sacrificing oneself for the Party," was the last incarnation of a form of transcendence, to the extent that individuals submitted their own judgment or will to the interests of a collectivity.

One observes the crumbling away of republican, indeed all, rituals. For a long time, the overall atmosphere of religious and republican holidays was different. In contrast to the solemnity and reverence expressed in religious or family holidays, public holidays were marked by much more exuberance (though it must be said that when religious holidays punctuated collective life, Easter pilgrimages could also be quite demonstrative in certain non-secular Mediterranean countries). Today, both kinds of holidays resemble each other in their loss of ardor. The religious and national holidays that once set apart, for the collectivity, a special period in which all social bonds could be strengthened still exist, but they henceforth induce less enthusiasm and participation than the sundry "theme-" days, holidays, weekends, weeks, or even months organized by the Cultural Providence State: the National Music Day ("Fête de la Musique") which was launched in 1982, corresponds to the summer solstice and encourages all sorts of professional and amateur musical groups to come out into the streets and give free concerts; the Historical and Cultural Heritage Days ("Journées du Patrimoine") during which monuments, both well-known and rare, both public and private, are open free-of-charge to the general public; the Museum Invitation Day ("Invitation au Musée"), which became The Spring of Museums ("Printemps des Musées") program in 1991 and which similarly encourages people to visit museums; the Art Rush project ("Ruée vers l'Art"), which began in 1985 and which is likewise designed to familiarize the general public with the art world; the Reading Fury

("Fureur de Lire") program, which was launched in 1989 and later rechristened A Time for Reading ("Le Temps de Lire"), and which aims at drawing the general public into libraries and bookstores; or The Spring of Poets ("Printemps des Poètes") project, which was initiated in 1999 and which promotes poetry throughout France through readings and other activities. This is not to forget spontaneous festive gatherings during which a town's athletic team is greeted when it returns home after a victory or even a glorious defeat. National holidays are now similarly replaced by demonstrations which employ well-practiced festive forms (parades, disguises, slogans, songs, banners, and the like) and in which specific groups defend their interests or identity. Such demonstrations may be staged by civil servants, farmers, hunters, or homosexuals gathered under the "gay pride" banner. All such demonstrations are transnational celebrations of a particularism that is put forward as a claim. Yet only the French victory in the 1998 World Soccer Cup, on 12 July, led to a truly national celebration; it was the first time since the Liberation that the churchbells of Paris tolled to celebrate a national event. This probably explains the mythical role that this victory still plays in the collective memory of the French.

Patriotism, and the internalization of this patriotism to the point of accepting to "die for one's fatherland" while singing *La Marseillaise*—which represented a sort of transfer of religious sacredness onto the nation (given value through the very word "fatherland")—have become so weak that their significance has become narrowly associated, at best, only with an individual's personal identity. The professionalization of the army is both an indication and instrument of this, even if a purely military rationale led to the decision to put an end to compulsory conscription. Athletic patriotism, based on local attachments, is a weakened symbolic form of national patriotic sentiment; yet it does not engage individuals in the same way. Soccer-team supporters display certain practices and emotions; they respect rituals that were long confined to religious and patriotic gatherings. They passionately identify with the victories and defeats of their team; they fashion domestic altars; they work hard to acquire sometimes very expensive relics; and they scrupulously respect the rituals that precede and follow the "ceremony." During the ceremony itself, they share strong emotions with others; they blend into the collectivity. They are not above wielding a certain violence against the supporters of the opposing team or even against the players of their own team when it loses. However, up to now, soccer fans have refused the supreme sacrifice. Despite the many qualities that soccer borrows from religious and patriotic rituals, it remains a "minor religion" which, in contrast to traditional and secular religions, formulates no "promise of a radiant future." Soccer does not claim to provide the ultimate meaning of existence, nor to ensure our salvation either here or in the beyond. It reflects the uncertainty and the fragility of the values and individual destinies in our societies.[48] Up to now, at least in Europe, deaths in soccer stadiums have not been caused by someone's willingness to make the supreme sacrifice, but rather by pure hooliganism or errors in security policy. One is not yet ready to die for the Marseilles "Olympique" or the Paris-Saint-Germain soccer teams.

Participatory Democracy

It is as a response to the democratic individual's aspiration to be represented only by himself that one now observes various demands for "participatory" democracy—an ambiguous term with nonetheless positive connotations. It implies both the idea of a direct exercise of citizenship as well as a criticism of representation. It also conveys the value of "proximity" (celebrated by politicians, political scientists, and sociologists alike), as opposed to the abstract, "imaginary"[49] or "tyrannical"[50] character of all that is national and republican.

It is no coincidence that political scientists have recently become interested in direct democracy.[51] Some predict and advocate its coming. According to Ian Budge, for example, the existence of the Internet and the development of mass education have outmoded the two arguments traditionally aimed against direct democracy: its impracticability, because of the number of people involved; and the "people's" lack of competence. In his view, thanks to the Internet, direct democracy could be the crowning achievement of the extension of the right to vote to ever broader categories of the population: a truly universal suffrage could take place at last. The Internet could be the new agora in which the entire population, despite its size, could meet freely and debate problems directly. Moreover—continues the argument—the people, because they have benefited from mass education, have become as competent as, if not more so than, professional politicians. What then can justify holding back genuine democracy—that is, direct democracy conducted through the

Internet—on the sidelines? This kind of thinking reflects the numerous books which, during the 1990s, theorized a new "tele-democracy" which would enable citizens to directly and permanently conduct the political affairs of the country. Through virtual "electronic town meetings" of everyone on the Web, and through Internet "televoting," immediate democracy could thereby recover the virtues of direct democracy and enable the people to act directly and immediately. This conception depends on the assumption that political abstention is actually caused by material difficulties preventing voters from getting to a polling place and from discussing political problems, and that problems related to political participation can be resolved by technical means. In a more traditional style, a more frequent use of referendums is again being discussed.

Similarly, the value of "mirror representation" is brought up by thinkers of a "communitarian" persuasion; in other words, a political system in which political institutions would represent a mirror image of the various categories of the population at large. This idea actually goes back to a concept formulated by John Adams. During the 1780s, in the great debates about representation in the United States, he defended the principle of "real" representation: "[The assembly] should be in miniature an exact portrait of the people at large. It should think, feel, reason, and act like them." One of his contemporaries also evoked the necessity of representatives being the "exact miniature of their constituents."[52] Yet at the same time, Adams let it be understood that representatives should also be the best and the wisest; in this sense, he followed the tradition of virtual representation. The idea of mirror representation, which has come back into discussion, calls into question the utopia of representation by which the representative is not supposed to represent such and such a category of the population, but rather to embody the general interest.

Political modernity indeed created confidence in the mechanisms enabling various peoples to live together, precisely because these mechanisms were abstract and universal. Political institutions had organized the shift from confidence in an *alter ego*—another person who is the same as oneself—to confidence in law, which organizes how public life is shared with others who are considered to be others. To have confidence in another person only to the extent that the other person is similar to oneself (that is, shares a common identity), calls into question how a common public realm of citizenship (as an instrument for the regulated management of various kinds of diversity) is constituted. Citizenship is not antagonistic to the existence or the expression of particular identities. It has always established a dialectic between "the ethnic" (relating to "identity") and "the civic" (which is "political"). However, by its very abstraction, citizenship creates a framework inside which particular identities are, in principle, controlled, organized, and limited by institutions enabling the most multifarious individuals to constitute a regulated society. Today, because of the pressures of democracy, this control exerted by the institutions of citizenship is losing its strength.

The appeal to universal reason, to the ability to detach oneself at least partly from one's origins, and to the legitimacy of law appears increasingly remote from the actual experiences of democratic individuals. The latter vigorously assert the positivism of a territorial identity and a specific origin, as well as the immediacy of their own actual experience—the only truth, in their view. They assert these claims against citizenship defined as a form of transcendence and an abstraction. "Against the old rule that one stripped oneself of private particularities in order to enter the public realm, today it is because of one's private identity that one intends to take one's place in the public realm."[53] In the dialectic between these two poles— identity (fact, memory, shared emotions, fusion with one's fellow man) and citizenship (history, choice, appeal to reason, self-detachment or impartiality)—the former is becoming preponderant. In other terms, "the ethnic" seems increasingly less controlled by the civic principle. To what extent does this precedence given to particularisms over the aspiration to transcendence, and to feeling and fervor at the expense of the control of reason and law, call into question the means—as had been elaborated by *liberalism* and citizenship—of living together with others?

Political Scientists, Sociologists, and Democracy

Analysts of contemporary citizenship allude to this depreciation of political transcendence. As was shown in the second chapter, debates about gender parity, alien residents' voting rights, or "residency citizenship" all invoke concrete, down-to-earth realities as much as democratic values. The argument in favor of gender parity asserted that humanity is divided into two, more or less equal, sexes, and that political institutions should therefore be equally composed of men and women. It was added that an equality of rights—or formal equality—had revealed the limits of its effectiveness, because de facto equality—or real equality—was far from being achieved. As for those who advocate giving the right to vote to aliens, they point out that foreigners live and participate de facto in national societies; consequently, they should be entitled to nationality and citizenship, without producing qualifications other than those of residency and daily participation in collective life. These arguments imply a conception of society according to which the political community coincides with the real, concrete society (which it no longer transcends). As we have seen, such arguments question the utopia of representation and the distinction developed by ancient Greek political philosophy between *genos* and *polis*; in other words, between real, living individuals, on the one hand, and the City or the people (in the political sense), on the other.[54]

As for sociologists, their criticism has unveiled the conventional and utopian nature of the republican idea. By definition, sociological analysis questions the "natural" character of institutions by revealing what they actually owe to the social and historical conditions in which they were conceived. Such analysis underscores the conventional nature of the principles upon which parliamentary practices are based: why, after all, should a decision voted through by half of the members of parliament, plus one, be imperatively imposed upon everyone? Can an election really be compared to an "unction" without appealing to pure myths? How can one accept, as an objectively established truth, that elected deputies are transfigured by universal suffrage, that they henceforth embody the General Will, and that their judgments are thereafter made independently of their real, tangible attachments, when one observes their behavior in their Paris office at the National Assembly and in their local headquarters in the provinces? No empirical study can definitively validate the conception according to which a local deputy embodies the general interest and does not have the essential role of responding to the immediate needs of his voters. Political scientists tend to dismiss the magical character of elections.[55] One can thus conclude that the very principle of traditional representation is a "'lure' (in the military sense of the term), in other words a decoy which perfectly resembles the general sum of all individual wills, but which is in fact not that general sum: it is only the will of the current political majority."[56] Without even having to denounce the impostures of "bourgeois citizenship," in the traditional Marxist sense of the expression, sociologists have the easy job of underscoring, and rightly, the conventional nature of the rules of representative democracy.

Moreover, the weakening of republican transcendence seems to be inscribed in an evolution whose stages have been defined by the English sociologist Terence Humphrey Marshall.[57] In a famous article published for the first time in 1949, Marshall suggested distinguishing three dimensions of citizenship. The first would be civil citizenship, which was obtained in the eighteenth century. He defined this kind of citizenship as the exercise of freedom rights (individual liberties, the freedoms of speech and ownership) guaranteed by a State which is based on law—an *État de droit*—and in which justice plays a preponderant role. The second kind of citizenship is political citizenship, which was obtained in the nineteenth century. Marshall defines it as the exercise of political rights (the rights to vote and be elected, to participate in political life, and to be informed) which are guaranteed by universal suffrage and the preponderant role of the Parliament. The third kind of citizenship is social citizenship, developed during the twentieth century. It is based on the preponderance of claim-rights (the rights to social protection, health, education, and work) which are organized and implemented by Providence State institutions. Today, more than fifty years after Marshall's article, it seems to many observers that we have entered a new phase, variously defined as "cultural democracy" (Alain Touraine), "the democracy of the public" (Bernard Manin), "continuous democracy" (Dominique Rousseau), "the democracy of public control" or "public opinion democracy" (Marcel Gauchet).

In their different ways, these sociologists all think that it is necessary to go beyond their respective analyses of the weakening of the civic spirit and the erosion of the republican transcendence, both of which once legitimated social organization. In their view, democracy has indeed become more democratic in the sense that those in power now immediately depend on society. In a certain sense, democracy develops when social citizenship shifts to a democracy in which civil society exerts a continuous control over those who govern. After the phases of "parliamentarism" (or the Republic of Notable Politicians) and political-party democracy (in which representatives were chosen from among the active members of the big political parties), today we are experiencing the democracy "of the public" or "continuous democracy." It follows that this kind of democracy should be distinguished from both representative democracy, in which representatives make decisions without consulting their voters, and direct democracy, which claims to abolish the distinction between voters and their representatives. It is not a weakened form of democracy, but rather, on the contrary, a new and genuinely democratic form of political modernity that has come into being. "What lies beyond representation is at once trivialized and pacified."[58]

Personality now plays a greater role than a candidate's affiliation with a party or the platform upon which he or she runs for election. Television "revives the face-to-face encounters that marked the bond between representatives and those whom they represented in the first form of representative government."[59] Public opinion democracy is the realm of the communications expert. An elite made up of pollsters, journalists, and politicians (in whom a talent for mass-media appearances becomes essential) has replaced the elite—made up of party bosses—which was characteristic of the preceding phase of democracy. Public-image counselors and communications specialists, as well as journalists and pollsters, have become more effective than political parties—their ideologies, platforms, and active members. It is they who henceforth shape and structure the political scene and its debates. Parties are reduced to maintaining a "stable of politicians" or, at best, a think tank designed to nourish the speeches, and ensure the election, of a presidential candidate. Like public opinion itself, voting becomes more spontaneous and emotional. Voters react in the same way that the public does to a commercial offer.

Hence, the "voice which—through opinion polls—the people retains and keeps apart from its representatives is now more constantly present than in parliamentarism. It can be heard not only in exceptional circumstances threatening the public order, but indeed daily."[60] Citizen pressure on those who govern is no longer exerted only sporadically, during election periods, but rather constantly or "continuously," as Léo Hamon phrases it. Street demonstrations, the publication of opinion polls, and the work of the mass media constitute genuine "political action" ensuring a "continuous and effective control, outside of election periods, over the action of those who govern."[62] Pollsters and journalists immediately communicate the evolution of public opinion, whereas members of parliament, who are elected every five years, by definition remain behind schedule. As for constitutional judges, they not only guarantee the application of the regulations of a State based on law (*État de droit*), but they also rival "directly the parliamentary institution in its claim to be the sole representative and express popular sovereignty."[63] Moreover, judges can chose, more readily than politicians dependent on the mass media, not to yield to the immediate emotional fluctuations of public opinion. Pollsters, journalists, and constitutional judges, not to mention professional lobbyists and members of advisory committees on important public questions, can therefore claim that, like—yet in fact better than—elected officials, they represent and express public opinion. Thanks to them, today the sovereignty of the people is exerted more directly. Continuous democracy thus "shatters the routines of representation, which had turned the people's elected officials into the only legitimate spokesmen of public opinion. Continuous democracy thus breaks up the unity of representation that had been formed by public opinion."[64]

These analyses can be associated with a critique of classic representation, such as that of Bernard Manin, by underscoring the antinomy between the very idea of representation (as it was elaborated in history) and democracy. In his view, "democracy of the public" thereby corrects the long-lasting aristocratic dimension of representation. According to Manin, representative government had been developed to eliminate the people; it is therefore anti-democratic as such. In one way or another, the idea of representation presupposes that the representative is superior to those who are represented. By asserting an essential difference between the representative and those who are represented, representation inevitably includes an aristocratic quality not entirely compensated for by the right to vote, which is granted to all citizens—such is the democratic dimension of representative government. As to the democratic idea, it posits an equivalence between the representative and those who are represented. The same inspiration has induced Dominique Rousseau to argue that the idea of representation serves only to justify the fact that the people, in a representative republic, are in fact deprived of sovereignty: "Constitutions probably enhance the image of the citizen . . . , but they devote the essential part of their articles to dispossessing the people of their power by organizing and legitimating the existence and the discourse of representatives and, consequently, the absence and silence of those who are represented."[65]

"The utopia of an *immediate democracy* indeed plays a role as decisive as that of direct democracy."[66] It conveys sociologists' and political scientists' efforts to theorize the weakening of republican transcendence, and the corresponding growth of the Providence State, which is a sort of outcast from the political Empyrean that the Republican State attempted to develop. The Providence State was directly established in order to respond to demands expressed by citizen-individuals in the public realm, and it increasingly draws its legitimacy from this one goal.

The weakening of republican transcendence through the extension of democratic ideas and values should be neither deplored, nor denounced, nor celebrated. Nor should it be used to justify a reactionary attitude, espousing the cause of an (in fact mythical) past that should be restored. When was the Republic ever totally faithful to its proclaimed values? Providential democracy indeed suits the aspirations of *homo democraticus*, who demands that his well-being be ensured and his dignity—expressed through his various proclaimed "identities"—be fully recognized.

Yet this acknowledgment does not exempt us from the duty of examining the fate of our societies and their capacity to preserve the sense of the political. No society can exist without its members sharing a common project borne by common values. These common values are necessary so that everyone will consider legitimate, and thus accept, the inevitable constraints of collective life and the redistribution of wealth organized by the Providence State in providential democracies. Political practices are transformed by the spreading of the democratic idea throughout all dimensions of social life, by the immediacy of information, and by the expression of "public opinion"—at any rate, what is generally accepted as the expression of this "opinion." This evolution involves risks. One may fear that bourgeois societies—pacified, tolerant, pleasure-seeking, and generally rich—become no longer concerned with defining values other than those relating to life itself: the comfort and moral development of its members. One may fear that such societies become incapable of adopting structural reforms, by definition unpopular with a "public opinion" attached to vested interests and little concerned with the future of the collectivity. Finally, one may fear the consequences of this egoism. Providential democracies risk forgetting that they are not alone in the world. The rest of the world is neither pacified nor rich. Will providential democracies be able to muster the willpower to defend themselves against outside dangers, if necessary, and to carry out the duty of practicing solidarity with other countries?

Notes

1. Agulhon, 1989, p. 9.
2. Isambert, 1982, pp. 167 ff.
3. Certeau-Julia-Revel, 1975, p. 10.
4. Certeau-Julia-Revel, 1975, p. 160.
5. Blais, 2000.
6. Agulhon, 1989, p. 130.
7. For this topic, see all the work by Yves Déloye and Olivier Ihl, summarized by Yves Déloye in the article "acte électoral," in Perrineau-Reynié, 2001.
8. Article 55 of the Electoral Code. If practical considerations are not to be excluded, they do not explain everything. In England, elections are generally held on Thursdays.
9. Ihl, 1993.
10. Today, church services have also lost their ceremoniousness, so much so that the difference between public and religious funerals tends to fade. This reveals the loss of the significance of ceremony in a providential democracy.
11. Yves Déloye and Olivier Ihl, "Deux figures singulières de l'universel: la république et le sacré," in Sadoun, 2000, vol. 1, p. 149.
12. Durkheim, 2000 (1912), p. 12.
13. Agulhon, 1989, p. 344 and *passim*.
14. This topic is developed in Schnapper, 1994 (chapter 4), as well as in Thiesse, 1999.
15. Chanet, 1996; Thiesse, 1997.
16. For this topic, see Manin, 1995, especially pp. 111 ff.
17. Gueniffey, 1993, pp. 41 and 76.
18. Sieyès, in *Orateurs*, 1989, pp. 1019 ff.
19. Wood, 1969, p. 175.
20. Wood, 1969, p. 174.
21. Wood, 1969, p. 164.
22. Wood, 1969, pp. 195-196, 596.
23. Wood, 1969, p. viii.
24. Yves Déloye, article "mandat impératif," in Perrineau-Reynié, 2001.
25. According to article 27 of the 1958 Constitution, imperial mandates are invalid.
26. Pierre Avril, "Notes sur les origines de la représentation," in d'Arcy, 1985, pp. 90-105 (p. 101).
27. Philippe Raynaud, article "souveraineté populaire," in Perrineau-Reynié, 2001.
28. Gauchet, 2001.
29. Rosanvallon, 2000, p. 256.
30. Aron, 1990 (1943), p. 769.
31. Raynaud, 1983.
32. Pierre Rosanvallon, "Malaise dans la représentation," in Furet-Julliard-Rosanvallon, 1988, p. 159.
33. For this topic, see Marcel Gauchet's remarks, in Gauchet, 1998, pp. 89 ff.
34. These kinds of behavior parallel the collapse of traditional religious practice: decrease in the number of people attending mass, decrease in the number of those aspiring to the priesthood, the withering away of the Catholic magisterium.
35. Cited by Élisabeth Dupoirier, article "vote," in Perrineau-Reynié, 2001.
36. Jérôme Jaffré, article "indécis," in Perrineau-Reynié, 2001.
37. Subileau-Toinet, 1993.
38. Muxel, 2001, pp. 119 ff.
39. Nor did Americans question the results, even when the voting conditions during the 2000 presidential elections revealed themselves to be highly dubious.

40. Muxel, 2001, p. 162.
41. Favre, 1990.
42. Manin, 1995, p. 300.
43. If Valéry Giscard d'Estaing was rejected to such a great extent by the public opinion, was it not because he did not really seem to be "like us," and because he too obviously brought himself forth as being more aristocratic and intelligent than his potential voters?
44. Koselleck, 1979.
45. Subileau-Toinet, 1990.
46. Jean-Louis Debré, leader of the RPR (the "Rassemblement pour la République" party) in the National Assembly, rarely mentioned his party during his campaign for the municipal elections of Évreux in 2001.
47. In a mission letter addressed to the President of the National Commission of the Public Debate Devoted to Informing the Prime Minister about the Third Paris Airport, the Prime Minister once again evokes "looking deeper into the idea of proximity democracy." Cf. *Le Monde*, 19 October 2001. Many other examples could be given.
48. Bromberger *et al.*, 1995, pp. 343, 348 and 340.
49. This is the meaning behind the success of the expression popularized by Benedict Anderson's book. Cf. Anderson, 1982.
50. Noiriel, 1991.
51. Budge, 1996; Papadopoulos, 1994 and Papadopoulos, 1998. See Morel, 2000.
52. Wood, 1969, pp. 165, 172.
53. Gauchet, 1998, p. 98.
54. See chapter 2 above.
55. Research devoted to de-mythologizing of the French deputy began with Cayrol-Parodi-Ysmal's book, 1973.
56. Dominique Rousseau, in Rousseau, 1995, p. 21.
57. Marshall, 1949.
58. Manin, 1995, p. 297. The expression "the beyondness of representation"—"l'au-delà de la représentation"—is found in Rousseau, 1995, pp. 16 and 25.
59. Manin, 1995, p. 281.
60. Manin, 1995, p. 297.
61. Hamon, 1984.
62. Rousseau, 1995, p. 25.
63. Rousseau, 1995, p. 10.
64. Rousseau, 1995, p. 13.
65. Rousseau, 1995, p. 6.
66. Rosanvallon, 2000, p. 409.

Conclusion
The Erosion of Collective Transcendence

Providential democracy assumes the legitimacy of ensuring the real equality of citizen-individuals. It favors all that is "real"—and thus whatever derives from economics, history, and ethnicity—as opposed to civic transcendence. In this regard, real freedoms tend to become more important than formal freedoms. Spurred by its internal dynamics and its Promethean ambition of ensuring equality for everyone, providential democracy always favors the quest of individual well-being and the acknowledgment of the historical rights of individuals and groups. It tends to reject all limits and barriers. It favors the inclusion of ever greater number of people in the political realm and granting them rights. In providential democracies, the aspiration to longer lifetimes and better living conditions should likewise have no limits; nor should the public recognition of the dignity of individuals and groups.

The previous chapters described how political modernity has been criticized in two important ways. Some critics have denounced the contradictions between the proclaimed freedom and equality of citizens—or formal equality—and the inequalities of their economic conditions—or real inequalities. Others have criticized the formal character of the political rights granted to all citizens and the real inequalities in the public acknowledgment of their historical and religious identities. These criticisms reveal at least the tensions, if not the contradictions, inherent in a society of citizens—tensions that the most clearsighted revolutionaries had already perceived in 1789. Providential democracy responds to these criticisms by giving an ever increasing preference to real equality.

Whether public rights or the rights to material and moral well-being are at stake, the democratic utopia entertains aspirations that cannot fully be satisfied. The body politic must be juridically defined; social and economic conditions will always be insufficient because humans needs constantly evolve; no public recognition of so-called "cultural" rights will ever fully satisfy human beings' aspirations to be acknowledged in accordance to what they consider to be their true value. Impatience when faced with the inevitable limits or barriers established for the subjective rights of individuals—be they political, economic, or cultural—and legitimate aspirations to well-being (which by definition ever remains inferior to individual expectations), fuel both demands and dissatisfaction. The political realm, even when conflictual, unites human beings forced by economic activity and the search for protection to compete with one another. The inevitable persistence of inequalities in social conditions and the impossibility of recognizing all collective identities within the same society induce indignation when all forms of collective transcendence have weakened.

The growing importance of "reality" in providential democracies erodes the two types of collective transcendence: religious and political transcendence. The idea of transcendence—through religion or politics—is not very familiar to *homo democraticus*, who lives amidst the daily positivism of economic and providential life, and in the immediacy of the here and now. Yet decent living conditions ensured by the Providence State do not by themselves give meaning to the existence of individuals.

The need to give a meaning to one's personal destiny, to individual and collective hardship, and to social injustice has obviously not disappeared with the fulfillment of the most immediate, basic needs. Democratic individuals have not ceased asking metaphysical questions. Yet today, each individual seeks out his own form of transcendence and fashions his own way of believing and expressing his beliefs. Institutionalized religions and classic institutions of citizenship henceforth have problems regulating individuals' relationship to the sacred and respond imperfectly to the aspirations of mankind. They no longer formulate a sense of living together which can be shared by everyone. The two widespread expressions that believers and patriots once mustered in order to give a meaning to death—"it pleased God to call his faithful servant back to Him" and "he died for France"—have almost completely disappeared from social parlance. Henceforth, relationships to the sacred, which are no longer expressed through recognized social forms, always risk being expressed in a tragic or uncontrolled manner. This is what developed in the secular, political "religions" that marked, for the worse, the destiny of the twentieth century. The ideological conflicts of the last century had the same characteristics as the religious wars of the sixteenth century: they were waged because of a certain conception of the good, even if "the good" was defined, no longer in religious, but rather in political terms. Today, in an obviously less dramatic manner, these needs for meaning are expressed in the new religious movements that are developing, in providential democracies, outside of the traditional religious institutions.[1] Spontaneous, temporary, and emotional group praying better respond to democratic individuals' needs to believe. Needs for meaning are also conveyed by various forms of infranational or supranational demands with respect to "identity" or "culture," ranging from those associated with the Corsicans in France and the Spanish Basque population in Spain to the kinds of solidarity networks that are established within various diasporas throughout the world. These demands are now more openly and vigorously expressed. In non-democratic countries, members of fundamentalist religious movements, by pointing to the irreligious nature of the secular, tolerant West, and to the imperative of fighting against the West in the name of the one true God, have made a sensational arrival in the very heart of world politics.

The great political and religious institutions have attempted to adapt themselves to this evolution, which can be viewed with either optimism or concern. Within providential democracies, which have made tolerance their cardinal virtue, major (ideological) conflicts no longer exist about how "the good" should be conceived. Secular or political "religions," organized and supported by a powerful State with totalitarian aims, have disappeared from the immediate political horizons of Europeans. The national, partisan patriotism that had led to the national, partisan excesses of the twentieth century—like the religious fervor which had justified, in past centuries, the horrors of religious wars—is now weakened and discredited. However, at the same time in providential democracies, there is no organized collective or institutional response to human beings' needs to find answers to their metaphysical questions and anguish. If the legitimacy of the political institutions inherited from the past is not recognized, providential democracies risk leaving the field open to kinds of political anarchy and to forms of religious fundamentalism no longer controlled by recognized historical and traditional religious institutions. When the same ideals and passions are not shared, providential democracies risk no longer being willing to defend themselves.

Providential democracy particularly challenges French society, because, more than other societies, it has gone farther in its attempt to create a form of political transcendence in accordance with a religious model as well as against it. The weakening of the Catholic Church as a social institution actually weakens the republican project at the same time, because the confrontation of the Church and the republic has shaped and structured French political life ever since the advent of political modernity.[2] It is in France that the alliance between nation and republic has been the closest. In contrast, the other big democratic countries (England, the Northern European countries, not to forget the United States) have been able to blend (at least until a recent date) monarchical and/or religious heritages—conveyed by national symbols and rituals—with *liberalism* in order to create a democratic public realm. The secularization of political institutions did not prevent genuine bonds between religion and politics from being maintained, and both religion and politics indeed continued to increase their integrative effects. In northern European democracies, religious practices still bear this out: they remain linked to daily social practices, and individuals belong to churches in the same manner that they belong to unions.[3] Whereas all European countries are faced with the necessity of calling into question the historical link between the nation and democratic institutions, they have approached this stage in different ways. Fundamentally liberal English-style citizenship, whose ambition is—to all appearances—less metaphysical than that of the republic by divine right that the French have endeavored to develop, and which is embodied in social practices inherited from a past without fundamental political ruptures, is probably better adapted to the demands of a providential democracy (in which individuals are anchored in reality, the concrete, and the immediate) than is the more transcendental—or republican—project of French-style citizenship, created and imposed against a royal absolutism allied with the Catholic Church, even as it was based on this very model.

Church and State, the two French institutions which shape and structure collective life and regulate practices in the name of common values, have both lost their strength. Religious transcendence is recycled into increasingly less metaphysical morals that pertain mostly to human relationships. For a while, Jesus was considered to be the archetypal social worker. A spiritual destiny is subordinated to living conditions in our world. Political transcendence, which was designed to replace religious transcendence, crumbles with the weakening of national patriotism. Is anyone still willing to die for the fatherland, or for the Party—that is, the Communist Party, whose first letters were capitalized in French as were those of State ("État") and Church ("Église")? Yet political transcendence is probably less instinctive than religious transcendence. Every individual wonders about the meaning of existence; no one has ever escaped metaphysical anguish for an entire lifetime. The idea of transcendence through politics, which was instituted by the Republic, derives neither from nature nor immediate social experience: asserting the civil and political equality, as well as the equal dignity, of a Nobel prizewinner and a homeless person—and the legitimacy of the institutions that substantiate this assertion—is neither spontaneous nor natural. It can only be the result of constant effort in the name of social justice values based on the idea of the equal dignity of all human beings, a form of transcendence inherited from the Judeo-Christian tradition and then secularized. In France more than elsewhere, the erosion of religious and political transcendence risks disintegrating the social bond.

The policies promulgated by European institutions in Brussels reinforce this evolution towards providential democracy. Although (as I have stated earlier) it is desirable that a united political Europe take shape, the elaboration of European institutions risks accentuating, in the first phase, the impact of the dynamics of democracy. Both collaboration among, and the economic and financial union of, European nations have gradually been accompanied by the development of a Providence State which is illustrated by the "recommendations"—a sort of "soft" regulation nonetheless sanctioned by the European Courts of Justice—designed to fight against poverty by imposing a minimum wage, to guarantee salaried employee rights and gender equality, to support agriculture and farmers, to adopt territory management policies, and to acknowledge and encourage regional identities. Is it not to be feared that this objective alliance of European institutions with regional political powers, which is inscribed in the overall project of constructing a united Europe, unwillingly contributes to the undermining of the historical locus of political transcendence and the practices of democracy?

However, no society—be it industrial, modern, post-industrial, post-modern, or providential—can evacuate politics as the realm where particular interests are transcended and legitimate collective choices are made, nor as the source of the society's willingness to defend itself against outside threats. Like all societies, European societies cannot exist without a political realm. Policy must bear on common values and willpower, not just on the production and redistribution of resources. The European system of political power must do more than regulate the economy, manage the Providence State, and control the application of human rights through the European Courts of Justice. If a redistribution of resources ensuring the dignity of all individuals is the prerequisite underlying the existence of a democratic society, then the existence of the community of citizens is also the necessary prerequisite enabling this redistribution to be accepted as legitimate. The republic—defined as the realm where citizenship is exercised and where collective decisions are made—is not necessarily national, as it has been up to now. Nationhood and citizenship coincided at a given moment of history; the nation-state does not imply the end of history. The link between nation-states and societies organized by citizenship is historical; it is neither logical nor necessary. Citizenship can be exercised at an infranational or a supranational level. Yet whatever level it is exercized at—national, infranational, or supranational—it is necessary to have a political realm where decisions and arbitration rulings can be made and which has the means and power of imposing them, in other words a realm where a population can express its willingness to live together and defend itself. In order for a united democratic Europe to exist, European citizens will have to accept, as legitimate, officials who are elected in European elections; that is, accept the decisions of these elected officials, even if they seem contrary to their immediate interests. The same legitimacy that Europeans currently grant to national governments and to decisions that they make will have to be given, by the same European citizens, to the officials that they elect to seats in European institutions and to the decisions that they make.

Up to now, democratic societies have benefited from the work of nation-building, from the ongoing heritage of national institutions (which has made them seem natural to citizens), and from the cultural homogeneity of the national population. Between immediate local realities and the utopia of humanity, nations offered the realm of political transcendence. The civic realm has benefited from social bonds developed throughout the gradual process of nation-building, through the centuries-long elaboration, by the great Western monarchies, of an abstract national body politic which was not to be confused with individuals—the prerequisite for a democratic public realm. As regards the near future, I find it difficult to see how the civic realm can continue to exist outside the national framework in which it was born in Europe. I find it difficult to see how European political institutions will be able to muster enough force to control fervor and zeal stemming from ethnico-religious attachments and loyalties, when the nation-state itself has never been able to achieve this fully. And I find it difficult to see how European political institutions will be able to mobilize the "European people" if they have to defend themselves against outside threats.

Indeed, the principle of citizenship does not take on genuine significance, nor truly shape and structure historical societies, unless it is inscribed in political institutions and social practices whose legitimacy has been internalized over the centuries. As a principle, citizenship has no impact on social life unless it becomes the practice of citizenship, and unless institutions give it a real, tangible meaning. Citizenship has no sense unless it is exercised through these institutions because democratic society is Janus-like: it is indissolubly ethnic and civic or, in other terms, national and civic, or still again, to use Jürgen Habermas's vocabulary, patriotic and constitutional. The idea of State abstention in religious life so that population groups of different religious faiths could live in the same State was originally formulated by Locke, but the actual possibility for a Jew to become a member of the British parliament was not granted de facto until the 1860s, two centuries later. It takes time before republican ideas can be inscribed in institutions and practices.[4] Up to now, these institutions have all been national ones.

The other reason making the construction of a European public realm difficult is the fragility of democratic society. A society based on the values and the institutions of citizenship is a form of organization that is as unlikely as it is fragile. Such a society functions in an acceptable manner only when a public realm has been built up which transcends the real society: its historical and religious diversities, its divisions and inequalities. The bonds linking human beings to each other are juridical and political; they are based on an abstract principle, one calling for equal rights for all citizens and their sovereignty. At stake is the creation of a social bond based upon this principle, whereas citizenship implies that individuals have the capacity to detach themselves from their particularisms and enter into relationships with others. Democratic society is also fragile because it is based on a utopia that inverts the social world, even if this utopia is creative. Against all real, concrete, down-to-earth social experience, democratic society asserts the civil, juridical, and political equality of individuals who are diverse and unequal in origin, capacity, and social conditions. It cannot help but be rightly criticized when daily social realities are compared to the values put forward by citizens and their elected officials. Whence the importance of these political institutions, which up to now have always been national and through which this blatantly abstract legitimacy principle can effectively organize the lives of individuals. Time has had to pass before such non-spontaneous and unnatural practices could be suitably internalized by all social participants and protagonists. Moreover, this is why the spreading of democratic models outside of Europe has always been difficult. The democratic sentiment is obviously not "natural"; it must be forged through the willingness of all—politicians, intellectuals, and citizens alike. A united Europe is no more natural than a nation or an ethnic group.

Democratic practices consist in managing conflicts of value — liberty and equality are not spontaneously harmonious; there is tension between them—and conflicts of interest among social groups. The method employed is compromise, not violence. In real terms, the public realm comprises all social practices—traditions and habits—through which all those acting and participating in society manage rivalries and conflicts by means of political institutions, by appealing to the principles of citizenship and of an *État de droit*, a State based on law. It is a real, concrete, down-to-earth realm inscribed within specific, well-defined borders—which is not the case of Europe. Individuals with their specific histories, feelings, and interests, can meet in this realm. These individuals are not only rational citizens; they also respect practices that they consider to be legitimate ones because the practices in question belong to long-standing institutions legitimized at once by time and—up to the present—indentification with a nationality. In our democratic age, will the abstraction of citizenship at the European level—without roots in national traditions and institutions—be sufficient for socially integrating individuals? Given the national character of democratic institutions, will it be possible to transpose the practices of citizenship to a European level in the foreseeable future?

By one of those typical tricks of history, the building of a united Europe, which was a grand political project in 1950, now risks contributing, in the twenty-first century, to the growing de-politicization of democratic societies. In 1989, European nations lost (or thought they had lost) their enemy; at the same time, they lost an essential factor motivating them to build a united Europe: waging war on neighbors, or defending oneself against them, has always united peoples. If, moreover, European nations no longer keep transcendence or common values alive, then what will continue to induce national States to yield a part of their sovereignty and power, when national political institutions have become familiar to the peoples of Europe and are thus perceived and experienced as natural? For the time being, European nations continue to express the identities and immediate interests of peoples more directly than the institutions of Europe. The "naturalization"—over the ages—of political practices, rites, and common symbols in nations cannot easily and rapidly be transposed to a European level without the collective participation and strong willpower of national governments and peoples. The prospect of constructing a form of political transcendence at the European level seems difficult—which means that it is desirable, yet unlikely in the near future. If such transcendence were to come into being one day, it would probably more resemble the English model; in other words, less ambitious and metaphysical than what the French Republic attempted to establish. It is possible to imagine such transcendence existing in a more distant future. Yet this presupposes that individuals work together at constructing it: transcendence is not forthcoming as such.

The study of providential democracy raises strictly political questions. To the extent that the development of the Intervention State was a political project—designed to give real meaning to citizenship in a political system based on political freedom—then its crisis, as it is experienced and expressed, is also political in nature. The legitimacy of the State increasingly depends on the action that it undertakes to enhance the production of wealth, to redistribute wealth among social groups, to stabilize economic growth, to cushion the social consequences of economic crises, and to ensure social solidarity and cohesion by intervening in economic and social life. Moreover, the sovereign power of the political State as a protagonist in the system of inter-State relations is dwindling.[5] Henceforth, to be a citizen still probably means possessing political rights, but it also means possessing rights within the social protection system. The Providence State has become an essential source of collective regulation and the construction of identities. Inscribed in the utopian democratic project, the willingness to ensure real freedoms reinforces an evolution towards the autonomy of the individual, at the expense of close-at-hand or face-to-face kinds of solidarity; it also trivializes social relationships, which tend to conform to the same model; it evacuates the idea of competence, and encourages countless demands which cannot all be satisfied. Yet is not the existence of a community of citizens necessary for legitimizing the wealth redistribution system?

This leads to a further question, now more deeply informed by historical experience, which was originally raised by Émile Durkheim at the dawn of modern sociology. He was concerned about social cohesion in modern societies and wondered how social bonds could be maintained and restored when religion and religious practices no longer linked individuals to each other. Today, it is not only religion which has trouble binding individuals, but also citizenship.

Is tolerance sufficient for uniting democratic individuals? Individuals continue to seek out a basis and justification for their common existence. Now that all forms of collective religious or political transcendence have weakened, they attempt to find this meaning elsewhere. Some look for it in philosophy, a phenomenon illustrated by the recent popularity of philosophy discussion groups that take place in cafés as well as of philosophy books designed for the general reader; other people look for it in morality, rechristened "ethics" (so as to remove its normative character), which leads to the creation of committees on ethical problems. Still other people get involved in astrology or spiritualism, ranging from Eastern religions to Western esoteric traditions and shamanism. For some, it is life itself, in the biological sense of the term, which has become the last sacred realm; beneath this realm, one departs from "the human." Yet human life *per se*, in other words biological life, cannot be sacred unless it is accompanied by references to shared values based on the idea of the absolute dignity of all human beings. One must ask whether a society can maintain bonds among individuals who do not share the same values and who do not express their conception of the world through the same symbols. Human societies need to maintain a certain cohesion which, in democracies, has until now been expressed in and through patriotism. How can a society that does not organize the ways in which individuals relate with the sacred and that no longer responds to metaphysical anguish, nor gives a meaning to individual and collective hardship, continue to "be held together"? In other words, how can such a society ensure the social bond or fabric, maintain the sense of common values and retain, if necessary, the willpower to defend itself? Does not such a society risk culminating in de-politicization?

It is indeed necessary to distinguish between, on the one hand, the real, tangible social bonds that are maintained by all the agents and managers of the Welfare State—the sundry educators, organizers, monitors, supervisors, all those who work in the fields of health and social care, not to forget media and communications people of all kinds and at all levels—who increasingly intervene in individual lives, and, on the other hand, the effectiveness of these social bonds as regards giving individuals in providential democracies a sense of their collective destiny and a willingness to defend their existence. Providential democracy seems to increasingly suit the freedom of the "moderns," as this concept was theorized by Benjamin Constant.[6] It tends to ignore the possibility of war. It is not excluded that a paradoxical mode of integration is at work, and that its very flexibility renders it resistant—which would explain the victory of providential democracy over the totalitarian political systems of the twentieth century. Providential democracy is adapted to the freedom of human beings through its acknowledgment of the kinds of tension that can exist among social individuals (the contradictions in their respective interests), and through the acceptance of all sorts of criticism. However, if it becomes necessary to defend society, through war, by risking one's life and showing solidarity with other peoples, one can imagine that loyalty as regards all that is collective will have its limits.

Up to now, peoples have always been more mobilized by their national identity than by their civic convictions. In the short history of democracies, democratic peoples have more often fought to defend their nation or fatherland than to assert their values. The victory of democracies in the Second World War was based on national feeling and pride more than on a willingness to spread the principles of democracy. During the winter of 1940-1, the English set forth the struggle of their country against one of their hereditary enemies, Germany, as much as, or more than, they fought in favor of Westminster democracy. Roosevelt was unable to convince Americans to intervene in the war until the Japanese attack on Pearl Harbor aggressed national pride. Many members of the French Résistance fought more against the Germans than the Nazis. The welcome peace that the building of a united Europe has created among democratic nations has made European peoples forget that the possibility of war still exists, that members of a society need to share common values—and not only a tolerance that risks becoming indifferent to all other values—and that they cannot cease defending these values, if they want to survive.

There is no essence of democracy. The crumbling away of the practices of the representative republican system implies the end neither of democracy nor history. Yet one can ask whether providential democracy is capable, in the name of social justice, of providing the means of regulating human conflicts in a manner that does not betray too deeply the values claimed by modern societies, and whether it is capable of maintaining genuine political willpower. Will providential democracy be able to satisfy the legitimate aspiration to equality that characterizes *homo democraticus,* without abandoning political freedom and without losing the willpower to defend that freedom?

Notes

1. One should obviously consult the work of Danièle Hervieu-Léger on this topic. In particular, see Hervieu-Léger, 1986; Hervieu-Léger, 1993; and "'Renouveaux' religieux et nationalistes: la double dérégulation," in Birnbaum, 1997, pp. 163-85.
2. For this topic, see the work of Marcel Gauchet, especially Gauchet, 1998.
3. Davie-Hervieu-Léger, 1996.
4. While citizenship structures how those who with different religious references live together, the European Union Monitoring Centre on Racism and Xenophobia (EUMC) published on 20 November 2000 the results of a survey of 17,000 people in European countries: "15% of the citizens of the European Union express a certain uneasiness with respect to other religions" than their own. The percentage rises to 32% in Denmark and 26% in Belgium. Cf. *Le Monde,* 22 December 2000.
5. For this topic, see the work of Bertrand Badie, especially Badie, 1998.
6. Constant, 1980 (1819).

Bibliography

Ageron, Charles Robert. *Les Algériens musulmans et la France: 1870-1919*. Paris: PUF, 1968.

Agulhon, Maurice. *Marianne au pouvoir: L'imagerie et la symbolique républicaine, 1780-1914*. Paris: Flammarion, 1989.

Aiach, Pierre and Fassin, Didier (eds.). *Les métiers de la santé: Enjeux de pouvoir et quête de légitimité*. Paris: Anthropos, 1994.

Alund, Aleksandra and Schierup, Carl-Urlik. *Paradoxes of Multiculturalism*. Avebury: Academic Publishing Group, 1991.

Anchard, David (ed.). *Philosophy and Pluralism*. Cambridge University Press, 1996.

Anderson, Benedict. *Imagined Community: Reflections on the Origin and Spread of Nationalism*. London: Verso, 1982. French translation: *L'imaginaire national: Réflexions sur l'origine et l'essor du nationalisme*. Paris: La Découverte, 1996.

Aarcy, François d' (ed.). *La représentation*. Paris: Économica, 1985.

Arendt, Hannah. *On Revolution*, New York: Viking, 1963. French translation: *Essai sur la révolution*. Paris: Gallimard ("Tel"), 1990.

Arnaud, Pierre (ed.). *Le sport en France: Une approche politique, économique et sociale*. Paris: La Documentation française, 2000.

Aron, Raymond. *Chroniques de guerre: La France libre, 1940-1945*. Paris: Gallimard, 1990 (August 1943).

Aron, Raymond. *Démocratie et totalitarisme*. Paris: Gallimard ("Idées"), 1965.

Aron, Raymond. *Dix-huit leçons sur la société industrielle*. Paris: Gallimard ("Idées"), 1962.

Aron, Raymond. *Essai sur les libertés*. Paris: Hachette ("Pluriel"), 1976 (1965).

Badie, Bertrand and Birnbaum, Pierre. *Sociologie de l'État*. Paris: Grasset, 1979.

Badie, Bertrand. *Un monde sans souveraineté: Les États entre ruse et responsabilité*. Paris: Fayard ("L'Espace du politique"), 1998.

Baverez, Nicolas. "La nouvelle question sociale," *Commentaire*, No. 92, Winter 2000-1, pp. 799-805.

Beaud, Stéphane and Pialoux, Michel. *Retour sur la condition ouvrière: Enquête aux usines Peugeot de Sochaux-Montbéliard*. Paris: Fayard, 1999.

Bell, Daniel. *The Coming of Postindustrial Society*. New York: Basic Books, 1973. French translation: *Vers la société postindustrielle*. Paris: Laffont, 1976.

Bergougnoux, Alain and Manin, Bernard. *La social-démocratie ou le compromis*. Paris: PUF, 1979.

Bertin, André, Da Silveira, Pablo, and Pourtois, Hervé (eds.). *Libéraux et communautariens*. Paris: PUF ("Philosophie morale"), 1997.

Binoche, Bertrand. *Critiques des droits de l'homme*. Paris: PUF ("Philosophies"), 1989.

Birnbaum, Pierre (ed.). *Sociologie des nationalismes*. Paris: PUF, 1997.

Blais, Marie-Claude. *Au principe de la République: Le cas Renouvier*. Paris: Gallimard ("Bibliothèque des idées"), 2000.

Boltanski, Luc and Thévenot, Laurent. *De la justification: Les économies de la grandeur*. Paris: Gallimard ("NRF/Essais"), 1991.

Boltanski, Luc and Chiapello, Ève. *Le nouvel esprit du capitalisme*. Paris: Gallimard ("NRF/Essais"), 1999.

Bourdieu, Pierre (ed.). *La misère du monde*. Paris: Seuil, 1993.

Bourdieu, Pierre. *La noblesse d'État: Grandes écoles et esprit de corps*. Paris: Minuit, 1989.

Boutin, Christine. *L'embryon citoyen*. Paris: Éditions du Sarment, 2001.

Bromberger, Christian, with Hayot, Alain and Mariottini, Jean-Marc. *Le match de football: Ethnologie d'une passion partisane à Marseille, Naples et Turin*. Paris: Éditions de la Maison des sciences de l'homme, 1995.

Brubaker, William R. *Immigration and the Politics of Citizenship in Europe and North America*. New York and London: University Press of America, 1989.

Brunschwig, Henri. *Noirs et Blancs dans l'Afrique noire française ou comment le colonisé devient le colonisateur: 1870-1914*. Paris: Flammarion, 1983.

Budge, Ian. *The New Challenge of Direct Democracy*. Cambridge: Polity Press, 1996.

Callede, Jean-Claude. *Les politiques publiques du sport en France: Essai de sociologie historique*. Paris: Économica, 2000.

Callede, Jean-Claude. "Destins du 'modèle français' du sport," *Pouvoirs locaux*, No. 49, November 2001.

Calvès, Gwénaële (ed.). *Les politiques de discrimination positive*. Paris: La Documentation française, 1999.

Calvès, Gwénaële. "Les politiques françaises de lutte contre le racisme, des politiques en mutation," *French Politics, Culture and Society*, Vol. 18, No. 3, Autumn 2000, pp. 75-81.

Carter, T., Dayan-Herzbrun, S. et al. *Genre et politique: Débats et perspectives*. Paris: Gallimard ("Folio"), 2000.

Castel, Robert. *Les métamorphoses de la question sociale: Une chronique du salariat*. Paris: Fayard ("L'Espace du politique"), 1995.

Cavalieri, Paola and Kymlicka, Will. "Expanding the Social Contract," *Etica e animali*, 1996/8, pp. 5-33.

Cavalieri, Paola and Singer, Peter (eds.). *The Great Ape Project: Equality beyond Humanity*. London: Fourth Estate, 1993. French translation: *La libération animale*. Paris: Grasset, 1993.

Cayrol, Roland, Parodi, Jean-Luc, and Ysmal, Colette. *Le député français*. Paris: Armand Colin ("Travaux et recherches de science politique"), 1973.

Certeau, Michel de, Julia, Dominique, and Revel, Jacques. *Une politique de la langue: La Révolution française et les patois*. Paris: Gallimard ("Bibliothèque des histoires"), 1975.

Chanet, Jean-François. *L'École républicaine et les petites patries*. Paris: Aubier, 1996.

Chazel, François (ed.). *Pratiques culturelles et politiques de la culture*. Bordeaux: Maison des Sciences de l'homme d'Aquitaine, 1987.

Condorcet, *Esquisse d'un tableau historique des progrès de l'esprit humain*. Paris: Garnier-Flammarion, 1988 (1794).

Conseil d'État. *Rapport public 1996*. Paris: La Documentation française, Études et documents du Conseil d'État, No. 48, 1997.

Constant, Benjamin. *La liberté des anciens et des modernes*. Paris: Hachette ("Pluriel"), 1980 (1819).

Costa-Lascoux, Jacqueline and Weil, Patrick (eds.). *Logiques d'États et immigrations*. Paris: Kimé, 1992.

Costa-Lascoux, Jacqueline. "L'Étranger dans la nation," *Raison Présente*, 106, 1992, pp. 79-93.

Dahl, Robert. *Who Governs? Democracy and Power in an American City*. New Haven: Yale University Press, 1965.

Davidson, Alastair. "Multiculturalism and Citizenship: Silencing the Migrant Voice," *Journal of Intercultural Studies*, Vol. 18, No. 2, 1997, pp. 77-92 (a).

Davidson, Alastair. *From Subject to Citizen: Australian Citizenship in the Twentieth Century*. Cambridge University Press, 1997 (b).

Davie, Grace and Hervieu-Léger, Danièle (eds.). *Identités religieuses en Europe*. Paris: La Découverte, 1996.

Demailly, Lise. "Les modes d'existence des techniques du social," *Cahiers internationaux de sociologie*, July 2000, pp. 103-124.

Demailly, Lise. *Le collège: Crise, mythes et métiers*. Lille: Presses Universitaires de Lille, 1991.

De Swann, Abram. *In Care of the State: Health Care, Education and Welfare in Europe and the USA in the Modern Era*. Amsterdam, Bakker, 1988. French translation: *Sous l'aile protectrice de l'État*. Paris: PUF ("Sociologies"), 1995.

Donzelot, Jacques. *La police des familles*. Paris: Minuit ("Critique"), 1977.

Dubar, Claude and Tripier, Pierre. *Sociologie des professions*. Paris: Armand Colin ("Collection U"), 1998.

Duhamel, Olivier and Meny, Yves (eds.). *Dictionnaire constitutionnel*. Paris: PUF, 1992.

Dumont, Louis. *Homo aequalis: Genèse et épanouissement de l'idéologie économique*. Paris: Gallimard ("Bibliothèque des sciences humaines"), 1977.

Duumont, Louis. *Homo hierarchicus: Essai sur le système des castes*. Paris: Gallimard ("Bibliothèque des sciences humaines"), 1967.

Dupuy, François and Thoenig, Jean-Claude. *Sociologie de l'administration*. Paris: Armand Colin ("Collection U"), 1983.

Durand, Patrice and Thoenig, Jean-Claude. "L'État et la gestion publique territoriale," *Revue française de science politique*, Vol. 46 (4), 1996, pp. 580-623.

Durkheim, Émile. *Les formes élémentaires de la vie religieuse.* Paris: PUF ("Quadridge"), 2000 (1912).

Émeri, Claude and Zylberberg, Jacques (eds.). *Citoyenneté et nationalité: Perspectives en France et au Québec.* Paris: PUF ("Politiques aujourd'hui"), 1991.

Esping-Andersen, Gosta. *The Three Worlds of Welfare Capitalism.* Cambridge: Polity Press, 1990. French translation: *Les trois mondes de l'État-providence: essai sur le capitalisme moderne.* Paris: PUF ("Le lien social"), 1999.

État-providence: Arguments pour une réforme. (Various authors). Paris: Gallimard ("Folio-actuel"), 1996.

Ewald, François. *L'État-providence.* Paris: Fayard, 1986.

Favre, Pierre (ed.). *La manifestation.* Paris: Presses de la Fondation des sciences politiques, 1990.

Ferry, Jean-Marc. *La question de l'État européen.* Paris: Gallimard ("NRF/Essais"), 2001.

Ferry, Jean-Marc. *L'allocation universelle: Pour une revenu de citoyenneté.* Paris: Cerf, 1995.

Ferry, Jean-Marc. *Les puissances de l'expérience.* Paris: Cerf, 1991.

Ferry, Luc and Renaut, Alain. *Philosophie politique, 3: Les droits de l'homme à l'idée républicaine.* Paris: PUF, 1985.

Ferry, Luc. *Le nouvel ordre écologique: L'arbre, l'animal et l'homme.* Paris: Grasset, 1992.

Fitoussi, Jean-Paul and Rosanvallon, Pierre. *Le nouvel âge des inégalités.* Paris: Seuil, 12996.

Fontenay, Élisabeth de. *Le silence des bêtes: La philosophie à l'épreuve de l'animalité.* Paris: Fayard, 1998.

Fontenay, Élisabeth de. "Pourquoi les animaux n'auraient-ils pas droit à un droit des animaux?", *Le Débat,* No. 109, 2000, pp. 138-155.

Fournier, Jacques and Questiaux, Nicole. *Traité du social: Situations, luttes, politiques, institutions.* Paris: Dalloz, 1984 (4th ed.).

Friedson, Eliot. "Les professions artistiques comme défi à l'analyse sociologique," *Revue française de sociologie,* 1986, pp. 431-443.

Furet, François, Julliard, Jacques and Rosanvallon, Pierre. *La République du centre: La fin de l'exception française.* Paris: Calmann-Lévy, 1988.

Galland, Olivier and Lemel, Yannick (eds.). *La nouvelle société française: Trente années de mutation.* Paris: Armand Colin ("Collection U"), 1998, pp. 146-180.

Gauchet, Marcel. "L'héritage jacobin et le problème de la représentation," *Le Débat,* No. 116, September-October 2001, pp. 32-46.

Gauchet, Marcel. *La religion dans la démocratie.* Paris: Gallimard ("Le Débat"), 1998.

Gauchet, Marcel. *La révolution des droits de l'homme.* Paris: Gallimard ("Bibliothèque des histoires"), 1989.

Gaxie, Daniel. *Le cens caché: Inégalités culturelles et ségrégation politique.* Paris: Seuil, 1978.

Gellner, Ernest. *Nations and Nationalism*. Oxford: Blackwell, 1983.

Girardet, Raoul. *L'idée coloniale en France de 1871 à 1962*. Paris: Hachette ("Pluriel"), 1983 (1972).

Goffi, Jean-Yves. *Le philosophe et ses animaux*. Nîmes: Jacqueline Chambon, 1994.

Grawitz, Madeleine and Leca, Jean (eds.). *Traité de science politique*, Vol. 4. Paris: PUF, 1985.

Grémion, Pierre. *Le pouvoir périphérique: Bureaucrates et notables dans le système politique français*. Paris: Fayard, 1976.

Gueniffey, Patrice. *Le nombre et la raison: La Révolution française et les élections*. Paris: Éditions de l'École des Hautes Études en sciences sociales, 1993.

Guillame, Pierre *et al. Minorités et État*. Bordeaux: Presses Universitaires de Bordeaux, 1986.

Guillemard, Anne-Marie. *La retraite, une mort sociale: Sociologie des conduites en situation de retraite*. Paris: Mouton, 1972.

Habermas, Jürgen. *Écrits politiques*. Paris: Cerf, 1990 (1985-1990).

Hammar, Tomas. *European Immigration Policy*. Cambridge University Press, 1985.

Hamon, Léo. "Du référendum à la démocratie continue," *Revue française de science politique*, August-October 1984, pp. 1084-1101.

Hassenteufel, Patrick. *Les médecins face à l'État: Une comparaison européenne*. Paris: Presses de sciences Po, 1997.

Hawkins, F., "Multiculturalism in Two Countries: The Canadian and Australian Experience," *Revue d'Études canadiennes*, Vol. 17, No. 1, 1982, pp. 64-80.

Helly, Denise, "Le multiculturalisme canadien: De la promotion des cultures immigrées à la cohésion sociale," *Cahiers de l'URMIS*, No. 6, November 1999.

Hervieu, Bertrand. *Les champs du future*. Paris: François Bourin, 1993.

Hervieu-Léger, Danièle. *La religion en miettes ou la question des sectes*. Paris: Calmann-Lévy, 2001.

Hervieu-Léger, Danièle. *La religion pour mémoire*. Paris: Cerf, 1993.

Hervieu-Léger, Danièle (with Champion, F.). *Vers un nouveau christianisme?*. Paris: Cerf, 1986.

Herzlich, Claudine *et al. Cinquante ans d'exercice de la médecine en France: Carrières et pratiques des médecins français 1930-1980*. Paris: INSERM / Doin, 1993.

Hobbes, Thomas. *Leviathan*. London: Dent, 1973 (1651). French translation: *Léviathan*. Paris: Gallimard ("Folio-Essais"), 2000.

Hoggart, Richard. *La culture du pauvre*. Paris: Minuit ("Le sens commun"), 1970 (1957).

Houle, François. "Citoyenneté, espace public et multiculturalisme: La politique canadienne de multiculturalisme," *Sociologie et sociétés*, Vol. 31, No. 2, Autumn 1999, pp. 101-125.

Ihl, Olivier. "L'urne électoral: Formes et usages d'une technique de vote," *Revue française de science politique*, I, 43, 1993, pp. 30-60.

Inglehart, Ronald, *Modernization and Postmodernization: Cultural, Economic and Political Change in 43 Societes*. Princeton, New Jersey: Princeton University Press, 1997.

Ion, Jacques and Tricart, Jean-Paul. *Les travailleurs sociaux*. Paris: La Découverte, 1992 (3rd ed.).

Isambert, François-André. *Le sens du sacré: Fête et religion populaire*. Paris: Minuit ("Le sens commun"), 1982.

Jobert, Michel and Muller, Pierre. *L'État en action: Politiques publiques et corporatismes*. Paris: PUF ("Recherches politiques"), 1987.

Juteau, Danièle. *L'ethnicité et ses frontières*. Montreal: Les Presses de l'Université de Montréal, 1999.

Kaltenbach, Pierre-Patrick. *Tartufe aux affaires: Génération morale et horreur politique 1980-2000*. Paris: Les Éditions de Paris, 2001.

Karpick, Lucien. *Les avocats entre l'État, le public et le marché: XIIIe-XXe siècle*. Paris: Gallimard ("Bibliothèque des sciences humaines"), 1995.

Kedourie, Elie. *Nationalism in Asia and Africa*. New York: World Publ., 1971.

Koselleck, Reinhart. *Le règne de la critique*. Paris: Minuit, 1979.

Kymlicka, Will. "Les droits des minorités et le multiculturalisme: L'évolution du débat anglo-américain," *Comprendre*, No. 1, Paris: PUF, 2000, pp. 141-171.

Kymlicka, Will. *Multinational Citizenship: A Liberal Theory of Minority Groups*. Oxford University Press, 1995. French translation: *La citoyenneté multiculturelle: Une théorie libérale du droit des minorités*. Paris: La Découverte ("Politique et sociétés"), 2001.

Lacorne, Denis. *La crise de l'identité américaine: Du melting-pot au multiculturalisme*. Paris: Fayard, 1997.

Lampué, Pierre and Rolland, Louis. *Précis de législation coloniale*. Paris: Dalloz, 1940 (3rd ed.).

Le Cour Grandmaison, Olivier and Withol de Wenden, Catherine (eds.). *Les étrangers dans la cité: Expériences européennes*. Paris: La Découverte,1993.

Leveau, Rémi and Schnapper, Dominique. "Religion et politique: Juifs et musulmans maghrébins en France," *Revue française de science politique*, 37, 6, December 1987, pp. 855-890.

Locke, John. *Two Treatises of Government*. London: Dent, 1975 (1924). French translation: *Deuxième Traité du gouvernement civil*. Paris: Vrin, 1977.

Lyotard, Jean-François. *La condition postmoderne*. Paris: Minuit, 1979.

Manin, Bernard. *Principes du gouvernment représentatif*. Paris: Calmann-Lévy, 1995.

Mariani, Margaret and Nicol-Drancourt, Chantal. *Au labeur des dames: Métiers masculins, emplois féminins*. Paris: Syros-Alternatives, 1989.

Marshall, Terence Humphrey. "Citizenship and Social Class," reprinted in *Class, Citizenship and Social Development*. New York: Anchor Book, 1965.

Meehan, Elizabeth. "Citizenship and the European Community," *Political Quarterly*, April-June 1993, pp. 172-186. (a).

Meehan, Elizabeth. *Citizenship and the European Community*. London: Sage, 1993 (b).

Mendras, Henri. *La seconde révolution française*. Paris: Gallimard ("Bibliothèque des sciences humaines"), 1988.

Mendras, Henri. *Les sociétés paysannes*. Paris: Gallimard ("Folio-Histoire"), 1995.

Menger, Piere-Michel. *La profession de comédien: Formations, activités et carrières dans la multiplication de soi*. Paris: La Documentation française, 1997.

Mesure, Sylvie and Renaut, Alain. *Alter ego: Les paradoxes de l'identité démocratique*. Paris: Aubier ("Alto"), 1999.

Montjardet, Dominique. "Le maintien de l'ordre: Technique et idéologie professionnelles des CRS," *Déviance et société*, 1988, pp. 101-126.

Morel, Laurence. "Vers une démocratie directe partisane?," *Revue française de science politique*, Vol. 50, Nos. 4-5, August-October 2000, pp. 765-778.

Mouffe, Chantal. "Éloge du pluralisme culturel," *Esprit*, April 1992.

Moulin, Raymonde *et al*. *Les architectes: Métamorphose d'une profession libérale*. Paris: Calmann-Lévy, 1973.

Moulin, Raymonde. *L'artiste, l'institution et le marché*. Paris: Flammarion ("Art, histoire, société"), 1992.

Muxel, Anne. *L'expérience politique des jeunes*. Paris: Presses de Sciences-Po, 2001.

Noirel, Gérard. *La tyrannie du national: Le droit d'asile en Europe*. Paris: Calmann-Lévy, 1991.

Noirel, Gérard. *Le creuset français: Histoire de l'immigration*. Paris: Seuil, 1988.

Octobre, Sylvie. "Profession, segments professionnels et identité: L'évolution des conservateurs de musée," *Revue française de sociologie*, Vol. 49, No. 3, June 1999, pp. 357-383.

Orateurs de la Révolution française. Paris: Gallimard ("La Pléiade"), 1989.

Oudghiri, Rémy and Sabbagh, Daniel. "Des usages de la 'diversité': Éléments pour une généalogie du multiculturalisme américain," *Revue française de science politique*, Vol. 49, No. 3, June 1999, pp. 443-468.

Papadopoulos, Yannis (ed.). *Présent et avenir de la démocratie directe*. Geneva: Georg, 1994.

Papadopoulos, Yannis. *Démocratie directe*. Paris: Économica, 1998.

Paradeise, Catherine. *Les comédiens: Profession et marchés du travail*. Paris: PUF, 1998.

Paugam, Serge (ed.). *L'exclusion: L'état des savoirs*. Paris: La Découverte, 1996.

Paugam, Serge. *L'ouvrier de la précarité: Les nouvelles formes de l'intégration profesionnelle*. Paris: PUF ("Le lien social"), 2000.

Paugam, Serge. *La disqualification sociale: Essai sur la nouvelle pauvreté*. Paris: PUF ("Sociologie"), 1991.

Perrineau, Pascal and Reynié, Dominique (eds.). *Dictionnaire du vote*. Paris: PUF, 2001.

Podselver, Laurence. "Sarcelles, une communauté bien dans sa peau," *Urbanisme*, No. 291, November-December 1996, pp. 77-81.

Pons, Xavier. *Le multiculturalisme en Australie: Au-delà de Babel*. Paris: L'Harmattan, 1996.

Raynaud, Philippe. "Droit naturel et souveraineté nationale: Remarques sur la théorie de l'État chez Carré de Malberg," *Commentaire*, 22, Summer 1983, pp. 384-393.

Renaut, Alain. *Les révolutions de l'université: Essai sur la modernisation de la culture*. Paris: Calmann-Lévy ("Liberté de l'esprit"), 1995.

Rosanvallon, Pierre. *L'État en France de 1789 à nos jours*. Paris: Seuil, 1990.

Rosanvallon, Pierre. *Le sacre du citoyen: Histoire du suffrage universel en France*. Paris: Gallimard ("Bibliothèque des histoires"), 1992.

Rosanvallon, Pierre. *Le peuple introuvable: Histoire de la représentation démocratique en France*. Paris: Gallimard ("Bibliothèque des histoires"), 1998.

Rosanvallon, Pierre. *La démocratie inachevée: Histoire de la souveraineté du peuple en France*. Paris: Gallimard ("Bibliothèque des histoires"), 2000.

Rostaing, Corinne. *La relation carcérale: Identités et rapports sociaux dans les prisons de femmes*. Paris: PUF ("Le lien social"), 1997.

Rousseau, Dominique (ed.). *La démocratie continue*. Paris: LGDJ-Bruylant, 1995.

Roussel, Louis. *L'enfance oubliée*. Paris: Odile Jacob, 2001.

Roy, Jean. *Le souffle de l'espérance: Le politique entre le rêve et la raison*. Quebec: Bellarmin, 2000.

Sadoun, Marc (ed.). *La démocratie en France. 1. Idéologies, 2. Limits*. Paris: Gallimard ("NRF/ Essais"), 2000.

Saint-Pulgent, Maryvonne de. *Le gouvernement de la culture*. Paris: Gallimard ("Le Débat"), 1999.

Schierup, Carl-Urlik. "Immigrants and Immigrant Policy in Denmark and Sweden: Failed Assimilation versus Corporatist Multiculturalism," *International Review of Comparative Public Policy*, 1989, pp. 223-288.

Schnapper, Dominique. *L'épreuve du chômage*. Paris: Gallimard ("Folio"), 1994 (1981).

Schnapper, Dominique. "De l'État-providence à la démocratie culturelle," *Commentaire*, No. 68, Winter 1994-5, pp. 889-895.

Schnapper, Dominique. "Le sens de l'ethnico-religieux," *Archives des sciences sociales des religions*, 1993, 1, pp. 149-163.

Schnapper, Dominique. "Rapport à l'emploi, protection sociale et statuts sociaux," *Revue française de sociologie*, I, 1989, pp. 3-29.

Schnapper, Dominique. *La communauté des citoyens: Sur l'idée moderne de nation*. Paris: Gallimard ("NRF/Essais"), 1994. English translation: *Community of Citizens: On the Modern Idea of Nationality*. Piscataway, New Jersey: Transaction, 1998.

Schnapper, Dominique. *La compréhension sociologique: Démarche de l'analyse typologique*. Paris: PUF ("Le lien social"), 1999.

Schnapper, Dominique. *La France de l'intégration: Sociologie de la nation en 1990*. Paris: Gallimard ("Bibliothèque des sciences humaines"), 1991.

Schnapper, Dominique. *La relation à l'autre: Au coeur de la pensée sociologique*. Gallimard ("NRF/Essais"), 1998.

Schuck, Peter and Smith, Rogers M. *Citizenship Without Consent: Illegal Aliens in the American Polity*. New Haven: Yale University Press, 1985.

Schweyer, François-Xavier and Binst, Marianne. *La santé otage de son système.* Paris: Économica, 1995.

Simmel, Georg. *Les pauvres.* Paris: PUF ("Quadrige"), 1998 (1908).

Singer, Peter. *Practical Ethics.* Cambridge University Press, 1993. French translation: *Questions d'éthique pratique.* Paris: Bayard, 1997 (1993).

Singly, François de. *Sociologie de la famille contemporaine.* Paris: Nathan ("128"), 1993.

Smith, Anthony D. *The Ethnic Origins of Nations.* Oxford: Blackwell, 1986.

Smith, Rogers M. *Civil Ideals: Conflicting Visions of Citizenship in U.S. History.* New Haven: Yale University Press, 1997.

Soysal, Yasemin Nuhoglu. *Limits of Citizenship: Migrants and Postnational Membership in Europe.* Chicago and London: The University of Chicago Press, 1994.

Spinner, Jeff. *The Boundaries of Citizenship: Race, Ethnicity and Nationality in the Liberal State.* Baltimore: Johns Hopkins University Press, 1994.

Subileau, Françoise and Toinet, Marie-France. *Les chemins de l'abstention: Une comparaison franco-américaine.* Paris: La Découverte, 1993.

Tamir, Yael. *Liberal Nationalism.* Princeton, New Jersey: Princeton University Press, 1993.

Taylor, Charles. "Politics of Recognition," in Gutman, Amy, *Multiculturalism: Examining the "Politics of Recognition".* Princeton, New Jersey: Princeton University Press, 1994. French translation: *Multiculturalisme: différence et démocratie.* Paris: Aubier, 1994.

Thiesse, Anne-Marie. *Ils apprenaient la France.* Paris: Éditions de la Maison des Sciences de l'Homme, 1997.

Thiesse, Anne-Marie. *La création des identités nationales: Europe XVIIIe-XXe siècle.* Paris: Seuil, 1999.

Tocqueville, Alexis de. *La démocratie en Amérique.* Paris: Michel Lévy, 1868 (1835). English translation: *Democracy in America*, translated by Henry Reeve and revised by Francis Bowen and Phillips Bradley, two volumes, New York: Vintage Books, 1945.

Topalov, Christian. *Naissance du chômeur: 1880-1910.* Paris: Albin Michel, 1994.

Touraine, Alain *et al. Le pays contre l'État: Luttes occitanes.* Paris: Seuil, 1981.

Touraine, Alain *et al. La prophétie antinucléaire.* Paris: Seuil, 1980.

Touraine, Alain *et al. Le mouvement ouvrier.* Paris: Seuil, 1984.

Touraine, Alain. "La séparation de l'État et de la nation," *Cahiers de l'URMIS*, No. 7, June 2001.

Touraine, Alain. *La société postindustrielle: Naissance d'une société.* Paris: Denoël, 1969.

Touraine, Alain. *Pourrons-nous vivre ensemble? Égaux et différents.* Paris: Fayard, 1997.

Turner, B. S. *Citizenship and Capitalism.* London: Allen and Unwin, 1986.

Urfalino, Philippe. *L'invention de la politique culturelle.* Paris: La Documentation française, 1996.

Verdès-Leroux, Jeanine. *Le travail social.* Paris: Minuit ("Le sens commun"), 1978.

Vers un revenu minimum inconditionnel? Paris: La Découverte/Mauss, No. 7, 1st semester, 1996.

Walzer, Michael. *Pluralisme et démocratie.* Paris: Esprit, 1997 (1992).

Waresquiel, Emmanuel de (ed.). *Dictionnaire des politiques culturelles depuis 1959.* Paris: Larousse/CNRS, 2001.

Weber, Max. *Essais sur la théorie de la science.* Paris: Armand Colin, 1992 (1920).

Weber, Max. *Le savant et le politique.* Paris: Plon ("10/18"), 1963 (1919).

Weil, Éric. *Essais et conférences.* Paris: Plon, 1971.

Wenden, Catherine de. *Citoyenneté, nationalité et immigration.* Paris: Arcantère, 1987.

Wenden, Catherine de. *La citoyenneté européenne.* Paris: Presses de Sciences-Po, 1997.

Wilson, William Julius. *The Truly Disadvantaged, the Inner City, the Underclass and Public Policy.* Chicago: The University of Chicago Press, 1987.

Wood, Gordon S. *The Creation of the American Republic, 1776-1787.* University of North Carolina Press, 1969. French translation: *La création de la République américaine.* Paris: Belin, 1991 (1969).

Name Index

Verdès-Leroux, Jeanine, 56 note 43
Vigne, Éric, 15

Walzer, Michael, 11 note 15, 16 note 15, 138, 157-158, 162 note 9
Waresquiel, Emmanuel de, 128 note 22
Weber, Max, 2, 4, 5, 7, 16 note 8, 107, 108, 110-111, 113, 116,128 note 34
Weil, Éric, 139 note 11, 162 note 11
Wenden, Catherine de, 81-82 note 47, 91 note 32, 92 notes 45-47

Wilson, William Julius, 42, 56 note 46
Wood, Gordon S., 90 note 2, 176-177 notes 19-23, 190 note 52, 197 notes 19-23, 198 note 52

Ysmal, Colette, 198 note 55

Zylberberg, Jacques, 90 note 16

Subject Index

.

For Product Safety Concerns and Information please contact our EU representative GPSR@taylorandfrancis.com Taylor & Francis Verlag GmbH, Kaufingerstraße 24, 80331 München, Germany

Batch number: 08158516

Printed by Printforce, the Netherlands